The Realm between Perfect Justice and Minimising Injustice

The Realm between Perfect Justice and Minimising Injustice

Ms. Ghazala Rizvi

KALPAZ

First Published, 2020
Published by

Kalpaz Publications
C-30, Satyawati Nagar,
Delhi – 110052
Ph.: 011-47034999, 9811692060
www.kalpazpublications.com
E-mail: kalpaz@hotmail.com

Printed at: Gyan Press, Delhi

Cataloging in Publication Data—DK
Courtesy: D.K. Agencies (P) Ltd. <docinfo@dkagencies.com>

Rizvi, Ghazala, 1990- **author.**
The realm between perfect justice and minimising injustice / Ms. Ghazala Rizvi.
pages cm
"Thesis submitted to Jawaharlal Nehru University for the award of the degree of Doctor of Philosophy."
Includes bibliographical references.
ISBN 9789353242893 (HB)

1. Kant, Immanuel, 1724-1804. 2. Rawls, John, 1921-2002. 3. Sen, Amartya, 1933- 4. Nussbaum, Martha C. (Martha Craven), 1947- 5. Justice. 6. Social justice. I. Title.

LCC B105.J87R59 2020 | DDC 190 23

Lady Justice depicts justice as equipped three symbols:
A Sword Symbolizing the court's coercive power;
A human scale weighing competing claims in each hand;
And a blindfold indicating impartiality.

Dedicated to
My Most Loving Parents

Late Reyaz Ahmad

&

Bibi Taslima

"Who have made me what I am and
Given me all that I have"

Contents

Preface 11
Introduction 13

1. Immanuel Kant on Perfect Justice 27
2. John Rawls on Distributive Justice: An Exposition 67
3. Amartya Sen on Justice as Welfare 103
4. Martha Nussbaum on Gender Justice 149

Conclusion 201
Bibliography & Webliography 213
Index 223

Preface

The present work is an attempt to discuss critically the concept of justice in the realms between perfect justice and minimizing injustices. This realm emerged from two streams of thinkers of enlightenment rationality during 18th and early 19th centuries in Europe. First; there are philosophers like Hobbes, Locke, Rousseau and Kant who have developed justice on the basis of hypothetical social contract theory. They have advocated an insight into the perfect, ideal or absolute justice which is required to understand the particular example of justice. In this context, I have taken into account, on the one hand, Kant's formulation of justice on the basis of human autonomy and dignity and, on the other, John Rawls who revitalizes the ideal justice. The second stream of philosophers include Adam Smith, Condorcet, Mary Wollstonecraft, Bentham, Mill and Marx, who have argued towards minimizing injustices in one way or another. MacIntyre, Amartya Sen and Martha Nussbaum have attempted to revitalize the same. On minimizing injustices, I have taken into account the positions of Amartya Sen and Martha Nussbaum.

I am grateful to the authors whose works have directly or indirectly helped me. I have always tried to supply exact quotations and full references to original works, and in the footnotes, I have also furnished suggestions for further reading. In referring to the works Plato, Aristotle, Immanuel Kant, John Rawls, Amartya Sen and Martha Nussbaum, I have used the most accurate available English translations. I am thankful to those translators of the texts. I have also taken help from online sources and articles. I am thankful to those authors too.

I would like to express my gratitude to my supervisor, Prof. R.P. Singh, without his support this work would never have been possible. He has been very generous with his time and suggestions, whenever I approached him. My interaction with him has greatly enriched my understanding of the issues related to this work.

My special thanks to Indian Council of Social Science Research, New Delhi, for the award of Post Doctoral Fellowship which helps me to the completion of this work and to Jawaharlal Nehru University, New Delhi for providing all the infrastructural facilities related to my research work. I am also thankful University Grants Commission and Indian Council of Philosophical Research for granting me fellowship during my M.Phil & Ph.D.

The constant support and encouragement that I received from my friends has been a source of motivation throughout this work. It would have been impossible to even think of this work, had there not been a strong support from my family. The patience and understanding shown by my mother and brother Mr. Dilshad Ghani even in the face of demanding situations and the way they handled things helped me immensely in concentrating on my work. A very special thanks to my friend, philosopher and mentor Dr. M.A. Wadood and Dr. Shiv Kumar Singh for their love, affection and constant moral support and encouragement. I thank to them for the unpredicted inspiration behind my every step in academic and personal life.

I would like to take this opportunity to express my thanks to Dr. Amit Garg of Gyan Publications, Delhi, for immense cooperation and timely publication of the work.

Lastly, but most importantly, I want to thank God for His blessing because of Him I have been able to complete my work on time.

Dr. Ghazala Rizvi
Postdoctoral Researcher
(ICSSR, New Delhi)
Centre for Philosophy
School of Social Sciences-1
Jawaharlal Nehru University
New Delhi-110067

Introduction

Historical and Methodological Seting to the Doctrine of Justice and Injustice

In this chapter, I shall discuss the historical and the methodological background concerning the concept of justice in the realm between perfect justice and minimizing injustice. This realm emerged from two streams of thinkers of enlightenment rationality during 18th and early 19th centuries in Europe. First; there are philosophers like Hobbes, Locke, Rousseau and Kant who have developed justice on the basis of hypothetical social contract theory. They have advocated an insight into the perfect, ideal or absolute justice which is required to understand the particular example of justice. In this context, I will be taking into account, on the one hand, Kant's formulation of justice on the basis of human autonomy and dignity and, on the other, John Rawls who revitalizes the ideal justice. The second stream of philosophers include Adam Smith, Condorcet, Mary Wollstonecraft, Bentham, Mill and Marx, who have argued towards minimizing injustices in one way or another. MacIntyre, Amartya Sen and Martha Nussbaum have attempted to revitalize the same. On minimizing injustices, i will be taking into account the positions of Amartya Sen and Martha Nussbaum.

The notion of justice has been a developing concept and it is in that process we corne across various discrepancies arising out of theological, moral, social, legal, political and economic aspects throughout history. So the concept of justice is dynamic in nature and the diversity of its connotation makes it difficult to lay down the precise meaning of justice. Moreover, there are numbers of important questions surrounding justice have been fiercely debated over the course of human history. These are namely, what is justice? What does justice demand of individuals and societies? What is a perfectly just society? How social benefits and burdens should be allocated? Is justice has much to do with being treated fairly? How can the form of injustices be removed? Is institutional approach to justice is sufficient to deliver justice? Therefore the concept of Justice can be analyzed from all these angles.

In general justice is a concept which deals with the fact that people should be treated fairly and impartially concerning their rights, freedom, need and choices. It is primarily concerned with the proper ordering of things which includes equitable distribution of social opportunities such as resources, goods, services and deterrence of crime and punishment within a society. Its main concern is the availability of equal social opportunities for the development of personality to all the people in the society without any discrimination on the basis of caste, color, sex or race.

The concept of justice has been analysed differently by philosophers at different ages and it changes from time to time depending upon the conditions and circumstances prevailing in each age. Historically, Plato (427-347 B.C.E) was the first philosopher who could give a systematic account of justice. In *Republic,* Plato's goal of whole discussion is to define justice. In Plato's view, justice is to have harmonious relations amongst the citizens and the state. A just society shall consist of just persons. For Plato, justice covers both the just person and the just city state. Justice consists in having and doing one's own duty. Everybody should mind his/her own business, i.e., that one should do the one job for which he is naturally best fitted and should not try to indulge in anyone else's job. In *Republic,* Plato's Socrates argues that justice is the harmony of the soul and the efficient functioning of a community based on contract. Plato makes the analogy of soul and state. According to Plato, "a person's soul has three parts - reason, desire and motive".[1] Similarly, the State has three parts - the rulers, soldiers and the workers. Plato says, "A city is just when its three natural constituents or capacities are each doing their job and it was self- disciplined, brave and wise in virtue of certain other states and dispositions of those constituents".[2]

On Plato's account, desire driven persons are workers, spirit driven persons are soldiers and reason driven persons are rulers. If a man is controlled by reason, with spirit and desire properly subordinated; he will act in a just manner. However, if a man is controlled by desire, or even spirit, he will act in an unjust manner. Just person is at peace with himself because his/her soul is well ordered; the unjust person is miserable because his soul is divided and disordered. And the proper order of the soul is for it to be governed by knowledge of the Good. Therefore, just person is on whose soul is guided by the vision of good and whose reason governs passion.

Carrying it further on the discussion of justice, Aristotle (384-322 B.C.E.) in Book V of *The Nichomachean Ethics,* discusses the concept of justice. He holds that, "in justice is summed up the whole of virtue. It is complete virtue in the fullest sense, because it is the active exercise of complete virtue; and it is complete because its possessor can exercise it in relation to other person and not only by himself'.[3] Aristotle argues that justice as a virtue must be something complete, that is not desired for some further end. So it seems that the virtue is the most complete virtue which is pursued wholly for itself. Aristotle claims that the most complete virtue is that which is always choice worthy in itself, which is just to say that the most complete virtue is intrinsically valuable. Aristotle proposes two conceptions of justice - general and particular. A general conception of justice is lawfulness where a particular conception of justice refers to what is fair and equal. Further, Aristotle divides particular conception of justice into distributive and certificatory. Distributive justice is concerned with what people deserve or else what one has the right to get. Aristotle linked the notion of distributive justice - offices and wealth, rewards and dues with the idea of proportionate equality, which in tum, connected to a theory of just rewards or equal shares according to the merit of its recipients. According to Aristotle, "what is just is what is proportional, and what is unjust is what violates the proportion".[4] Thus, Aristotle 's notion of Justice deals with good judgment and sense of fairness .

In the European modernity, it is the enlightenment that has played the most important role in formulating the notion of justice on the basis of the autonomy of the individuals in the civil and democratic society. This stage was the beginning of a just society where individuals were free to pursue natural rights, happiness, liberty, equality and justice. During this time great changes occurred in scientific thought and exploration. New ideas filled the horizon and man was eager to explore these ideas freely. It also brought about a great change in the social relationship because at this time, reason, rationality, freedom, equality, justice became the central part of human affairs. Man began to embrace an exaggerated belief in the perfection of humanity based on reason, clear thinking. They happily left the medieval extremism of mysticism and superstitions and they changed their opinion to the other extremes of reason, rationality, science and technology. Enlightenment has played most important role in making a society just by criticizing king's special right.

The enlightenment thinkers, namely, Thomas Hobbes, John Locke and Jean- Jacques Rousseau who have adopted the method of social contract to repudiate feudal monarchy and aristocracy by using the natural right that is freedom to enter into civil society to protect their natural rights especially right to life, liberty and property. Thomas Hobbes is the foremost enlightenment thinker who expanded the idea of social contract. He wrote *Leviathan* in response to the English Civil War. In this book, he wrote that in the earliest days there was no government. Instead, those who were the strongest could take control and use their power at any time over others. Hobbes's theory was that the people mutually agreed to create a state, only giving the state enough power to provide protection of their well-beings. However, in Hobbes' theory, once the power was given to the state, the people then surrendered any right to that power. Hobbes thinks that the lives of individuals in the state of nature were solitary, poor, nasty, brutish and short, a state in which self-interest and the absence of rights and contracts prevented the 'social', or society. Life was anarchic and full of injustices. Individuals in the state of nature were apolitical and asocial. This state of nature is followed by the social contract. Hobbes's *Leviathan* rested his despotism on consent. He assumed that,

> Without the restraints of government men would be in a constant of war and insecurity. They are by nature so quarrelsome and competitive that only the strongest rule will restrain them. The choice between despotism and anarchy, and this should be apparent in everyone's thinking.[5]

Here the state system, which grew out of the social contract, was anarchic or without leadership. For instance, the individuals in the state of nature had been sovereigns and thus guided by self-interest and the absence of rights, so the individuals now acted in their self-interest in competition with each other. Just like the state of nature, states were thus bound to be in conflict because there was no sovereign over and above the state i.e. more powerful capable of imposing social-contract laws. The social contract gained importance when individuals came together and gave up some of their individual rights and others will also do the same. This entails the establishment of a just state. The state acts as a sovereign power to protect these rights which regulate societal justice. Society was thus no longer anarchic because political authority was based on the individuals self-interest to choose their authority with mutual consent by surrendering their rights and live themselves under the shadow of monarch who was sovereign must give up to absolute authority in the form of king or head if a society to be created and he can only do justice. Liberal tradition of justice is based on the social contract. The social contract theory of the state implies that there was a time when men lived without any recognised civil law or without the state. That's why Hobbes advocated justice in absolute monarchy.

However, Hobbes' social contract was not mature because he focused on authoritarian regime that could deliver justice. It was John Locke whose liberal and anti-authoritarian theory of the state led to the overthrow of the system of absolute monarchy. Locke criticized Robert Filmer's views in *Patriarcha or The Natural Power ofKings* that a king's authority was vested in him or her by God, that such authority was absolute, and therefore that the basis of political obligation lay in our obligation to obey God absolutely.[6] Locke repudiated king's divine rights in his *First Treatise of Government.* He denied that king has any special power. There is no divine right of King to rule human beings and God did not appoint Adam and his decedents to rule over the world. In this way Locke has repudiated king's hereditary right and states that every man has a natural right that is right to life, liberty and property. The principle of consent plays an important role in any social contract theory. He says,

> Men being, as has been said, by nature, all free, equal, and independent, no one can be put out of this estate, and subjected to the political power of another, without his own consent. The only way whereby anyone divests himself of his natural liberty, and puts on the bonds of civil society, is by agreeing with other men to join and unite into a community for their comfortable, safe, and peaceable living one amongst another, in a secure enjoyment of their properties, and a greater security against any injustices. When number of men consented to make one community or government, thereby incorporated to make one body politic, wherein the majority has a right to act and conclude the rest. For when any number of men have, by the consent of every individual, made a community, they have thereby made that community one body, with a power to act as one body, which is only by the will and determination of the majority. And thus every man, by consenting with others to make one body politic under one government, puts himself under an obligation, to every one of that society, to submit to the determination of the majority of the social agreement in any institutions for enhancing justice.[7]

Social contract theory applies the concept of social consent in its description of the behavior of individuals in the state of nature as they come together in a context of consent to form social, political, and legal associations and institutions to make just. Locke's social contract was sufficient to overthrow authoritarian regime completely. It is the natural right to enter into social contract to form civil society in which natural right i.e. right to life, freedom and property are protected by the government established to enforce laws protecting rights and its related disputes. Justice lies in protecting the rights of the individuals. Rousseau also applied social contract approach in the form of general will i.e. will of majority. Rousseau's concept of general will is not merely the sum of all the individual wills that enter into the social contract but the will of all should give consent. In this way by entering into the original agreement confirmed to seek to consensus regarding the welfare of all and this was the vision underlying justice. On Rousseau's view, "The social contract is a genuine and legitimate contract, which is to the benefit of everyone, since it unites liberty with law and utility with right".[8] The social contract approach is beneficial to all the members of the society or the state. It is a genuine and legitimate contract as it unites liberty with law and utility with right. The state of *The Social Contract* is a community united by the general will and the sense of a community on the part of its citizen is necessary for the maintenance and well-being of all.[9] In the social contract the general will is the moral sovereignty to give impartial laws for all.

In the modem times, there are various notions of justice. For instance, Utilitarianism is a form of consequentialism where justice is based on the maximization of usefulness. Utilitarian tradition of justice requires the maximization of the total or average welfare across all relevant individuals. Thus, utilitarian tradition of justice is based on welfare maximization where some individuals are used as a means for the good of others. Mill's utilitarianism is a form of consequentialism where the moral worth of an action is determined by its outcome. According to Mill,

> Justice is not as fundamental as we often think. Rather, it is derived from the more basic standard of rightness, i.e., consequentialism: what is right is what has the best consequences (usually measured by the total or average welfare caused). So, the proper principles of justice are those which tend to have the best consequences.[10]

For Mill, justice is derived from the basic standard of rightness implies what is right is what has the best consequences. The proper principles of Justice are those which tend to have the best consequences. In this way the principle of utility introduces system into our judgments of justice.

Though the concept of Justice has been in debate for centuries, it may not be possible for me to go into all the details of these theories of justice evolved at different stages of the social development. However, I am not going to discuss in detail about the above philosopher's and their conception of justice. My concern is to see how they have apprehended the conception of Justice.

The notion of perfect justice in Immanuel Kant can be elaborated in the context of his critical appreciation of social contract theory as only regulative on the one hand and on the other hand the concepts of autonomy and dignity formulated in terms of enlightenment rationality and the maxims of categorical imperative. "Enlightenment is man's release from his self incurred tutelage. Tutelage is man's inability to make use of his understanding without direction from another".[11] For Kant, once humanity coming out from their self-imposed immaturity reaches at the stage of enlightenment and develops reason to the extent that they becomes autonomous and dignified to perform juridical and ethical duties. Enlightened being acts in the conformity of categorical imperative, realises an ideal such as universality, end-in-itself and kingdom of ends. This ideal reaches at the notion of a just society wherein every enlightened being makes a general consent in formulating the principles of justice. At this stage human being can realize his own betterment and for the sake of entire society. Thus, the principle of perfect justice transforms an individual behaviour in such a way that everyone can act rationally to transform oneself and society as well. This is the philosophical vision for perfect justice.

It is Kant's philosophical insight into perfect justice that has been carried forward by John Rawls by modifying social contract theory and by reformulating the principles of justice to be applied to the institutions. According to Rawls, the principles for determining the basic institutions of a society as to what is just are:

> First: each person is to have an equal right to the most extensive basic liberty compatible with similar liberty for others.
>
> Second: Social and economic inequalities are to be arranged so that they are both (a) reasonably expected to be to everyone's advantage, and (b) attached to positions and offices open to all.[12]

Rawls calls principle I the principle of equal liberty, principle 2(a) the difference principle, and principle 2(b) the principle of fair equality of opportunity. Rawls's notion of 'justice as fairness' focuses on 'just institutions' rather than concentrating on 'just individuals and societies' as it is in Kant which can help to create effective institutions and reduce injustices and inequality as well. This position has been criticized by Rawls in his later work *Political Liberalism.* However Rawls' own criticism of his earlier position still amounts to the fairness of the institutions with liberal values. There is still a lack of the realization of the sense of justice not as a matter of judging institutions and principles for distributing primary goods but minimising injustices at individual and social level.

It may be emphasized that institutional choice and arrangement focused approaches to justice are not sufficient conditions because society consists of human beings who are outside of the institutions and the latter gets affected by the former. The notion of minimizing injustice is very necessary wherein less people are capable to use their freedom, rights and toleration. More importantly, the search for perfect justice could distract us from tackling real-life, immediate injustices such as discrimination relating to education, skill, health, environment, etc. for women, tribal people and marginalized community who are deprived of all these.

In recent times, Amartya Sen and Martha Nussbaum have developed justice as welfare through capability approach.[13] There is an attempt to tackle the issues of minimizing injustices by highlighting that human being has a dignity with their ability to pursue their own ends. Sen's notion of minimizing injustice is a dynamic departure in the debate on justice which concentrates on the well being of each and every individual. It does not concentrate on the means of primary goods and just institutions but minimizing injustices by removing obstacles in actual opportunities in day to day life. Sen has brought a new conception of justice as welfare through freedom, capability and public enlightenment. Instead of institutional mechanism which governs collective choices, Sen's minimizing injustices make each and every individual to act on his/her own choices.

Carrying out further the notion of minimizing injustice, Martha Nussbaum considers the quest for justice and equality of opportunities between genders. She tries to establish an inclusive society and the possibility of feminist perspective on justice. In order to minimize social injustice, we must incorporate the historical and cultural circumstances of different people. For Nussbaum, "the need to recognize that the lives of women are highly varied, that women live within a variety of traditions, and that the best account of human justice is not one that merely projects western values onto groups with different concerns".[14] Her main concern is to pay attention to the actual experiences and circumstances of individual women. The majority of women across the world are deprived of legal, political, social and economic status enjoyed by men. This discrimination and their deprived situation is due to their cultural traditions and practices that mould their lives. The conflict between cultural practices and women's rights has been prevalent as a social phenomena and it has to be interrogated. The question arises - are we going to minimize women's injustice and bring gender equality under the purview of human rights or let the culture or tradition decide their lives?

The main objective of the thesis will be to fill the gap between 'perfect justice and minimising injustice' and develop an inclusive notion of justice. The purpose of this study is first of all to show the deep and subtle differences which led them to obviously divergent views on justice and secondly to show how we should think about the inclusive notion of justice. It may pave the way for a constructive integration by clarifying those issues which remain in need of resolution.

In order to proceed in this direction, there are, as a matter of fact, certain discrepancies in the notion of justice itself when we discuss the theories like distributive, rectificatory/ reformative, retributive, restorative, etc., or concepts like goodness, *eudaemonia,* dignity, fairness, harmony, etc. or minimizing injustices in terms of capability, welfare, gender equality, etc. These theories and concepts have evolved to address particular aspects of justice concerning institutions, distribution of resources, deterrence of crime and theories of punishment, and so on. There are numbers of important questions surrounding justice have been fiercely debated over the course of human history: What is justice? What does it demand of individuals and societies? What is the proper distribution of wealth and resources in society: equal, meritocratic, according to status, or some other arrangement? There are number of possible answers to these questions from divergent perspectives on the philosophical, political and economic spectrum. There is a contestation on the idea of perfect justice advocated by Kant and Rawls derived from hypothetical social contract theory on the one hand and the concepts like autonomy, dignity, fairness, etc. on the other. Just as on the idea of perfect justice, similarly on minimizing injustice, there are contending claims between Amartya Sen and Martha Nussbaum. I am going to examine and address this problematic in the following four chapters:

1. The social contract theory propounded by Hobbes, Locke and Rousseau introduced justice by way of a hypothetical contract

for mutual advantage to have a just society. For Hobbes justice lies in the hands of the Monarch whereas for Locke justice consists in the form of individual rights related to life, freedom and property. For Rousseau, it is the general will or moral collective will of the individuals in the society who will shape the laws of institutions which will deliver justice. Kant has attempted to re-visit social contract theory not as a historical phenomenon but as a regulative mechanism to be used as the device to explain the origins of the state, the nature of autonomy and dignity of the individuals. I will try to examine contending claims on social contract theory and the emergence of perfect justice.

2. Rawls has revived social contract theory not to explain the origin of the state and its sovereignty or autonomy of the individuals, but as transcendental mechanism to explain the principle of distributive justice with reference to institutions. Individuals and their actions are just insofar as they conform to the demands of just institutions. Then the question arises: is justice the realization of institutions and rules or principles or is it concerned with the society as well? I will try to attempt to vindicate Rawls' position on justice and bring out its shortcomings in two fold manner; first the way Rawls has criticized his own earlier position in his later work and secondly the way his successors like Sen, Martha Nussbaum and others have criticized the positions of Rawls.
3. In *The Idea of Justice,* Sen criticizes the original position, i.e. veil of ignorance of Rawls' theory of justice which amounts to the lack of genuine information concerning injustice. Sen argues that Kant and Rawls have developed perfect justice to concentrate primarily on getting the institutions right with transcendental institutionalism, and it is not directly focused on the actual societies that would ultimately emerge. I have to bring out the discrepancies and the implications between well-being (collective) and happiness (individualistic) to substantiate minimizing injustice in Sen.
4. Martha Nussbaum further develops the capability approach, not as a procedural justice but as an outcome-oriented approach that gives impartial account of justice as welfare. I will attempt to bring out the close relationship between the institutional and

constitutional design in Martha Nussbaum with the quest for justice and equality of opportunities between genders. I will address the questions concerning minimizing injustice in terms of discrimination, particularly gender discrimination in the cultural practices of different people on the one hand and legal, political, social and economic status of women on the other. With feminist perspective, Martha Nussbaum attempts to establish an inclusive society which not only incorporates the basic philosophic visions of Kant, Rawls and Sen but also transcends it.

In order to sort out problematic area mentioned above, I propose to adopt a method which is analytical, critical, comparative and normative. It is analytical because I shall develop an understanding about various concepts in the realm of justice like autonomy, dignity, fairness, welfare, capability, etc. These concepts can be contextualized in terms of the respective theories on justice with their representative thinkers. It is critical and comparative because I will be discussing the positions as distinct as Aristotle, Kant, John Rawls, Amartya Sen and Martha Nussbaum. The normative aspect of my approach has a reference to the ideas of goodness, happiness, well- being, equality, etc., in general and also in relation to particular philosophers. I will also critically evaluate the utilitarian approach taken by Mill and contrast it from the pragmatic approaches taken by Sen and Martha Nussbaum.

In order to organise my study, I propose to divide my study III the fallowing chapter:

In Chapter I, shall analyse Kant's position on justice in the context of the social contract theory advocated by Hobbes, Locke and Rousseau. I will develop perfect justice with reference to Kant's enlightenment rationality and morality. The former gives rise to human rights, toleration and public reason to enter into contract to secure one another's autonomy and dignity. The latter gives the vision of perfect justice that *how* justice ought to be under all circumstances through categorical imperative; namely, universality, end in itself and kingdom of end.

In Chapter II, I will critically examine Rawls' theory of justice to create institutions wherein every individual abides by the rules of social contract to formulate the principle of justice behind a 'veil of ignorance'. I'll analyse Rawls' justice as fairness in terms of just institutions where fair distribution of social goods to all human being with the exception of those who are less well off. Moreover institutional based perfect justice is not sufficient because society consists of actual human beings.

In Chapter-III, I shall discuss Amartya Sen on minimizing injustice in the form of injustices, freedom and capability, well being and public enlightenment. It is attend by welfare mechanism through enhancement of individual and collective quality of life in the form of freedom, capability and public enlightenment; each individual has dignity and is worthy to pursue his well being. I will take up freedom as wellbeing as an alternative approach which emphasizes that people, instead of resources, are the real wealth and the purpose of justice is to create an enabling society wherein each individual becomes capable to make decision about issues that affect their lives and minimize injustice to that extent.

In Chapter IV, I will discuss Martha Nussbaum's conception of gender justice based on women as entitled to use human rights, removal of their poverty and inequality followed by their capabilities to construct an inclusive society. In order to minimize social injustice particularly gender justice, we must recognise the historical and cultural circumstances of individual women. I will go into the details of the conflict between cultural practices and women's rights which have been prevailing since the society has evolved.

References

Plato. *The Republic.* Translated by Desmond Lee. England: Penguin Groups, 1987.

Aristotle. *Nichomachean Ethics.* Translated by J. A. K. Thompson. London: Penguin Books, 2004.

Hobbes, Thomas. *Leviathan.* Edited by Richard Tuck. London: Cambridge University Press, 1991.

Locke, John. *First Treatise on Civil Government.* Edited by Ashcraft, Richard. London: Rutledge University Press, 1991.

Locke, John. *The Second Treatise of Government.* Edited by Laslett Peter. U.K: Cambridge University Press, 1960.

Rousseau, Jacques Jean. *The Social Contract.* Translated by Maurice Cranston. England: Penguin Books Limited, 1968.

Levine, Andrew. *The General Will: Rousseau, Marx, communism.* USA: Cambridge University Press, 1993.

Mill, Stuart John. "Utilitarianism". *On Liberty and Other Essays.* Edited by Gray, John. Oxford: OUP, 1991.

Kant, Immanuel. "What is Enlightenment"? (1784). *On History.* Edited & Translated by Lewis White Beck. New York: Macmillan, 1963.

Rawls, John. *A Theory of Justice.* Cambridge: Harvard University Press, 1971.

Sen, Amartya. *The Idea of Justice.* London: Penguin Books, 2009.

Nussbaum. Martha. *Sex and Social Justice.* Oxford: Oxford University Press, 1999.

Notes

1. Plato, *The Republic.* p. 207.
2. Ibid, p. 209.
3. Aristotle, *Nichomachean Ethics.* p. 115.
4. Ibid. p. 120.
5. Hobbes, *Leviathan.* p. 45.
6. Locke, *First Treatise on Civil Government.* p. 28.
7. Locke, *The Second Treatise ofGovernment.* pp. 54-55.
8. Rousseau, *The Social Contract.* pp. 27-28.
9. Levine, *The General Will: Rousseau, Marx, communism,* p. 40.
10. Mill, "Utilitarianism" *On Liberty and Other Essays.* Gray. p. 5.
11. Kant, "What is Enlightenment?" *On History.* p. 35.
12. Rawls, *A Theory of Justice.* p. 60.
13. Sen, *The Idea of Justice.* p. 225.
14. Nussbaum, *Sex and Social Justice.* pp. 6-8.

Chapter - 1

Immanuel Kant on Perfect Justice

In this Chapter, I will develop the notion of perfect justice with reference to Immanuel Kant's enlightenment rationality and morality. The enlightenment rationality gives rise to human rights, toleration and public reason to enter into contract to secure one another's autonomy and dignity. Kantian morality gives the vision of perfect justice that *how* justice ought to be under all circumstances through categorical imperative; namely, universality, end in itself and kingdom of ends. In formulating the notion of perfect justice in Kantian perspective, enlightenment rationality has played an important rôle because it is the stage at which human beings recognize their freedom, rationality, right, dignity, autonomy and sovereignty. It is the enlightenment and morality which awakens individuals to become autonomous to formulate self-imposed laws of morality and justice. It also encourage to adopt the method of social contract to repudiate feudal monarchy and aristocracy by using their rights, to enter into contract within civil society to protect their basic rights especially right to freedom, autonomy and dignity. The sense of autonomy requires individuals to make self-imposed laws which ought to be compatible with categorical imperative of the moral law. It is the moral law of categorical imperative that would harmonise with the maxims of self and other enlightened beings. It is our duty as an enlightened and moral being to examine our action in such a manner that is compatible with universal law so that it would be valid for all and under all circumstances.

Kant's principle of perfect justice revolves around the concept of individual autonomy, sovereignty and dignity. His principle of justice is meant to regulate and safeguard individual autonomy and dignity on the basis of moral law namely; 'universality' 'end in itself and 'kingdom of ends' so that the principle of human autonomy and dignity ought to be universalized. It is the Kant's enlightenment rationality bestowed with public reason to enter into social contract to create an institution which safeguards our autonomy and dignity. It is public reason which commands each autonomous being to enter into an agreement to formulate institutional principles which deliver justice in the form of categorical imperative to reach to the perfect justice.

For clarity and precision, I shall divide the present chapter into three parts. In Part-I; I will discuss social contract theory of Hobbes, Locke and Rousseau and the notion of perfect justice that has evolved out of the institutional mechanism. In Part-II; I will discuss autonomy and dignity as the foundational principle in formulating perfect justice. In Part-III; I will discuss Kant's notion of Categorical Imperative in the form of Universality, End in itself and Kingdom of Ends wherein human autonomy and dignity ought to be universalized. The notion of autonomy and dignity becomes the very foundation of a perfectly just society where every enlightened person inculcates the habit of moral and juridical responsibility to promote justice for oneself and the society as well.

Before coming to the basic issues which I shall be dealing in the above three parts, I would like to point out that Kant's enlightenment philosophy is preoccupied with the concept of a 'just man' who has come out of his immaturity by using his own reason securing sufficient freedom, equality, rights and autonomy. Enlightenment rationality and morality in the context of freedom is an important concern for the image of a just and a moral man. Kant says, "Enlightenment underlies in the idea of *Sapere aude;* Think boldly, take courage, and use your own understanding to serve".[1] It is the duty of each individual to inculcate the habit which serves the condition of enlighten and moral being. As James Schmidt interpreted the *Critique of Judgment,* the phrase Kant had employed as the motto of enlightenment serves as the first of his three maxim of understanding: Firstly, think for oneself; secondly, think from the standpoint of everyone else; and thirdly, think always consistently. The first is the maxim of an unprejudiced, the second of a broadened, and the third of a consistent way of thinking.[2] Further, James Schmidt also says that it is only by becoming skilled at the first two which Kant's enabled the maxims of understanding and of judgment-that we become proficient in the third, which he called the maxim of reason.[3]

Once individuals become enlightened and moral inculcate the virtue of just man such as reasonable thinking, from the standpoint of everyone else, and thinking consistently for the betterment of themselves and humanity as a whole.

Here I, propose to explain enlightenment rationality becomes the foundational pillars in formulating the notion of perfect justice through an understanding of Kant's essay on enlightenment. For Kant,

> Enlightenment is man's emergence from his self-incurred immaturity. Immaturity is the ability to use one's own understanding without the guidance of another. This immaturity is self-imposed, because reason itself languishes not in lack of understanding but only of resolve and courage to solve oneselfwithout direction from another.[4]

It can be argued that once a person become enlighten get away from his/her selfincurred habits and to use his/her understanding without the guidance of another. In other words, it is the point at which a person recognizes his or her own autonomy and rights. It develops reason to the extent that it becomes autonomous and gets rid of restraints from tradition and authority. As professor Singh has pointed out, "The way to enlightenment for Kant is not to seek a mentor or authority in thinking, in willing and in feeling".[5] Enlightenment rationality inculcates the habit of autonomy and sovereignty in individuals thinking, willing and feeling. It is the ultimate outcome of just man by giving right, tolerance, autonomy, equality, fraternity, justice, public and private reason. It also focuses that human beings are free to make and transform their institutions in accordance with their own critical rationality to enter into contract and formulate universal principle which promotes fair and impartial treatment concerning their freedom and dignity.

Enlightenment brought great changes in the society through "scientific thought and exploration. New ideas filled the horizon and people were eager to explore these ideas freely. It also brought change in the social relationship as reason, rationality, freedom, equality and justice became the central part of human affairs. Human began to embrace an exaggerated belief in the perfection of humanity based on reason, and clear thinking. They happily left the medieval extremism of mysticism and superstitions and they changed their opinion to the other extremes of reason, rationality, science and technology. The advancement in science in the form of Copernicus revolution also contributed in shaping the thoughts of enlightenment rationality. With this brief remark regarding enlightenment rationality which is the most operative term in Kant's perfect justice; I shall come to the Part I of the chapter.

Part - I

An Examination of Social Contract Theory

The social contract theory propounded by Hobbes, Locke and Rousseau introduced justice by way of a hypothetical contract for mutual advantage to have a just society. For Hobbes justice lies in the hands of the Monarch whereas for Locke justice consists in the form of individual rights related to life, freedom and property. For Rousseau, it is the general will or moral collective will of the individuals in the society who will shape the laws of institutions which will deliver justice. The social contract theory was repudiated by Hume on the ground that there is no historical evidence to any contract, original or otherwise. His account of 'justice is based on convention and customs."[6] Kant has attempted to re-visit social contract theory not as a historical phenomenon but as a regulative mechanism to be used as the device to explain the origins of the state, the nature of autonomy and dignity of the individuals. I will try to examine contending claims on social contract theory and the emergence of perfect justice

Kant's conception of perfect justice can be elaborated in the context of his critical appreciation of social contract theory as only regulative principle that helps to organize social affairs. It has been the dominant theory and it turns out to be the most appropriate normative model for the Vision of perfect justice in today's world because it tries to protect individual's autonomy and dignity through institutional mechanism. Kant rightly argues in *Perpetual Peace,*

> In this civil union, self-sought, yet sought reluctantly, man is able to tum his most unlovable equalities to a profitable use. They bind this society together. They are the instruments by which he wins for himself self-culture. It is here with men as it is with the trees in a forest: just because each one strives to deprive the other of air and sun, they compel each other to seek both above, and thus they grow beautiful and straight. Whereas those that, in freedom and isolation from one another, shoot out their branches and at will, grow stunted and crooked and awry.[7]

These mutual advantages encourage and provide a sufficient motive for entering into contact to form an institution which protects individual's autonomy and dignity.

The social contract has rich history and it rejected the traditional theory of divine rights. It played an important historical role in the emergence of the idea that political authority or institution must be derived from people's consent. According to them, a person's moral or political obligations are dependent upon a contract or agreement made among them to form the society in which they live. Since ancient times the social contract idea has been used as a progressive intellectual tradition that has questioned authority in all its guises. In fact it has been used since ancient times that social arrangements were not the products of nature but consent and contract. It developed through the centuries as criteria of distinguishing a just contract from an unjust contract. The search for such criteria continues in recent attempts to apply social contract theory to any just organisations and institutions. Moreover, Socrates uses social contract argument to explain to Crito, "why he must remain in prison and accept the death penalty rather than escape because he makes an agreement to obey the laws of his country".[8] He was morally bound to follow the laws of his country because he makes an agreement to obey. However, Edward Harris points out that, "Socrates presents his analysis of political obligation in the form of an imaginary discussion between him and the laws of Athens".[9] Socrates offers an argument that rests on the notion of a social contract existing between him and the city-state of Athens and having made a mutual consent that was itself just. Further he argues in *Crito,* "We must have experience of the manner in which we order justice and administer the State, and still remains, has entered into an implied contract that he will do as society commands".[10] Socrates asserts that he must keep to this agreement that he has made and obeys the laws in this case by not escaping and accepting the death penalty

Bringing forward Socrates view of social contract into the modem times, the concept of social contract theory gets mentioned in its first sufficient description by Thomas Hobbes, John Locke and Jean-Jacques Rousseau. They are the best known promoters of this influential theory to make a just society. However, each of them drew different viewpoint on the nature of political authority and how justice to be delivered within social institutions. Hobbes's idea about social contract is that in a state of nature men lived in lawless and unjust society, not just because of things were not equally distributed but lack of rules and regulations. Hobbes says in *Leviathan,*

> The condition of man is a condition of war of every one against everyone, in which case everyone is governed by his own reason; and there is nothing he can make use of, that may not be a help unto him, in preserving his life against his enemies; it fallowed, that in

such a condition, every man has a right to everything; even to one another's body. And therefore as long as this natural right of every man to everything endures, there can be no security to any man."[11]

Through social contract, human beings were able to move from the 'state of nature' to civil society because they are free to form a state with the support of their freedom and reason. People wanted a ruler of a sovereign or political body in order to be able to live in a civil society. It is the rational human who overcomes the unjust state of nature to formulate the just society wherein individual rights are protected by the state.

Locke in *Two Treatises of Government* offers a substantial theory of social contract. He says that,

> In the 'state of nature', every man was equal. But there was no guarantee of individual rights. However, people live unsecure and unstable life, but they realized that they can enjoy their life if they can come together by means of contract. The purpose of contract is to form a civil society in which natural rights are guaranteed under a government established to enforce laws protecting natural right."[12]

Hobbes makes clear that the journey from 'state of nature' to the 'social contract' has been remarkable in establishing the civil society. The social contract guaranteed the formation of a just government to enforce laws for protecting natural right. Locke's conception of institution provides a powerful tool for the just arrangement to provide each and every person with what they need such as equal rights, freedom, dignity and the right to enter into contract. In formulating the status of justice in Locke, social contract was a very powerful approach. This approach was inspired by the background of the unjust society in the form of monarch's hereditary privileges. It was the time where all opportunities were distributed unequally to people according to class and their inherited status. He tried to establish an equal society through the method of maintaining individual rights, equality, and toleration. His vision of justice represents a synthesis of the principle of autonomy, individualism, equability, liberty and toleration and it is the function of the institution or government (ruler) to provide the sufficient conditions under which individuals can enjoy their natural rights. If the government is unable to provide a just condition under which people may enjoy their right then they are entitled to over throw the governing authority.

The idea of social contract, however, took a highly philosophical form at the hands of Rousseau who reposed the fact of political obligation in the name of general will. He argues,

> The movement from the state of nature to the civil state produces a very remarkable change in man by substituting justice for instincts in his conduct, and giving his actions the morality they had formerly lacked. Then only when the voice of duty takes the place of impulses and appetites, does man, who so far had considered only himself, find that he is forced to act on different principles, and to consult his reason before listening to his inclinations.[13]

In this way after entering into a "civil society, man is no longer the slave of his mere impulses of appetite, he becomes the bound to obey the law of the general will which he prescribes to all including himself and that constitute his real liberty".[14] Social contract is the method on which a civil society and its terms and condition have been formulated by an agreement among its members that determines the laws of their association. Rousseau further says,

> The social contract discovers a form of association which will defend and protect with the whole common force the person and goods of each associate and while uniting himself with all, may still obey himself alone and remain as before. This the fundamental problem of which the social contract provides the solution.[15]

By giving up their rights, they actually create a new entity in the form of a public reason that would be directed by a general will. When people join the community, they willingly agree to comply with the general will of the community. The general will becomes the source of procedural norms and it implies to the general interest of the entire society. The fundamental question is that why do we need to institutionalise the normative principle of justice with the consent of all autonomous beings.

However, there have been disagreements among philosophers to implement social contract to establish civil society or state or any institution as a necessary tool to deliver justice. "The social contract theory was repudiated by Hume on the ground that there is no historical evidence to any contract, original or otherwise. His account of justice is based on convention and customs".[16] Hume's and his social contract theory does not have any historical and philosophical ground. Martha C. Nussbaum observes the lacuna in Hume's argument on justice. In *Frontiers of Justice,* Nussbaum writes, "Like the contractarians, Hume relies on mutual advantage as the key to the emergence and maintenance of justice".[17] Whereas, the rule of justice depends on the particular state and conditions in which men are placed. For instance, the sense of justice will prevail when the condition is moderate in wealth and possessions once the rules of justice are framed and people see the usefulness of the rule that provide justice to all. That is why for Hume; justice is convention whose usefulness is directly proportional to the situation and circumstances wherein people are placed.

> Government for Hume is not always necessary nor is it possible for primitive societies to live without consent of the governed, neither are all men created free and equal. In the same way the foundations of government and the reason for its sovereignty and stability rest upon a far broader basis in the human nature than the simplest consent of the governed.[18]

For Hume, history does not reveal the origin of government and it is clear that to maintain justice in the state we don't need to enter into the contract to form a government. The authority of government is derived from force, custom and historic continuity.

Advancing Hume's criticism on social contract theory and the emergence of perfect justice, Hegel also strongly opposed the social contract because it has no historical foundation and the notion of justice is based on individual efforts towards absolute spirit through social interaction. Civil society is not based on institutional mechanism rather it is guided with human struggle for their rights. "Social contract theory could be explanatory as an ethical and logical advanced to provide a moral evaluation and reconstruction of constitution to justify an evaluation. But it certainly has no historical evidence".[19] Hegel was anti contracterian because he had a different understanding of the relationship between the individual and the civil society. According to Christopher J. Berry,

> Hegel's argument for the dismissal of the Social Contract is cantered on his depiction of the relationship between the individual, or citizen, and the State. To him, we are already citizens of the State by birth and given that the State is no mere administrative organ but mind or *Geist* objectified wherein freedom is actualized.[20]

In Hegel, state is nothing but mere agglomeration of individuals and the relation between them as a part and whole. He believes, "since the state is *Geist* objectified, it is only as one of its members that the individual himself has objectivity, genuine individuality, and an ethical life".[21] It is the individual as a member of the state that makes him spiritual and concrete universal. Hegel's chief criticism to the notion of the social contract is that,

> It operates with an abstract, a cultural and non-contextual view of man. That is to say that the idea of social contract has cogency only because it assumes that the individual (the outer), so that from this putative separateness, membership of the state can be optional and a matter of voluntary choice. This means that the state's existence now depends on the individual's capricious will through his individuality given consent.[23]

Hegel regarded *Geist* as the centre of the state. Since *Geist* is rational and the basic feature of rationality is its universality, therefore, the laws of the state should be known to all. In spite of criticism by Hume and Hegel on social contract, Kant uses this theory as a regulative mechanism in formulating the notion of perfect justice. Kant has argued social contract as an indispensible part for a perfect society in his work entitled "The Contractual Basis for a Just Society",

> In all social contracts, we find a union of many individuals for some common end which they all share. But a union as an end in itself which they all ought to share and which is thus an absolute and primary duty in all external relationships whatsoever among human beings (who cannot avoid mutually influencing one another), is only found in a society insofar as it constitutes a civil state, i.e. a commonwealth.[24]

It can be argue that among all the contracts by which people unites to form a society to establish an institution to have a just society. Kant holds civil state is regarded as purely a lawful state which is based on the fallowing *a priori* principles:

1. The *freedom* of every member of a society as a *human being*
2. The *equality* of each with all the others as a *subject*
3. The *independence* of each member of a commonwealth as a *citizen.*[25]

The first principle embodies the right of freedom belonging to each person as a member of the civil state, in so far as each is a being capable of possessing rights. The second principle is the idea of the equality of men as subjects in a civil state. Civil state is characterised by equality in the effects of freely willed actions which limit one another in accordance with the general law of freedom. Thus the birth right of each individual in such a state is absolutely equal and no members of the commonwealth can have hereditary privileges as against others. The third principle is the 'independence of a member of the commonwealth i.e., as a co legislator. Kant argues, "An individual will cannot legislate for a commonwealth. For this requires freedom, equality and unity of the will of all the members. And the prerequisite for unity, since it necessitates a general vote (if freedom and equality are both present), is independence".[25] A just society ought to be based on a fair system of cooperation among free and autonomous beings and the function of social contract is to protect individual's autonomy *for all and not for few.*

In Kant's view, social contract acts like the idea of reason rather than historically and empirically oriented concept. Kant's use of social contract as a public reason has brought common agreement and its legitimacy based on each and everyone's consent. Kant says in *Rechtslehre,* about the insight of social contract and why he has formulated social contract theory. Kant asserts that, "morality consists in the set of rules governing behaviour that rational people would accept, on the condition that others accept them as well".[26] It makes clear that, Kantian social agreement brings out from the morality that we ought to make an agreement so that it delivers impartial justice to all human beings. His entire theory of Justice is based on the consent of practical reason of enlightened being who makes a common principle for the welfare of a perfectly just society. He emphasizes that the individuals in the original contract are rational in the sense that they prefer to become members of a society whom they represent to obtain a greater rather than a lesser share of the benefit of social cooperation. The fact that the individuals are rational does not entail that they as the members of a society whom they represent are egoistic. Those members may, for example, wish to use a portion of their shares to promote for others benefit. He also emphasizes that the enlightened individuals are reasonable and they must be willing to reach to agreement with their counterparts on fair terms.

Kant's perfect justice presupposes by public right or autonomy to use public reason to enter into contract because public right is one of the necessary tools to evaluate if the formulated principle would be compatible for the betterment of society or not, just as the categorical imperative evaluates whether our action is compatible with universal code of conduct. As Jonathan David has argued in *A Brief History of Justice,*

> Public right by invoking the idea of the original contract is to test and evaluate the public laws and policies. If it is plausible to suppose that

the law or policy in question would have received the approval of all the members of a society in an original contract, then according to Kant, we must assume that that law or policy is just. If this supposition is implausible, then we may conclude that the law or policy is unjust.[27]

Kantian perfect justice evolved out of social consent to form an institution wherein sovereign and autonomous being makes an agreement about the principle of justice that acts only on that maxim through which you can at the same time will that it should become a universal law of justice. It is intended to explain the appropriate relationship between individuals and the society and their terms and conditions of the institution. It also implies that enlighten and moral being unite into political societies by a process of mutual consent to abide by the common rules and accept certain duties to protect themselves and others from any kind of injustices, violence and other kinds of harm, It is one of the vehicles in the civil society which promotes justice.

Kant's perfect justice implies that every enlightened and moral being in the society is represented by an end in itself or autonomous and sovereign being. It ensures that each and every individual ought to get equal treatment and value as a human and come together to reach an agreement for instance, principle of universal autonomy and dignity while treating humanity as an end rather as a means so that it can become universal principle of justice that shapes the very foundation in Kant's commonwealth or civil society. The method of social contract is to imagine that a commonwealth or civil society must be founded by an agreement among its members that determines the terms of their association. In ideal society everyone tries to inculcate the habit of enlightened and moral to formulate normative principle which could be applicable in the form of institutional mechanism to deliver universal justice. Kantian notion of contract is one of the foundational parameter to assess whether formulated norms are just or unjust. "For Kant, the idea of the original contract is the vehicle for determining whether or not laws and policies are just, much as the categorical imperative is the test for ascertaining whether or not individuals' maxims and discrete actions are rightful".[28] In perfect justice, social contract becomes evaluative tool to assess whether formulated principle is just or unjust. In the same way, Kant's categorical imperative becomes universal law of morality or moral code of conduct to assess individual's action is either right or wrong.

Thus social contract has been the dominant theory and it turns out to be the most appropriate normative model in the emergence of perfect society in today's world because it tries to protect individual's autonomy and dignity through institutional mechanism. However, social contract theory is in itself contested in the emergence of perfect justice because Hobbes's conception of justice underlies lies in the hands of the Monarch whereas for Locke justice consists in the form of individual rights related to life, freedom and property. In other way, Rousseau regards it is the general will or moral collective will of the individuals in the society who will shape the laws of institutions which will deliver justice. Indeed the social contract theory was repudiated by Hume on the ground that there is no historical evidence to any contract, original or otherwise and his conception of justice is based on convention and customs. Despite of all criticism and contestation about social contract theory, Kant has used it as a regulative mechanism that helps to organize social affairs. In other words, social contract theory helps us to unite together to form an institution for a just society to protects individual's autonomy and dignity.

Part - II

Autonomy and Dignity as the Operative Terms for Perfect Justice

In formulating Kant's perfect justice, enlightenment rationality of autonomy and dignity play an important role. It is the stage where human autonomy and dignity ought to be treated equally in terms of their rights, freedom and moral worthiness. In Kant's view, freedom is a universal concept and it should not be restricted at personal level as it is a necessary presupposition of all action as well as of all thinking. Kant has argued in his article entitled "The Contractual Basis for a Just Society" that the freedom of every member of society as a human being and it is the principle for the constitution of a civil state.

> No one can compel me to be happy in accordance with his conception of the welfare of others, for each may seek his happiness in whatever way he sees fit, so long as he does not infringe upon the freedom of others to pursue a similar end which can be reconciled with the freedom of everyone else within a workable general law i. e., he must accord to others the same right as he enjoys himself.[29]

Freedom of man is the most essential basis to constitute a civil state where man's freedom can be expressed in the concept of human rights. It can be argue that each person has a right to dignity, and just treatment and reciprocal responsibility to ensure justice for others. By freedom,

Kant meant objective freedom of human beings who is free when he gladly wills to follow the laws of his own rational soul and the moral order of cosmos. Freedom does not mean the subjective freedom driven by desire for pleasure and feels free only when able to do whatever he wants. However, the notion of freedom is a complex concept throughout Kant's philosophy. "Within Kant's moral theory there are two main types of freedom: inner and outer freedom. Inner freedom is the primary subject of Kant's ethical theory while external freedom is the primary subject of Kant's theory of justice".[30] It may be pointed out that Kant's external freedom in the most general sense is independence of constraints imposed by others which makes an autonomous human being. Moreover from normative perspective, freedom is divided into two further categories; rightful external freedom and lawless or wild external freedom. The rightful external freedom is freedom of action circumscribed by law of justice. On the other hand, the lawless freedom is the unrestricted anarchic liberty of the state of nature. The purpose of justice for Kant is to distinguish right from lawless external freedom and to determine that which makes rightful freedom possible.

Kant's perfect justice presupposes on the principle of human freedom rather than principle of utility and happiness. In perfect justice utility cannot help to formulate the universal principle because it is unreliable in the way that no empirical foundation can secure the primacy of justice and sanctity of individual rights. It minimizes injustices and will be discussed later. As utilitarianism is a form of consequentialism where justice is based on the maximization of usefulness and welfare maximization where some individuals are used as a means for the good of others. According to Mill,

> Justice is not as fundamental as we often think. Rather, it is derived from the more basic standard of rightness, i.e., consequentialism: what is right is what has the best consequences (usually measured by the total or average welfare caused). So, the proper principles of justice are those which tend to have the best consequences.[31]

The sense of justice derived from the basic standard of rightness implies what is right is what has the best consequences. The proper principles of Justice are those which tend to have the best consequences. In this way the principle of utility introduces system into our judgments of justice where the moral worth of an action is determined by its outcome. Kant criticizes utilitarian conception of justice because it is unreliable in the way that no empirical foundation can secure the primacy of justice and sanctity of individual rights. According to Johnstone, "Kant empathetically rejected the assumption that the promotion of human enjoyment or happiness can never serve as a foundation for sound ideas about justice".[32] The notion of happiness varies from person to person, for instance, if A's interest is in playing football and B's interest is in studying then A will find his or her joy or happiness in playing football and B's happiness will depend on how well he or she studies. Individuals' views on the empirical end of happiness and their subjective desires can be brought neither under any common principle nor under any external law harmonising with the autonomy of everyone. Kant argues that "no general or universal conclusion about morality can be reached on the basis of happiness as the precepts of morality must by nature be universal commanding every person in the same way and taking no account on inclinations that vary from person to person".[33] It is moral and just for each human being to be allowed to pursue happiness in his or her own way and it is unjust to attempt to impose on human beings any particular conception of happiness.

Perfect justice in the form of autonomy evolved out of the universal principle of morality that is called categorical imperative. Kamenka Eugene has argued in her essay entitled "What is justice?"

> Justice is an act externally so that free exercises of your personal will could be brought under general law together with the freedom of everyone-consummates the separation between law and justice on the one hand as concerned only with external behaviour, and morality on the other hand as concerned with inner life.[34]

To Kamenka, justice and morality are inseparable from each other. Both are like the two sides of same coin, justice is primarily based on external life while morality is based on inner life. The morality deals with inner sense and justice deals with external behaviour of individual's. In other way, justice is not concerned with the feelings, wishes and desires of individual but relationship applies to external relation between individuals in so far as their action may affect each other directly or indirectly. In this way Kant's perfect justice is surrounded with autonomy of will and not heteronomy of will. Indeed justice underlies in autonomy of will so that person's autonomy can be universalised. "Justice is concerned simply with the problem of harmonizing individual wills by giving them universal autonomy compatible with similar autonomy for others".[35] Justice tries to give grounds for equal autonomy and dignity to build a society wherein each one would get equal opportunities to act on self imposed laws that would be consistent with universal principle of morality.

Perfect justice demands that people ought to be treated equally in terms of their rights namely autonomy and dignity and emphasises that enlightenment and moral ingredient ought to be universally applicable to all human being irrespective of any differences. These opportunities ought to be evaluated by a single universal law, that is, categorical imperative of moral principle so that each one would live a dignified life in the society. According to Rosen "Kantian justice is the aggregate of those conditions under which will of one person can be conjoined with the will of another in accordance with a universal law of freedom".[36] Its concern is to evolve the notion of universal autonomy so that everyone will get equal chance to become enlightened and moral. He further identifies three main characteristics in the concept of Kant's perfect justice.

> Firstly; the sense of justice applies to only external relation between individuals in so far as their action may affect each other directly or indirectly. Secondly, it is not concerned with the wishes or desire of an individual but solely with the relationship of will to another person's will. Thirdly, it deals only with the form of the relations between the will in so far as they are regarded as free. Synthesizing these three characteristics, Kant reaches to his definition of universal justice.[37]

The first principle of perfect justice consists in the notion of autonomy that each person must lead an autonomous life and there should be an institutional mechanism to preserve and protect their autonomy and sovereignty. In fact, Kant has developed individuals at the level of autonomy, sovereignty and dignity in order to substantiate the maxim of universality, end in itself and kingdom of ends in the doctrine of categorical imperatives. The categorical imperative is the most fundamental principle of morality that can be derived from the good will. Kant argued that we must have free will to follow the principle of categorical imperative. Perfect justice evolve at the notion of autonomy of every member of a society as a human being and its purpose is to demarcate an area of personal autonomy within which individuals are free to act as they want but it ought to be guided with moral law of categorical imperative.

Perfect justice is surrounded with free will or autonomy which Kant defines as, "free will as a kind of causality or a power of causal action belonging to living beings so far as they are rational. To describe such a will as free would be to say that it can act causally without being caused to do so by something other than itself."[38] However, it may be pointed out that person's free will in terms of practical reason follows its own commands to become just. In other way, it should not act for an inclination or passion or law which is not given by it to itself. When practical reason is free from passions and inclinations, it only has laws or, in practical terms, maxims as moral laws.

Free will is always law oriented but this law is not imposed by something other than itself. If laws would be other than itself, then they would merely be the laws of natural necessity. Kant says, "Free will is nothing but autonomy of the will is self-legislative. To escape the heteronomy of will, man acts in accordance with a law he gives himself. The only rational law man can abide is the categorical imperative".[39] Free will acts in accordance with moral reasoning and that's why individuals distinguish themselves from other life forms, and reach to some conclusions about rightness or wrongness of moral actions. This habit of moral reasoning provides individuals with some understanding of the categorical imperative. The sense of distinguishing between just and unjust action is evident through rational comprehension of the universal law which aims to protect freedom. Free will is the principle of moral laws and it will act under moral laws that what ought to be just under all circumstances.

To define autonomy in Kant's view, categorical imperative is one of the principles that could be taken into account. Kant's maxims of categorical imperative cannot be strange to any culture because they are universal. One can easily imagine that the absence of any maxim could be tantamount to the denial of the human rights in the form of autonomy and dignity. Therefore maxims could be regarded as the necessary principles for any study of human right. Now the basic question arises- what is a right and what is the right of humanity? Kant sometimes speaks of the right of humanity as the autonomy of each "to seek his happiness in whatever way seems best to him".[40] Every individual should lead an autonomous life and free to pursue one's own ends. As Kant has pointed in his book *The Moral Law: Groundwork of the Metaphysic of Morals,* "The literal meaning of autonomy is obedience to a self-imposed law".[41] It is clear that person's autonomy underlies in self imposed laws. In general sense, autonomy is regarded as basic human right particularly a right to determine oneself independent of other imposed laws. It is also called as self rule and self determination as it is based on the individual's ability to direct one's life according to rational principles of categorical imperative. Kant says, "Reason determines the will in a practical law that directly, not through an intervening feeling of pleasure or displeasure, even if this pleasure is taken in the law itself'.[42] It is clear that sense of autonomy is always guided through rational principle of human will. Moreover one can say that rationality is an autonomous source of individual's action. It is the property of rational being. Autonomy of human being is the property of it by which it is a law to itself independently of any property of objects of volition. In this regard Oliver Sensen also has argued in his book on *Kant on Moral Autonomy* that,

> Autonomy understood as individual independence from coercion in making decision- is variously considered to be a capacity all normal adults have, a goal one should strive for and especially a moral right one can claim. To violate a person's autonomy is considered to be a serious moral offense. Autonomy is put forth as a fundamental principle of human rights."[43]

The rights of autonomy help an individual to get rid of tradition and superstition and lead an authentic life. It also helps men to come out from ignorance to reach in the age of enlightened where autonomy guides how to use understanding. It gives men the capacity to engage in a continuing process of criticism and reevaluation in men. It provides the higher order capacity to choose his or her ends. The main requirement of enlightened and just man is that the choices be truly one's own that one must not have been manipulated, brainwashed or conditioned into making them. On the other hand, Jonathan Peterson argues in his article that is "Enlightenment and Freedom" that, "right of humanity is not defined as a right to the pursuit of happiness, but as a right not to be subject to the will of others".[44]

Moreover, Kantian notion of freedom implies in the act of independence from constrained by other's choices of individuals. Kant argues in *Science of* Right,

> The only original right, belonging to each man in virtue of his humanity is freedom .... And there is only one innate right, the birth right of freedom. Freedom is independence of the compulsory will of another; and in so far as it can coexist with the freedom of all according to a universal law, it is the one sole original, inborn right belonging to every man in virtue of his humanity. There is, indeed, an innate equality belonging to every man which consists in his right to be independent of being bound by others to anything more than that to which he may also reciprocally bind them.[45]

Freedom is the only original right that belongs to every individual by virtue of his humanity. Every human being has natural right i.e. right to freedom which ought not to be constrained by other human being. Each and every man is equal in terms of rights and the master of one's own right as a rational being. "Freedom which is independence from being constrained by another's choice insofar as it can coexist with the freedom of every other in accordance with a universallaw".[46] We can infer from the above statement that when Kant develops freedom as the only original right of man, and he proposes to limit that freedom in the case of each individual solely by the demand for an equal freedom on the part of all other individuals.

Freedom is independence of the heteronomy of the will of another and it can coexist with the freedom of all according to a universal law, that is, categorical imperative. The universal principle of rights assert that, "Every action is right which in itself, or in the maxim, on which it proceeds, is such that it can coexist along with the freedom of the will of each and all in action, according to a universal law".[47] It means that, one's autonomous action generally can coexist with the autonomy of others in according to a universal law. For instance, if any one does wrong to me and curtails or hinders me in the performance of this action then such hindrance and obstruction cannot coexist in accordance with the freedom of universal laws. It is evident for Kant that an action would be contrary to right if it interferes with the formal freedom of one's neighbour. For constructing the formula of autonomy, H J Paton says,

> Autonomy is derived from combining the formula of universal law and the end in itself. We have not only seen that we are bound to obey the law in virtue of its universality, we have also seen that rational agents are subjects are the ground of this categorical imperative. If this is so, the law of which we are bound to obey must be the product of our own will (so far as we are rational agents) - that is to say, it rests on 'the idea of the will of every rational being as a will which makes universal law.[48]

Autonomous being is capable to act in accordance with their maxim to make universal law of rights which make them to obey that law which is good for the sake of him and society as well. Kant has clearly made a distinction of autonomy of public and private rights in *Science of Rights,* "The right of freedom in terms of independence leads first to private right, which governs the interaction of free persons, and then to public right, which requires the creation of constitutional state".[49] Independence from external constraint is the basic principle of fundamental right. It guarantees equal freedom, and it requires that no person should be subject to the will of another. The core idea of autonomy here is an articulation of the distinction between persons and things. Human beings are possessed with will or practical reason whereas thing does not have will or practical reason. For Kant,

> Will is a kind of causality (a power of casual action) belonging to living being so far as they are rational. To describe such a will free would be to say that it can act causally without being caused to do so by something other than itself. Non rational beings can act causally only so far as they are caused to do so by something other than themselves. And this is what meant by natural necessity as opposed to freedom.[50]

A person is a being capable of setting his or her own purposes, while a thing is something that can be used in pursuit of purposes. It is well known saying that if 'A' causes 'B' to move because former has itself being caused to move by latter rather himself or herself caused would not acquire the sense of autonomy.

In the formulation of Kant's justice, nothing is required but autonomy of public use of one's reason at every point. Now the question arises what kind of freedom becomes barrier in the way of enlightenment? It is the restriction of freedom to use public reason which becomes obstacle in the process of enlightenment. Kant has rightly said,

> I hear on all sides, 'Do not argue' The Officer says: 'Do not argue but drill'. The tax collector: 'Do not argue but pay'. The cleric: 'Do not argue but believe!' Only one ruler in the world says, 'Argue as much as you will, and about what you will, but obey'. So, everywhere there is restriction on freedom. Which restriction is an obstacle to enlightenment, and which is not an obstacle but a promoter of it? I answer: The public use of one's reason must always be free, and it alone can bring about enlightenment among men. The private use of reason, on the other hand, may often be very narrowly restricted without particularly hindering the progress of enlightenment. By the public use of one's reason I understand the use, which a person makes of it as a scholar before the reading public. Private use I call that which one may make of it in a particular civilpost or office, whichis entrusted.[51]

If we undermine the autonomy of public use of reason by intolerance, Kant's enlightenment and perfect justice would be unachievable. Now it's necessary to discuss the distinction between public and private reason and what kind of freedom or autonomy promotes enlightenment and perfect justice. The private use of reason is the use of reason in the context of a civil or official role to which Kant expressed, "What I call the private use of reason is that which one may make of it in a certain civil post or office with which he is entrusted".[52] In contrast to private use of reason, the public use of one's reason deals with oneself as a freethinker. This type of reason is non-restrictive to the individual.

The autonomy of public use of reason ought to be free and not restricted by the authority. If the public use of reason is curtailed then individuals cannot become enlightened. It is one of the important rights of a person which helps a person to apply one's own reason for the betterment for him as well as humanity as a whole. Public use of reason is the moral obligation of authority to make public use of reason free so that each individual acts autonomously to become the member of Kant's enlightened age rather than age of enlightenment. It builds an autonomous nature to make a self-legislative law and is to rely on self-imposed laws that are evaluated with categorical imperative rather than hypothetical imperative. Unlike public use of reason, autonomy in the use of private reason is required when there is need to take a decision regarding official matters. For instance, the roles in which one can implement the private use of reason are army officer, and citizen as taxpayer and clergy man etc. In the case of the citizen as taxpayer and army officer is probably the most general example. The obedient citizen as a taxpayer has the duty to pay and obey the authority. It shows that the private use of reason is a matter of structures and relations of authority.

Kant has rightly said in his discussion, "example of clergy man and citizen as a taxpayer involves acting in the name of another and carrying out another's commission't.[53] In case of private use of reason, an individual act in accordance with the rule of authority. Although this does not preclude that someone in an official role may be required to exercise judgment in carrying out his or her tasks. It is clear that individual's uses of private reasons are bound to some extent. In the case of the citizens as a taxpayer, are to be bound by to pay and they will be bound by the law of authority. As a citizen, it is the moral and legal obligation to pay tax to the authority and follow the tax rule at any cost.

In Kant's perfect justice, autonomy in public use of reason shapes the foundation in constructing its principle because it evaluates whether formulated maxim would be compatible with the moral code of conduct or not. It becomes a foundational principle in the fallowing way:

1. "Public reason identifies the status of those who reason publicly in terms of membership in a community. In public reason, you regard yourself as a member of a whole commonwealth, even of the society of citizens of the world".[54] It ought to be free for every individual as members of society where they are living. It is quite general for the betterment for humanity as a whole.
2. Autonomous being regarded as an audience of public reason. Kant says, "Insofar as you see yourself as a member of the commonwealth of public reason, you address a public in the proper sense of the word. You speak for the betterment of public enlightenment to the public in the strict sense, that is, the world".[55] 69 Every enlightened person is free to use public reason to speak against government, if the authority is curtailing public rights of the individual.
3. "Kant elucidates the notion of private reason with the example of clergy. Like the first feature, it focuses on status and on the capacities to act that go along with that status".[56] In the case of clergy, the cleric propagates the idea of believe and not to argue, thereby, curtailing the freedom to clarify doubt. Hence, public reason cannot be realised in the case of clergy, unlike cases where one can argue with authority and clarify the doubt.
4. In the public use of reason, you speak in your own person. This feature of the account of public reason is particularly important, for it allows a clear distinction to be drawn between the public and private use of reason. The private use of reason is carried on in the name of another and involves carrying out another's commission, whereas the public use of reason is a matter of acting on your own[57] autonomy so that it becomes the universal law of autonomy.

In Kant's notion of perfect justice enlightenment and moral ingredient is an awakening call or message for each enlightened person ought to perform moral duty to bring humanity at the stage of progress. This can be possible when each autonomous being ought to impose a maxim such as the duty to use one's own understanding to make one's own progress and perfection as an end. It also states that one should acquire the duty of virtue to enhance oneself in terms of consciousness and other's consciousness as well with the help of public reason.

Kant's justice in the form of humanity and dignity has evolved out of free will, categorical imperative and finally culminates into good will which gives the vision on how human behaviour ought to be just and moral under all circumstances. Once individual become enlighten and moral, the habit of good will can be acquired. It inculcates the habit of moral and just to act in accordance with the universal principle of morality i.e. categorical imperative. Individual good will is the only jewel that shines intrinsically and it commands that one has to be just under all circumstances. It commands to act in accordance with the consciousness of duty and always act rationally for themselves and for others. Although, freedom can be misused, yet it is one feature that gives an insight of universal human dignity which promotes peace and harmony among all nations.

Kant's Good will is one of the foundational pillars of his notion of perfect justice especially in the form of autonomy and dignity. It gives the vision of perfect justice that can be applied under all circumstances. The principles of perfect justice are self-imposed laws and justice consists in obeying self-imposed laws which are coexistent with other rational self-imposed laws to fulfil the condition of universality and end in itself. Justice belongs to good will or rational will because it is the rational will that would autonomously act on self-imposed laws contributes in formulating the notion of perfect justice. According to Kant, "good will acts under the laws, but these laws could not be imposed on it by something other than itself; for if they were, they would merely be laws of necessity. If the laws of freedom cannot be other imposed they must be selfimposed".[58] That is to say that autonomy and dignity is identical with goodness and sense of justice. Indeed, Kant's absolute justice is possible with good will because it is guided with perfect and imperfect duty. Good will is surrounded with moral obligation to act in accordance with which one ought to be just. As Kant rightly said,

> Good will is unconditionally good and the absolutely good if it cannot be evil- i.e., if its maxim when made into a universal law can never be variance with itself. This principle is therefore also its supreme principle: Act always on the maxim whose universality as a law you can at the same time will.[59]

Dignity is also one of the foundational pillars in formulating the principle of perfect justice. The sense of dignity in Kant's perfect justice implies two senses namely; individual respect as a person and treatment of individual as an end. The notion of dignity has been deduced from second maxim of categorical imperative which asserts that we ought not to treat humanity as a means for something else. Kant argues, "Act in such a way that you always treat humanity, whether in your own person or in the person of any other, never simply as a means but always at the same time as an end".[60] However, it is important to clarify the distinction between means and ends while treating humanity. Human beings, at times are used as means to obtain some ends. Contrary to this, when human beings are understood as ends in themselves they are viewed with ultimate respect and moral worth. Objects and inclinations have only a conditional worth; their worth depends on the particular need with which they are linked. If that need becomes disassociated from inclination then it ceases to have value. That is why Kant holds that all objects have a conditional worth and makes a distinction between persons and objects. Persons are worthy of respect and dignity as an ends in themselves while objects exists solely to serve as means.

Kant's conception of dignity also teaches self-dignity as well as dignity of others. It is suggested that each individual is valuable in itself therefore; the act of suicide or killing of oneself is condemned. Apart from self dignity justice demands that people should be treated equally as an end in themselves rather than means to some end. This rationality would promote equality and justice, because the first duty of justice is never to treat people as a means to one's own end. But treating persons as an end in themselves is to do more than respect this duty and it is also to assist them in achieving their moral lawful ends.

Justice as a human dignity asserts that treating any individual as a means for oneself will not be compatible with the universal principle of moral code of conduct. As Kant rightly argued that, "the rights of human beings are rooted in the original right to freedom, which belongs to every human being by virtue of his or her humanity".[61] Each individual has inherent dignity in the form of basic right and it has to be respected by the individual and institutional level. He also argued that all human beings are inherently equal, in the sense that individual is entitled not to be bound by others. He asserts that all individuals of a state are entitled to being treated as equals by the laws, so that none should receive special privileges or be subject to unfavourable discrimination which entails injustice. It is the moral obligation to follow the laws of categorical imperative to treat humanity as an end so that the principle dignity can be universalized under all circumstances without discrimination. The categorical imperative is the universal moral code of conduct which commands that perfect justice could be achieved only while treating humanity equally. Its principle ought to underpin equal dignity for all persons regardless of any differences and it should be governed by the principle of reciprocity.

However treating humanity as an end is a matter of debate; why one should respect others? Is to respect others because of an absolute worth that is freedom or rational capacity to set ends? or because of the value of moral good will that they possess? Martha Nussbaum critiquing Kant's conception of dignity and respect is entirely dependent on person's rational capacity rather than emotional capacity in her recent book that is *Political Emotions Why Love Matters for Justice,*

> At the heart of our societies' conception is the idea of human equality. All human beings are of equal worth, and that worth is inherent or intrinsic: it does not depend on a relationship to others (such as being the wife of X, or the vessel of Y). This worth is equal: all human beings are worthy of equal respect or regard, just in virtue of their humanity. Although some past conceptions have held that this worth is dependent upon the possessions of some specific capacity, such as rational capacity, or a rather sophisticated ability to make moral choices, our nations do not say this. They are aware that humanity comes in many forms, and human beings with profound cognitive impairment are not less human or non human simply because they have little or no calculative capacity and little or no sophisticated moral capacity. Perhaps they lack those capacities, but possess the capacity for affection and delight, or the ability to perceive and respond to beauty - and it is invidious to say that those capacities are less worthy of our humanity than calculative capacities.[62]

Nussbaum further argues, the core values ofjust society is to respect equally to all human being which implies dignity of people who have any kind of impairment and provide them suitable support and care to live lives equally worthy of human dignity.

> In order to live well, people need food, care, protection and sustenance of many kinds. They also have deep needs for protected spheres of activity, such as religious freedom and the freedom of speech. It is not trivial, then, but profoundly damaging, to refuse people such

support. Thus deprived, people retain human dignity, since that is inalienable, but in the absence of suitable support and care they will not be able to live lives worthy of human dignity.[63]

Despite these criticisms, Kantian notion of dignity inculcates duty to live autonomously by accepting others as an autonomous being and promotes the habit of tolerance to live to get along and learning to get along. The sense of human dignity develops the concept of tolerance which states that one should respect others right and it should be reciprocal. Tolerance regulates human affairs in accordance with the principle of human rights, human goods and human bonds. The sense of toleration developed the concept of justice by setting human affairs in accordance with the principle of human rights and human bonds. It is a set of social or political practices of the acceptance of other's autonomy and dignity. The sense of justice would come if people will live peacefully and tolerate one another's way of life. It inculcates the habit of toleration and it makes individual to be a just by tolerating and giving respect to others right and freedom so that everyone irrespective of cast, creed, sex, and religion coexist and live peacefully and just fully. It is the enlightenment rationality presupposes human dignity which encourages each one ought to be tolerant towards other and accept their differences.

Kant's concept of tolerance is a duty to respect other's right which in return, allows them to have the same right to their beliefs, opinions, race, caste, creed, and sexuality and others. Respecting individuals means respecting individual's rationality, freedom and right. We must respect person because of their rationality."[64] It emphasised that each individual ought to be treated equally and can lead their life according to their self-interest. Monique Deveaux says,

> "Toleration, both historically and today, refers to the principle and practice of non-interference. A person or institution exercises tolerance by refraining from interfering with, and/or by extending a kind of permission to, practices or beliefs with which they disagree."[65] Tolerance is generally considered as the conditional acceptance of or non-interference of beliefs, actions or practices of others. The contemporary commentator on Kant, Onora O'Neill writes in book, *Constructions of Reason,*

> Toleration in the Kantian picture is then not only merely a political virtue or practice that would have to be a part of any achieved just polity or society. It is the only matrix within which a plurality

> of potentially reasoning beings can constitute the full authority of reason and so become able to debate without restrictions what a just political constitution might be."[66]

Tolerance is always right centric and has a permissive and reciprocal attitude toward others rights. It has the potential to debate without any restriction and reach to consensus through reasoning in formulating any political constitution. This shows that toleration unites and binds all human being into a just society where all human being can express themselves properly.

Thus perfect justice is the ultimate outcome of just man by giving equal autonomy and dignity to each and every individual as a human being. It focuses on human beings as free to make and transform themselves in accordance with their own critical rationality. In one aspect enlightenment rationality helps us to become just man by using one's own autonomy; the other aspect morality justifies the sense of human dignity. Kant's enlightenment rationality and morality gives us the value of autonomy and dignity to have a just society. The enlightenment rationality provides us freedom, equality, fraternity and justice by emphasising on equal freedom, universal right, and tolerance for others right, autonomy, public and private reason to every person as a human. Morality provides us a vision of human dignity which asserts everyone gets equal treatment in terms of their autonomy and dignity to become the enlightened man. Once the person leads his life autonomous and dignified, the person creates the habit of tolerance to live peacefully by accepting others autonomy and dignity.

Part - III

Universality, End in itself and Kingdom of ends as the Imperative for Perfect Justice

In Kant's perfect justice, once humanity reaches the stage of enlightenment and morality develops themselves to become autonomous and sovereign to act in conformity of categorical imperative, they realises ideals such as universality, end-in-itself, and kingdom of ends. This ideals impact a just society where each enlightened being can realize his/her betterment and betterment of the entire society. In *Groundwork oj Metaphysic oj Morals* Kant offered "three universal moral codes namely universality, end in itself and kingdom of ends"[67] as the imperative for Kant's perfect society. In fact his notion of just society is based on deontological view that asserts each individual should act in such a way so that their action can be compatible with the maxims of categorical imperative namely universality, end in itself and kingdom of ends.

Kantian notion of justice is looking for some insight to make people autonomous and sovereign so that their maxim becomes the foundational principle. Perfect justice in the principle of universality demands that individual action and social institution ought not to be based on the principle of inclination, coercion, inequality, violence and deception because it cannot be universalized.

Those who are at a given time the victims of coercion cannot act freely therefore, they cannot make coercion their own principle. Equally, action on a principle of violence or inequality damages or curtails the autonomy of individuals to some extent and so it cannot be universally acted on. There should be no occasion under which an exception of injustice regarding discrimination on individual's autonomy is made. It deals with the principle of common autonomy on the basis of general law which applies to everyone under all circumstances.

The universality of morality shapes the foundation of perfect justice. Justice in the form of universality implies that autonomy and dignity ought to be guided in such a way that it becomes the universal law of autonomy. Kant's principle of justice deduced from the formula of universal law of categorical imperative states, "so act that the maxim of your will could always hold at the same time through which you can as a principle establishing universal law".[68] It is proposed that we ask ourselves whether the maxim by which we propose to guide our actions can simultaneously will that all others should act on. The point is to consider what we can consistently will, must be done, not only by ourselves but also by all others. In accepting and fallowing the categorical imperative we accept the moral reality and the principle of perfect justice.

It is the universality which becomes the guidelines of our action and it can simultaneously encourage the others ought to act in such a manner and can be share by all. In formulating principle of universal justice, Kant's perfect duties play an important role because it does not allows any exception in the interests of inclination. The question is what is perfect and imperfect duty? Perfect duty is the duty towards self and imperfect duty is towards others. According to Kant,

> A perfect duty is one which admits of no exception in the interests of inclination. Under this heading the examples given are the ban on

> suicide and on making a false promise in order to receive a loan. We are not entitled to commit suicide because we have a strong inclination to do so, nor are we entitled to pay our debt to one man and not to another because we happen to like him better. In the case of imperfect duties the position is different: we are bound only to adopt the maxim of developing our talents and of helping others and we are to some extent entitled to decide arbitrarily which talents we develop and which persons we will help.[69]

Perfect and imperfect duties serve as the criteria for maxim of universality. Onara O'Neill writes,

> These two aspects of formula for universal law are to serve as the criteria for maxims of strict (or perfect), and of wide (or imperfect) duties. Kant brings duties of justice and of respect for self and others under the first heading, and duties of beneficence and self-development under the second.[70]

With the performance of perfect duties, enlightened being can bring sense of equality, peace, harmony, dignity and justice for themselves and others as well. On other hand, imperfect duties of beneficence and self-development also contribute in bringing enlightenment and justice by using their autonomy in just manner.

Universality in perfect justice categorically commands that enlightened persons ought to perform perfect duties not only in external sense but in inner sense as well. It states that enlightened and moral persons ought to act on that maxim through perfect and imperfect duties which will become the universal principle of justice. However, "principle of justice could be fixed by constructing principle of obligation rather than of entitlement".[71] As in the tradition of social contract approach, the principle of Justice gets formulated in obligation rather than entitlements. Kant's constructivist approach to justice lies in the principle of obligation and its reciprocal attitude of enlightened being. Thus, Kant's categorical imperative commands that every individual ought to perform the perfect and imperfect duties for maintaining just to him/her and for the sake of society as well.

Kant's perfect justice concerns in self-imposed laws by one enlightened person that ought to coexist with others self-imposed laws to formulate a universal law of justice that enables freedom, right, autonomy and respect for others should universally manifest in the hands of all human beings. The purpose of Justice is to make people autonomous so that they can act according to the selfimposed maxims that coexists with others maxim to become universal principle of justice. Perfect justice implies in the sense of human autonomy and it is deduced formula of universal law of categorical imperative of the moral law. "Act only on that maxim through which you can at the same time will that it should become a universal law".[72] It commands that we always act in such a manner so that it universalize. It also presupposes that human autonomy ought to be regulated and governed with practical rule determined by reason and not from ignorance and lack of understanding so that autonomous action can fulfil the universal law of nature. For Kant, "Act as if the maxim of your action were to become through your will a universal law of nature".[73] Justice in the form of universality asserts that we ought to fulfil the condition of universality in dealing with perfect duties or duties towards self and imperfect duty or duty towards others. H. J. Paton says,

> A man feels sick of life as the result of series of misfortunes that has mounted to the point of despair but he is still so far in possession of his reason as to ask himself whether taking his own life may not be contrary to his duty to himself. He now applies the test 'can the maxim of my action really becomes a universal law of nature?[74]

In this way, any person can kill him/ her out of misfortune and his/ her self love maxim of action cannot become universal law of nature. This subjective maxim done out of inclination and consequences in the form of misfortune is not compatible with moral duty especially duties towards self. It is the perfect justice which is not concerned with the protection and regulation of juridical duties but ethical duties as well. It tells that enlighten and moral being to act rationally so that their autonomous subjective maxim can be compatible with other autonomous being and finally it lead an universal law of autonomy.

Kant's purpose is to universalise autonomy of will rather than heteronomy of will because latter cannot be harmonised with other's autonomy in formulating perfect justice. As Kantian justice is presupposed in universality of right, autonomy, toleration and other social opportunities, to make individual autonomous and dignified to act on the universal maxim of action so that it becomes the principle of perfect justice. Justice evolved out of universality which eradicates all kinds of discrimination in the context of enlightenment ingredient such as right, autonomy, toleration public and private use of reason. It is unjust to deprive other's autonomy and dignity because in that case the right of autonomy cannot be universalised. If it was made a universal rule then inequality in terms of autonomy has to be removed. The maxim makes it clear that it is unjust to curtail or not tolerate others autonomy and dignity because it cannot become the universal principle of justice. And if this inequality would be removed then one's autonomy would be compatible with others autonomy to fulfil certain condition of the universality. If intolerable attitude would be practice by all persons then there would be no person left to tolerate other's autonomy and dignity. That is why Kant's notion of justice states that to tolerate other's autonomy in such a way that everyone else should tolerate and give respect to each other under the same general condition. This is the first maxim of absolute justice that commands each enlightened and moral person to tolerate others autonomy, right and not to act in such a way that can curtail others freedom which culminate in the form of dignified lives in a just society. Otherwise, Kant's vision of justice in the form of universality would be unachievable.

The idea of second maxims that is, 'end in itself underlies the vision of perfect justice in the form of human dignity and their value. It implies the notion that humanity has a right of autonomy and their treatment as an end in itself. It commands that humanity has absolute right of autonomy and their absolute worthiness. Kant considered "All enlightened persons, regarded as *hominess noumena,* should be equally treated".[75] This treatment ought to be regulated in the form of balanced reciprocity as the basis of just relations among all people. We can achieve the sense of justice in the society wherein every member reciprocally respect each other's autonomy and dignity and by refraining from violations of their rights. It is clear that the attitude of reciprocity plays an important role in just treatment. For Kant, "all our ethical duties arise from the obligation to make each human being's capacity for autonomous choice the condition of the value of every other end".[76] A person can be made enlightened and perfect because the person can control his/her will and make it conform to the moral law. However one can never make other individual autonomous and enlightened because one could not control others wills. Autonomous and sovereign will can only be cultivated by a person himself. Perfection and enlightenment is to be achieved and not to be given. Kant's principle of end in itself underlies in perfect society where every enlightened being makes a general consent in formulating the principles of Justice which transforms an individual behaviour in such a way that they can act rationally to transform oneself and the society as well.

Perfect justice demands that people should be treated equally as this rationality would promote harmony and justice, because the first duty of

Justice is never to treat people as a means to one's own end. Treating persons as an end in themselves is to do more respect and it is also to assist them in achieving their moral lawful ends. On this subject matter, Kant writes,

> The categorical imperative in the maxim of end-in-itself states that in the order of ends, man and every rational being is an end in itself i.e. he is never to be used merely as a means for someone (even for God) without at the same time being himself an end, and that thus the humanity in our person must itself be holy to us, because man is subject to the moral law and therefore to the subject to that which is of itself holy and it is only on account of this and in agreement with this that anything can be called holy.[77]

The attitude towards end in itself IS deduced from the categorical imperative based on the autonomy of a person's will as a free will which ought to be compatible with treating others as an autonomous being. Its massage is to give all enlightened individuals what they ought to do to maintain harmony and justice among individuals by respecting their dignity as a human being. It states that willing a just maxim on the basis of universal law, it has to be maintained that the willing of this kind is always to be considered as an absolute end and never simply as a means. Kant mentions, "Every human being exists as an end in itself, not merely as a means for arbitrary use of will; he must in all his actions, whether they are directed to himself or to other beings always viewed as the same time as an end".[78] It is the moral law in the form of perfect and imperfect duties that commands us always to treat others as an end in themselves or equal absolute worth, and not merely as a means or worth for the sake of something else. However this maxim does not forbid us to use others enlightened being so long as their fundamental autonomy is not curtailed and abused by others. Our equal and just relation to others form the matter or basis for the principle of perfect justice. It gives the matter of universal principle of justice that how to treat and respect others with dignity as an objective reality rather as a subjective reality so that it ought to universalized. Its purpose would be achieved when every enlightened being treats other being with respect and dignity and never try to use them for the sake of one's own ends. For example, if I am treating others as forced labour and coerce them to do what I want them to do, then I am treating them as a means for the sake of my own needs, which is unjust and cannot be universalized. The maxim of treating people as an end in itself is to treat them with respect and dignity which contributes in the Kant's kingdom of ends.

Following the principle of end in itself, Kant's third maxim i.e. 'kingdom of ends' underlies the vision of perfect society where everyone would become enlighten and moral. Kant says, "Kingdom as a systematic union of different rational beings under common laws"[79]. It is an enlightened society where every autonomous being derives their action from the maxim of universal law and considers themselves and others in this society as an end not as means to maintain peace and harmony. It attempts to bring out complete justice and harmony between the maxim of universal law and the maxim of end in itself which commands rational being in the maxim: "So act as if you were through your maxims a law making member of a kingdom of an ends"80. This means that the action should be consistent with universal law in which people are treated as an end in themselves. It is a harmony of ends in that its member can act only on the maxims that can meet everyone's consent and they respect one another as a rational self-determining agent.

The kingdom of ends promotes a just society or an idea of intelligible world where every individual acts as an enlightened being so that we would live in enlightened age or society. Kant's just society ought to be realized when everyone perform their duties namely, ethical duties and juridical duties. The former is duty to oneself and the latter is duty to others. Ethical duties to oneself include both perfect and imperfect, and also duties of respect to others. This duty inculcates the habit of mutual relation among all individual irrespective of any differences of caste, creed, race, sex and religion. Kant's kingdom of ends is the vision of perfect and enlightened society that encourage each autonomous person what one ought to perform ethical and juridical duty to bring humanity at the stage of progress. It states that one should acquire the duty of virtue to become enlighten and moral, realise own goodness, and promote goodness of others also.

In the kingdom of ends, enlightened being dissolves all kind of prejudices and discriminations because they combine the principle of universal law and end in itself to construct the common laws that unites every human being. The former specifying the form that maxim of duty must have, and latter determining matter or end that they must have. It creates such society where the particular objects of desire that autonomous being pursues are constrained by the universally willed categorical imperative. In this way enlightened person construct the principle of justice that could be absolute in nature. They realize that everything in nature works in accordance with laws. It is moral obligation to follow the laws of categorical imperative to maintain a just society where enlightened person does not consider himself as a part of sensible world from which their inclinations and heteronomy of will as moral principles derive as a result of natural causality.

On the other hand they can think of themselves as belonging to an "intelligible world from which their duties derive as a result of the moral law"81. This intelligible society would inculcate moral responsibility and juridical responsibility to promotes justice for himself and the society as well. It fills the gap between Kant's age of enlightenment and enlightened age where everyone becomes enlightened rather than few. In this society each enlightened and moral person act in their subjective maxim in such a way that to will their maxim would be objectified with universal law of categorical imperative. It inculcates the reciprocal attitude toward others right, autonomy, freedom and especially to respect others who have different opinions, religious belief, race and practices. Thus, Kantian notion of kingdom of ends help each individual to become just man by inculcating the habit of autonomy, tolerance and dignified life to lead peacefully by accepting others. It promotes virtue that inculcates the habit to live peacefully and to get along with others.

Kant's perfect justice transform each and every individual into enlightened and moral being to act in the conformity of categorical imperative to accept an ideal such as universality, end in itself, and the kingdom of ends. It is true that once each individual becomes enlightened and moral, they can act in such a way that their subjective maxim contributes in fulfilling the criteria of universality while treating oneself and others as a moral worth which leads Kingdom of ends. It is the universality and human value as an end in itself to construct a just society which automatically fulfils the purpose of Kant's kingdom of ends where every enlightened being would be free and equal to each other to pursue their wellbeing for themselves and society as well. This perfect society will reaches at the level of well-ordered society where each one will act in conformity of Kant's perfect and imperfect duty for the betterment for himself and others.

To bring this chapter an end, I can say that, perfect justice is one of the important notions in its debate that how *justice ought* to be rather than *what is just?* Kant's contribution lies in formulating justice in terms of perfect, and ideal could be presupposed in making any judgment on justice. This concept of justice is surrounded with human relation and their value rather than the distribution of resources. It lies at the centre of individual's concern and how humanity understands their relations with one another in terms of autonomy and dignity. In fact Kant's enlightenment rationality encourages us to become enlightened by overcoming immaturity and self-incurred habit while using one's own understanding to use their autonomy and dignity for the sake of themselves and others. The vision of perfect society could be achieved when everyone would become enlightened and act in such a manner so that their action ought to be compatible with universal law of nature.

Perfect justice evolved out of enlightened and moral being to reach in a mutual consensus through contract to formulate the principle of justicebetterment for the sake of the individual and also for the entire society. Its purpose is to maintain social relation of mutual respect, human dignity, tolerance, right and reciprocity among autonomous and equal individuals in the society. InKant's view, a just institution or society is one whose principal goal is to maintain social relations of autonomy, mutual respect and toleration among free and equal citizens with the help of social contract to formulate institutional norms which ensure impartial justice to all.

At the time of pre-enlightenment the human society was under monarchy system where rights and privileges were found in the hands of very few people, *not all.* It was Hobbes, Locke and Rousseau who brought the concept of social contract in the form of human rights to establish an institution which deliver justice *for all,* not *few.* They propounded that people should have natural right to enter into social agreement to establish institutions. Their notion of justice emerged in the struggle against monarchy and hereditary privileges. However, Kant uses social contract method as regulative mechanism which regulates social affairs just as categorical imperative evaluates individual action whether just or unjust. So justice in Kant's is based on the institutional mechanism by the enlightened and moral being that evolves from immaturity to maturity and formulates principle of justice. This kind of justice as an institution tries to remove discrimination among human beings on the ground of individual's caste, creed, sex, race, and treats them with equal dignity and moral worth of all being. It regulates the mutual toleration between individuals and groups and builds an environment conducive for everyone to get equal opportunities to become just for themselves and others as well.

In Kant, the quest of justice is to aim at evolving reasonable rules on human autonomy, toleration and dignity it should be applied impartially to all. Here, the core commitments of perfect justice. Justice consists of applying general rules impartially to all human regardless of their circumstances or differences in the society. In other way justice in the principle of universal norms that is the concept of justice regulated in the form institutional mechanism and it exists in institution or rules of law. It can also be argue that justice entails about basic individual rights such as right to autonomy, toleration, dignity and the autonomy public right.

Last but not least, perfect justice tries to explicate Kant's project of age of enlightened wherein each individual pursue their lives with rationality and morality to become just for themselves and others at large. It underlies the vision of the moral and enlightened man to construct such a society where every individual ought to lead their life for the betterment of themselves and the society. This would be possible once humanity becomes autonomous and sovereign to act freely and acquire the habit of tolerance because tolerance is the reciprocal attitude toward others who have different opinions, religious belief, race and practices. Perfect justice shapes the very foundation of Kant's enlightened society to inculcate the habit of tolerance and respect to live peacefully by accepting others' dignity, right and autonomy. It acts as a virtue which promotes social justice to live and get along with others.

References

Kant, Immanuel. "What is Enlightenment"? (1784). *On History.* Edited & Translated by Lewis White Beck. New York: Macmillan, 1963.

Kant, Immanuel. *Critique of Judgment.* Translated by Welner S Pulhar. New York: Indianapolis, 1987.

Schmidt, James. "On the Question What is Enlightenment"? *What Is* Enlightenment? Eighteenth Century Answers and Twentieth-Century Questions. edited by Moses Mendelssohn. 53-57. London: University of California Press, 1996.

Singh, R P. *Freedom and Causation with Special Reference to Hegel's Overcoming ofKant.* New Delhi: Om Publications, 2000.

Hume, David. *Political Essays.* New York: The Liberal Arts Press, 1953.

Kant, Immanuel. *Perpetual Peace: A Philosophical Essay.* Translated by Marry Campbell Smith. London: George Allen and Unwin Ltd, 1795.

Harris, A Edward. "From Social Contract to Hypothetical Agreement: Consent and the Obligation to Obey the Law," *Columbia Law Review* 92, no. 3,1992: 651683.

Irwin, Edman. *The Works of Plato.* Translated by Benjamin Jowett. UK: The Modem Library, 1965.

Hobbes, Thomas. *Leviathan.* Edited by Richard Tuck. UK: Cambridge University Press, 1991.

Locke, John. *Two Treatises of Government.* Edited by Laslett Peter. U.K: Cambridge University Press, 1960.

Rousseau, Jacques Jean. *The Social Contract.* Translated by Maurice Cranston. England: Penguin Books Limited, 1968.

Nussbaum, C Martha. "Social Contract and Three Unsolved Problems of Justice," *Frontiers of Justice Disability, Nationality, Species Membership.* New Delhi: Oxford University Press, 2006.

Christopher J Berry. "From Hume to Hegel: The Case of the Social Contract. *Journal of the History of Ideas* 38, *noA.* 1977: 691-703.

Kant, "The Contractual Basis for a Just Society" in *Justice : Alternative Political Perspectives. Justice: Alternative Political Perspectives.* Edited by James P. Sterba. Canada: Wodswort/ Thomson Learning, 2003.

Kant, Immanuel. *Rechtslehre Einleitung, pAO,* Quatation taken from Vaughan, C.E. *Studies in the history of Political Philosophy before and After Rousseau.* Manchester: Manchester University Press, 1939.

Johnston, David. "Kant's Theory of Justice," *A BriefHistory of Justice.* Edited by David Johnston. 143-165. United Kingdom: Willy Blackwell, 2011.

Kant, Immanuel. *The Doctrine of Virtue: Part 2 of the Metaphysic of Morals.* Translated by Mary J. Gregor. Philadelphia: University of Pennsylvania Press, 1964.

Kamenka, Eugene. "What is justice?". *Ideas and Ideologies Justice.* Edited by Eugene Kamenka. London: Edward Arnold Ltd, 1979.

Rosen, D Allen. *Kant's Theory of Justice.* Itchaca: Cornell U.P, 1993.

Kant, Immanuel. *The Moral Law: Groundwork of the Metaphysic of Morals.* Edited by H. J Paton. London: Hutchinson University Library, 1969.

Peterson, Jonathon. Enlightenment and Freedom. *Journal of the History of Philosophy* 46, no. 2, 2008: 223-44.

Kant, Immanuel. *Critique of Practical Reason.* Translated by L.W. Beck. New York: Liberal Arts Press, 1956.

Sensen, Oliver. "Kantian Autonomy and Contemporaries Ideas of Autonomy", *Kant on Moral Autonomy.* Edited by Thomas E Hill Jr. 15-30. New York: Cambridge University Press, 2013.

Kant, Immanuel. 1790. *Science of Right* Translated by W, Hasti. e:Books@Adelaide 2009.

Kant, Immanuel. *The Moral Law: Groundwork of the Metaphysic of Morals.* Edited by H. J Paton. London: Hutchinson University Library, 1969.

Nussbaum, C Martha. *Political Emotions Why Love Matters for Justice.* Cambridge: Harvard University Press, 2013.

Noggle. "Kantian Respect and Particular Person". *Canadian Journal of Philosophy* 29, no.3, 1999: 449-478.

Deveaux, Monique "Toleration and Respect", *Public Affairs Quarterly,* Vol. 12, No. 4, 1998, pp. 407-427.

O'Neill, Onora. *Constructions of Reason: Explorations of Kant's Practical Philosophy.* USA: Cambridge University Press, 1989.

Kant, Immanuel. *Critique of Practical Reason.* Translated by L.W. Beck. New York: Liberal Arts Press, 1956.

Korsgaard, M Christine. *The Sources of Normativity.* Cambridge: Cambridge University Press, 1996.

Kant, Immanuel. *Practical Philosophy.* Edited by M. Gregor. U.K: Cambridge University Press, 1996.

Notes

1. Kant. "What is Enlightenment?". *On History* . p. 36.
2. Kant. *Critique of Judgment.* pp. 160-161.
3. Schmidt, James. "On the Question: What is Enlightenment"? *What* is *Enlightenment Eighteenth Century Answers and Twentieth-Century Questions.* p. 30.
4. *Ibid,* p. 58.
5. Singh, R P. *Freedom and Causation with Special Reference to Hegel's Overcoming of Kant.* p. 32.
6. Hume, *Political Essays.* p. 21.
7. Kant, *Perpetual Peace: A Philosophical Essay.* (1795). p. 54.
8. Harris, A Edward. "From Social Contract to Hypothetical Agreement: Consent and the Obligation to Obey the Law". pp. 651-683.
9. *Ibid,* p. 652.
10. Irwin, *The Works ofPlato.* p. 102.
11. Hobbes. *Leviathan.* p. 91.
12. Locke. *Two Treatises ofGovernment.* p. 52.
13. Rousseau. *The Social Contract.* p. 46.
14. *Ibid.* pp. 46-48.
15. *Ibid.* p. 49.
16. Hume, *Political Essays.* p. 21.
17. Nussbaum. "Social Contract and Three Unsolved Problems of Justice," *Frontiers of Justice Disability, Nationality, Species Membership.* p. 46.
18. Singh, R P. *Freedom and Causation with Special Reference to Hegel's Overcoming of Kant.* p. 104.
19. *Ibid,* p. 102.
20. Christopher. "From Hume to Hegel: The Case of the Social Contract". pp. 691-703.
21. Singh, R P. *Freedom and Causation with Special Reference to Hegel's Overcoming of Kant.* p. 103.
22. *Ibid.* p. 103.
23. Kant, "The Contractual Basis for a Just Society" in *Justice : Alternative Political Perspectives.* p. 102.
24. *Ibid,* p. 102.
25. *Ibid,* p .l 04.

26. Kant, *Rechtslehre Einleitung.* Quatation taken from Vaughan, CE. *Studies in the history of* Political Philosophy before and After Rousseau. p. 40.
27. Johnston, "Kant's Theory of Justice," *A Brief History of Justice.* p. 210.
28. *Ibid,* p. 164.
29. Kant, "The Contractual Basis for a Just Society" *Justice: Alternative Political Perspectives.* p. 102.
30. Kant, *Doctrine of Virtue. Part 2 of the Metaphysic of Morals.* p. 213.
31. Mill, "Utilitarianism", *On Liberty and Other Essay.* p. 5.
32. Johnston. "Kant's Theory of Justice", *A Brief History of Justice.* p. 142.
33. *Ibid,* p. 144.
34. Kamenka, Eugene. "What is justice?" *Ideas and Ideologies Justice.* p. 21.
35. *Ibid,* p. 22.
36. Rosen. *Kant's Theory of Justice.* p. 75.
37. *Ibid.,* pp. 75-76.
38. Kant, *The Moral Law: Groundwork of the Metaphysic of Morals.* p. 41.
39. *Ibid,* p. 49.
40. Peterson, Jonathon. "Enlightenment and Freedom". pp. 223-44.
41. Kant. *The Moral Law: Groundwork of the Metaphysic of Morals.* pp. 54-55.
42. Kant. *Critique of Practical Reason* . p. 24.
43. Sensen, Oliver. "Kantian Autonomy and Contemporaries Ideas of Autonomy", *Kant on Moral Autonomy.* p. 29.
44. Peterson. "Enlightenment and Freedom". pp. 223-44.
45. Kant. *Science of Right.* p. 6.
46. Kant. *The Moral Law: Groundwork of the Metaphysic of Morals.* p. 12.
47. *Ibid,* p. 2.
48. *Ibid,* p. 34.
49. Kant. *Science of Right.* p. 12.
50. Kant. *The Moral Law: Groundwork of the Metaphysic of Morals.* p. 41.
51. Kant. "An Answer to the Question: What is Enlightenment?". pp. 58-60.
52. *Ibid,* p. 60.
53. *Ibid.* p. 63.
54. Peterson, "Enlightenment and Freedom". pp. 223-44.
55. *Ibid,* p. 228.
56. *Ibid,* pp. 228-230.
57. Kant. "An Answer to the Question: What is Enlightenment?". pp. 58-62.
58. *Ibid,* p. 39.
59. Kant. *The Moral Law: Kant's Groundwork of Metaphysic of Morals.* p. 104.
60. Kant. *The Moral Law: Groundwork of the Metaphysic of Morals.* p. 32.
61. Kant. *Science of Right.* p. 6.
62. Nussbaum, *Political Emotions Why Love Matters for Justice.* pp. 119-120.
63. *Ibid,* p. 120.

64. Noggle."Kantian Respect and Particular Person". pp. 449-478.
65. Deveaux, Monique. "Toleration and Respect". pp. 407-427.
66. O'Neill. *Constructions of Reason: Explorations of Kant's Practical Philosophy.* p. 50.
67. Kant. *The Moral Law: Ground Work of Metaphysic of Morals.* p. 29.
68. Kant. *Critique of Practical Reason.* p. 30.
69. Kant. *The Moral Law: Ground Work of Metaphysic of Morals.* p. 31.
70. O'Neill. *Constructions of Reason: Explorations of Kant's Practical Philosophy.* pp. 2013-14.
71. *Ibid,* p. 214.
72. Kant, *The Moral Law: Ground Work of Metaphysic of Morals.* p. 29.
73. *Ibid,* p. 88.
74. *Ibid,* p. 89.
75. Johnston. "Kant's Theory of Justice". *A Brief History of Justice.* p. 164.
76. Korsgaard, M Christine. *The Sources of Normativity.* p. 331.
77. Kant. *The Moral Law: Ground Work of Metaphysic of Morals.* p. 136.
78. *Ibid.* p. 101.
79. *Ibid,* p. 33.
80. *Ibid,* p. 34.
81. Kant. *Practical Philosophy.* p. 99.

Chapter - 2

John Rawls on Distributive Justice: An Exposition

Distributive justice is concerned with the question of how benefits and burdens, and in particular how economic resources, should be allocated. Rawls has revived social contract theory as transcendental mechanism to explain the principle of distributive justice with reference to institutions. In Rawls's "justice as fairness"[1] concerned about 'just institutions' rather than focusing on 'just societies' which help to create effective intuitions and reduce injustices and inequality as well. The institutions are specified and integrated into a social system which deeply affects people's characters, desires, and plans and their future prospects as well as the kind of persons they aspire to be. Then the question arises: is justice the realization of institutions and rules or principles or is it concerned with the society as well? I will try to attempt to vindicate Rawls' position on justice and bring out its shortcomings in two fold manner; first the way Rawls has criticized his own earlier position in his later work and secondly the way his successors like Amartya Sen, Alasdair MacIntyre and others have criticized the positions of Rawls.

Rawls's central concept of perfect justice revolves around the idea of fair institutional arrangements and according to him, "justice is the first virtue of social institutions, as truth is of system of thought."[2] Justice as a virtue implies norms that enable us in assessing how societies ought to be fair in terms of distribution of resources, exactly in the way truth is the criteria that assesses the validity of judgments, discourses, arguments, theories etc. Justice demands that social institutions must be well organized and arranged so that members of the society would get equitable distribution of resources to fulfill their expectations and aspirations at individual and social level.

Rawls's distributive justice underlies in the form of perfect society where rights and liberties ought to be fairly distributed because justice is distinct from benevolence, charity, mercy, generosity or compassion. It presupposes fair or just distribution of wealth and resources in society, however; fair or just distribution consists in various institutional arrangements of equal, meritocratic, according to status or some other ways. His vision of perfect justice underlies about organizing and governing a society wherein people would cultivate the virtue of cooperation to enter into mutual consensus to have the sense of justice. He believed that "society as a fair system of cooperation. It is a cooperative venture between free and equal persons for the purpose of mutual advantage".[3] In this way Cooperation is one of the basic requirements of any society because it makes social life better.

For the sake of clarity and precision, I shall divide the present chapter into three parts. In Part I, I will examine Rawls's theory of distributive justice with reference to institutions where, every individual abides by the rules of social contract in the form of original position to establish a well ordered society. In Part II, I will analyze Rawls's justice as fairness with the help of "original position behind a veil of ignorance in formulating two principles of justice".[4] The sense of fairness presupposes under veil of ignorance with the focuses on just institutions. In Part III, I will develop Rawls's notion of Justice in the form of liberty, equality and fraternity. While analyzing the contents of Rawls' two principles of justice i.e. liberty and equality, I will substantiate not only the notion of liberty and equality but the values of fraternity which is one of the important condition in order to have a sense of Justice.

Before coming to the basic issues which I shall be dealing in the above three parts, I would like to point out that perfect justice has been carried forward by Rawls by modifying social contract theory to formulate the principles of distributive justice. Rawls's distributive justice primarily concerned with the fair allocation of resources among diverse members of a community. For Rawls, the general conception of distributive justice is that, "all social primary goods liberty and opportunity, income and wealth, and the bases of self-respect-are to be distributed equally unless an unequal distribution of any or all of these goods is to the advantage of the least favoured".[5] Fair allocation implies "social goods to be distributed equally" among all individuals with the exception of those who are *less well off* so that the vision of fairness could be achieved.

Historically, Aristotle is the first philosopher who has developed distributive justice, in Book V of *The Nichomachean Ethics,* where he says that, "justice is summed up the whole of virtue. It is complete virtue in the fullest sense, because it is the active exercise of complete virtue and it is complete because its possessor can exercise it in relation to other person and not only by himself".[6] Aristotle argues that justice as a virtue must be something complete, that is not desired for some other end. So it seems that justice is the most complete virtue which is pursued wholly for itself and not for any other particular end. Aristotle claims that the most complete virtue is that which is intrinsically valuable. Justice as a virtue in itself relates to all human beings because its possessor practices in its relation to other person as well as for himself. In other words, person has the sense of justice to act virtuously towards other people. For Aristotle, justice is that which relates to all human beings because its possessor can exercise it in relation to other person and not only by himself. In this way a person is said to be just if he/she is moral towards state laws because he/she agreed to obey the law.

Carrying justice as a virtue ill itself, he proposes two conceptions of justice i.e. general and particular. A general conception of justice is lawfulness. Whereas a particular conception of justice refers to what is fair and equal. On the other hand, Aristotle divides particular conception of justice into distributive and rectificatory. In the conception of distributive justice, merit or desert and proportionate is one of the foundational principle to justify the distribution of resources. Here distributive justice concerned with what people deserves or else what one has the right to get. Aristotle linked the notion of distributive justice offices and wealth, rewards and dues with the idea of proportionate equality, which in tum, connected to a theory of just rewards or equal shares according to the merit of its recipients. According to Aristotle, "what is just is what is proportional, and what is unjust is what violates the proportion".[7] He believed in proportionality as one of the just principle in the distribution of resources belonging to the community. For instance, it is considered to be just when distribution of resources from any public funds follow the same proportion and unjust when it is not distributed in proportionate way. Thus, Aristotle's notion of distributive justice deals with good judgment and sense of fairness.

Fallowing Aristotle's distributive justice, in modem times, there has been strong tradition of two representative criteria ofjust distribution of social goods in the conception of distributive justice. One of which is distribution in accordance with individual worth, merit, ability and contributions while the other being equal distribution with regard to individual needs. The former justifies distribution of benefits and responsibilities through merit and competitive mechanism. The latter criterion justifies resource allocations through human equality and needs. It makes equality as a foundation and focuses on the needs of the most disadvantaged people. This conception of distributive justice plays an important role in judging what the resource allocation policies are justifiable to achieve social equity and security.

John Rawls's conception of justice is surrounded on the basis of equalityneed principle which justifies the departure from human equality to the needs of the *less well off people.* Rawls's distributive justice concerns for the perfectly just society under fair system of social cooperation as our society consists of inequalities of misfortune that some people are blessed with good fortune and some are with bad fortune. At this stage where social inequalities prevail it would not be considered a just society until it is not guided by the principle of fair distributive justice. It is Rawls who tried to remove inequalities between rich and poor and tries to establish a just society through a process by which social goods are to be distributed fairly so that each one will get justice. He tries to seek for the perfectly just society where various social arrangements determine fair institutional principle on proper distributive shares. Moreover, such institutional principles underlie social justice for appropriate distribution of the benefits and burdens of social cooperation. With this brief remark regarding fairness and equality in distributive justice in Rawls's perfect justice; I shall come to the Part I of the chapter.

Part - I

Re-visiting Social Contract Theory

John Rawls has revived social contract theory not to explain the origin of the state and its sovereignty or autonomy of the individuals, but as transcendental mechanism to explain the principle of distributive justice with reference to institutions. Though, he has revisited the social contract tradition of theorizing about justice associated with Locke, Rousseau and Kant in a very different manner because his predecessor has been used it to justify political and social obligation to obey the laws of the state and the society.

> The contractual approach exemplifies consent and voluntarism by trying to show how self-interested persons, with legitimate competing

claims arnve at naturally acceptable social arrangements. Unlike the social contracttheory that uses the device to explain the origins of the state and the nature of sovereignty, Rawls revived it to explainprinciple of Justice.[8]

Rawls says, "In order to do this we are not to think of the original contract as one to enter a particular society or to set up a particular form of government. Rather, the guiding idea is that the principles of justice for the basic structure of society are the object of the original agreement".[9] For him, social contract serves as a thought experiment to construct a just society where free individuals come together to have cooperation to choose institutional principle in a well ordered society. In a well ordered society each and every individual would be free and equal so that social benefits and burdens should be fairly distributed. Moreover, Rawls has revived social contract in the form of original position of equality which corresponds to the state of nature in Hobbes, Locke, and Rousseau. According to Samuel Freeman,

> The original position develops the basic idea underlying the liberal and democratic social contract traditions stemming from Locke, Rousseau and Kant that just laws, constitutions, or principles are those that could or would be agreed to among free persons from a position of equal rights. Like his predecessors, Rawls's social contract is hypothetical. It is not an actual agreement made at some point in history; rather it is a kind of thought experiment where hypothetical people, described as fairly situated as free, equal and rational, are given the task of coming to a unanimous agreement upon principle of justice that are to be applied within their ongoing society.[10]

Rawls's original position can be understood as a hypothetical contract not as a historical contract so that social and political institution is ought to be just under all circumstances and "laws and institutions no matter how efficient and well arranged must be reformed if they are unjust".[11] In formulating an intuitive idea of distributive justice as fairness is to think of an institutional arrangement which is an object of fair agreement. On Rawls view, hypothetical social contract asserts that rational person makes an agreement about the fair institutional principle which helps to establish a just society where fair institutional arrangements protects individual rights and liberties irrespective of caste, creed, religion and sex etc.

For Rawls, society is a cooperative venture for mutual advantage and this venture is surrounded with individual's conflicting interests as well as shared interests. Social cooperation enhances living standard to such a level which is unattainable for the individual to reach by its own effort. For the sake of mutual advantage, each individual enter into cooperative venture that binds members of the society and makes life better. As cooperation promotes their goodness of society and benefits all member of the society irrespective of whatever else its member wants. Rawls argues about social contract in *Justice as Fairness A Restatement,*

> ...as a device of representation and the original position models two things. Firstly as a fair condition under which the representatives of citizens, viewed slowly as free and equal person, are to agree to the fair terms of social cooperation whereby the basic structure is to be regulated. Second....as acceptable restriction on the reasons on the basis of which the parties, situated in those fair conditions may properly put forward certain principles of justice and reject others.[12]

The original position serves various purposes because it provides an evaluative tool to assess parties' recommended principle and bring out the mutual consensus of institutional principle that enables justice as fairness . Rawls's idea of original position is the most influential one because social contract addresses the problem of Justice directly and not via social welfare as in utilitarianism. While criticizing utilitarianism, he developed contractual liberal conception of justice in which justice is not understood as maximum welfare or efficiency but as the "first virtue of social institution".[13] Rawls says,

> Utilitarianism is a teleological whereas justice as fairness is a deontological.. ...which does not specify the good independently from the right, or does not interpret the right as maximizing the good. ...it does not characterize the rightness of institutions and acts independently from their consequences.[14]

The utilitarian principle is based on teleological theory which states the sense of good that is independent from the right which maximizes the good. Utilitarianism tries to seek such institutional arrangement which maximizes the good in the form of utility. In fact, utilitarianism proposes a standard of welfare in terms of individual's happiness over unhappiness and guided with the principle of consequentiality to individual's right and wrong action. For utilitarianism, social institutions are arranged in such a manner that brings out greatest happiness for the greatest number of people. Moreover, Rawls has not concerned with such institutional arrangement and offers a series of criticisms against utilitarianism. Rawls has pointed out, "The parties in the original position would reject the classical principle in favor of that of maximizing average utility. Since they are concerned to advance their own interests, they have no desire to maximize the total (or the net balance) of satisfactions".[15] As he argues, utilitarianism does not protect the liberty of people because it justifies the majority's happiness over minority's happiness. In such situation, "the greatest happiness principle would justify the minority's loss of liberty".[16] Hence, Rawls regards, such institutional arrangements are considered to be flawed in a well ordered society.

Rawls believed in a just society where, free and equal persons would choose its institutional principle which has to be fair. That's why Rawls's theory of distributive justice underlies in social contract because justice is viewed as a fair system of cooperation between free and equal persons and not of maximum utility. Moreover, Samuel has also has sided with Rawls's critique of utilitarianism, "His discussion and argument against utilitarianism provides a pattern of argument that can be applied to many other teleological conceptions, i.e. those which hold that it is right and just to always act to maximize the good".[17] It is one of the main reasons that Rawls has not supported institutional principle of utilitarianism because of inappropriate and favors unjust institutions.

As Prof. R P Singh writes in *Morality and Social Justice* that, "Rawls argues that each of us would reject the utilitarian theory of justice that we should maximize welfare because of the risk that we might tum out to be someone whose own good is sacrificed for greater benefits for others".[18] Moreover, utilitarian principle concerned about wealth maximization which ignores the individual's endowments and capacities. Richard has also criticizes about wealth maximization in *The Economic of Justice,*

> The implication of the wealth maximization is that people who lack sufficient earning power to support even a minimum decent standard of living are entitled to no say in the allocation of resources unless they are the part of utility function of someone who has wealth. This seems to weight too heavily the individual's particular endowment of capacities. If he happens to be born feeble-minded and his net social product is negative, he would have no right to the means of support even though there was nothing blame worthy in his inability to support himself.[19]

Moreover, utilitarianism fails to recognize that people have variety of interests in which happiness may be the only one. Hence, "utilitarianism does not take seriously the distinction between persons".[20] For instance, each person distinct to one another in their personal interest because some people believe in life of happiness and life of integrity and others may hold different interest about the aims of life. This varied interest would ultimately leads interpersonal conflicts of interest in maximizing aggregate benefit when it comes to individual and social interest. In other way, utilitarian does not recognize the plurality of human interest which is the central question about justice. Hence, utilitarianism is against the ethos of institution because its basis of interpersonal comparison for social justice is not based upon social goods but entirely based on utility. Further utilitarianism and its flawed, Rawls combines several criteria of justice under the idea of contract in the form of initial situation. For him, "Initial situation is described in which rational individuals with certain ends and related to each other in certain ways are to choose among various courses of action in view of their knowledge of the circumstances".[21] In original position, each rational person makes a rational choice to promote their interest.

> We might then imagine that each party in the original position has a good idea what they want accomplish in life (through a career or avocation), as well as an idea of personal relationships (friendships, families, children and so on), of their identity as a members of various groups (ethnic, religious, political, and so on), and more generally of the kind of values and pursuit that give their lives meamng for them. These aims, convictions, ambitions, and commitments are among the primary motivation of the parties in the original position.[22]

This intuitive idea becomes one of the foundational tools in formulating fair institutional arrangements where rational persons concerned about the advancement of the society and not their own interest. As Rawls has emphasized that,

> The conception of the original position embodies features peculiar to moral theory. Its aim is to characterize this situation so that the principles that would be chosen, whatever they turn out to be, are accepted from a moral point of view. The original position characterized as a status quo in which any agreements reached are fair.[23]

In original position, persons are conceived as a moral point of view with regard to their moral capacity for the conception of good and the sense of Justice because it is assumed that "parties in the original position are rational".[24] This moral or rational capacity for sense of good is what Rawls believes, "the content of morality characterized by the cooperative virtues: those of justice and fairness, fidelity and trust, integrity and impartiality".[25] By virtue of these capacities a person becomes aware about what is their advantage so they conceive original position as a system of cooperation to formulate an institutional principle for the good of its member. On the other hand, persons in original position conceived as "one another as equals, as friends and associates, joined together in a system of cooperation and governed by the common conception of justice".[26] In this situation person possess with the capacity for sense of justice in the form of mutual trust, bond of friendship, absence of envy so that he/she can act in a state of morality where each one would be equally represented as a moral person to construct a procedural justice in terms of fairness. Such hypothetical situation reaches at moral reasoning about basic principles of social and political justice. Rawls use of social contract in distributive justice has been the most noble and striking features which asserts that each and every person would get equal opportunities in public goods so that the vision of fairness can be achieved. However, free and equal person have different values and beliefs, and in this way Rawls has brought an idea of people's consent and agreement so that institutional arrangements have a sense of fair justice. It is the social contract that unites each individual through association and develops friendly feelings towards each other. It promotes a system of social cooperation to have a sense of fellow feelings and mutual trust. As Samuel Freeman says,

> "What makes an agreement appropriate is that the principle of justice behind coercive laws should be acceptable to a free and equal person whose conduct is regulated by them. This is fundamental assumption of social contract views. There is no commonly accepted moral, religious, or philosophical authority that otherwise could be consulted to decide rights or settle disagreement about justice and principle of justice. Thus the only way for principle of justice to be acceptable to everyone is by a social contract".[27]

For Rawls, persons in the original position are rational, capable of conception of good and have a sense of justice. They are rational with the capacity for intelligent pursuit of one's own interests to enter into an agreement to decide whether a conception of Justice is fair under such conditions that adhere and fulfill in a "well ordered society". Furthermore, the parties are not in a position to coerce anyone, thus ensuring that agreement is voluntarily. For Rawls, distributive justice has to be understood in terms of institutional principle. These principles are the best formulation of a social system which applies to basic structure of society. Rawls has pointed out in his book- *A Theory of Justice* about justice, "The primary subject of justice is the basic structure of society, or more exactly, the way in which the major social institutions distribute fundamental rights and duties and determine the division of advantages from social cooperation".[28] As he argues,

> "The basic structure is the primary subject of justice because its effects are so profound and present from the start. The intuitive notion here is that this structure contains various social positions and that men born into different positions have different expectations of life determined, in part, by the political system as well as by economic and social circumstances. In this way the institutions of society favor certain starting places over others. These are especially deep inequalities. Not only are they pervasive, but they affect men's initial chances in life; yet they cannot possibly be justified by an appeal to the notions of merit and desert. It is these inequalities, presumably inevitable in the basic structure of any society, to which the principles of social justice apply".[29]

However, the basic structure of society" is not based upon personal interests or specific moral doctrines but it can be constructed through social cooperation where justice is defined through institutional procedure that claims to be fair. In other way, sense of fair cooperation plays an important role in society's sociopolitical and economic institutional arrangements. Rawls says,

> I characterized a well ordered society as one designed to advance the good of its members and effectively regulated by a public conception of justice. Thus it is a society which everyone accepts and knows that the other accept the same principles of justice, and the basic social institution satisfy are known to satisfy these principles.[30]

A well ordered society regulates, promotes sense of justice because each individual in original position or hypothetical situation assumes that the principle of justice are chosen with the mutual consent of its members. Rawls regards, institution is nothing but the basic structure of the society which specifies public rules as the result of social agreement. He argues,

> A person taking part in an institution knows what the rules demand of him and of the others. He also knows that the others know this and

that they know that he knows this, and so on. The principles of justice are to apply social arrangements understood to be public in this sense.[31]

Rawls conception of justice is governed with an institutional mechanism where public rules and regulations specify certain form of action as permissible and forbidden. Hence he has chosen principle of justice in social arrangement which could determine the division of advantages. In this way problem for choosing between various social arrangements could be solved by defining a set of principle which determines the division of advantage. To overcome the problem of conflicting principles, Rawls breaks down his conception of justice into two components and arranges them according to the lexical principle which I will discuss in next part.

Rawls's distributive justice is a type of procedural justice where justice lies in fair principles which regulate social practice and institutions. Moreover, contracterian approach to justice has been subject to a lot of criticisms because the participants of the 'social contract' are mutually disinterested in identifying just institutional arrangements for a perfectly just society. It focuses on "identifying fair institutional arrangement in the basic structure of society and can be called transcendental institutionalism".[32] It is transcendental because it is looking for an ideal society which is regulated by fair institutional arrangements and just principles. Then, the question arises: is justice the realization of institutions and rules or principles or is it concerned with the society as well? Moreover, Rawls himself criticized in his later work. Rawls in his later work *Political Liberalism* where he criticizes justice fairness through original position by arguing that, "... is a political conception and it is justified by reference to political values and should not be presented as part of a more comprehensive moral, religious, or philosophical doctrine".[33] In other way, Rawls' own criticism of his earlier position still amounts to the fairness of the institutions with liberal values. There is still a lack of the realization of the sense of justice not as a matter of judging institutions and principles for distributing primary goods but minimizing injustices at individual and social level. It may be emphasized that institutional choice and arrangement focused approaches to justice are not sufficient conditions because society consists of human beings who are outside of the institutions and the latter gets affected by the former.

In his recent book, *The Idea of Justice,* Amartya Sen criticizes the contractarian approach because they have developed justice on the basis of hypothetical social contract" which has an insight into perfect or an ideal justice. "Their use of social contract underlies in perfect institutional arrangement can also be called transcendental institutionalism".[34] For him transcendental institutionalism concentrates on perfect justice in terms of fair institutional principle rather on relative comparisons of justice and injustice. The enquiry is "aimed at identifying the nature of the just, rather than finding some criteria for an alternative being less unjust. Sen argues, "Rawls original position is searching for perfection and it concentrates primarily on getting the institution right and it is not directly focused on the actual societies that would ultimately emerge".[35] More importantly, the search for perfect justice could distract us from tackling real-life, immediate injustices such as discrimination relating to education, skill, health, environment, etc. for women, tribal people and marginalized community who are deprived of all these. Moreover, Sen is not interested in proposing a theory of perfect justice rather he is interested to minimizes injustices from the society. Hence, he proposes *realization focused comparison*[36] to justice where justice concentrates on the actual society related to human problems. Despite of all criticism about Rawls's transcendental mechanism to construct a perfect institution, contracterian approach to justice plays an important role because it address the problem of Justice directly and not via social welfare.

Therefore, social contract in the form of original position has immense effect to construct a well ordered society where justice is considered to be the first virtue of social institution. In other way, social contract as a device of representation in the original position" plays an important role in the fallowing way:

> First, it models what we regard- here and now - as fair conditions under which the representatives of citizens, viewed solely as free and equal persons, are to agree to the fair terms of social cooperation (as expressed by principles of justice) whereby the basic structure is to be regulated.
>
> Second, it models what we regard - here and now - as acceptable restrictions on the reasons on the basis of which the parties (as citizens' representatives), situated in those fair conditions, may properly put forward certain principles of Justice and rejects others.[37]

Hence, social contract theory in the form of original position ensures each and every individual would be free and equal as a basic criterion for an impartial distribution of social benefits and opportunities under Rawls' innovative device i.e. veil of ignorance.

Part - II

Procedure of Veil of Ignorance and the Concept of Fairness

The procedure of veil of ignorance underlies the concept of fairness in Rawls's distributive justice. It is one of the essential devices through which Rawls' places on the knowledge of persons in the original position. "In original position, the participants are all faced with veil of ignorance about particular facts on the one hand and person conceived with regard to moral capacity for the conception of good and the sense of Justice on the other".[38] In other way, Rawls's specification of justice emerges out of his constructive idea of the original position or hypothetical situation under veil of ignorance.[39] Veil of ignorance denies the knowledge of person's social status, moral characters, wealth, talents, life plans.[40] It is one of the fundamental conditions which does not misled the contracting parties to favor a principle which is considered as unjust and unfair. Now the question arises, why he uses the device of veil of ignorance to construct fair principle of justice? One reason for Rawls' proposing the veil of ignorance is that he wants participants in the original position were presumed to be unaware of individual interest, wants, skill and abilities as well as other conditions which mislead them to construct a principle of distribution which is partial for the betterment of some people and not for all. Moreover the impartial institutional principle fills the gap between privileged and underprivileged and reduces discrimination, inequality and conflict in society.

Before discussing about veil of ignorance III distributive justice, it is imperative to discuss about the idea of fairness which is equivalent to the idea of justice. When we think about justice, one of the basic questions that come to our mind is: what does fairness implies and what makes a fair or just society? What rules a society should fallow to have fair distribution? These are of course, one of the important concerns for distributive justice when we speak of fair and unfair distribution of public goods that are scarce. Moreover, if there would be sufficient resources for the betterment of everyone then there would be no question of distributive justice. So, distributive justice in Rawls explicitly asserts on the "equal distribution of social goods so that each citizen adequately develop and fully exercise their moral powers".[41] Then the first question is that what does social goods consists? For Rawls, social goods consist in the following:

1. Basic liberties and rights.

2. Freedom of movement and free choice of occupation against a background of diverse opportunities.
3. Powers and prerogatives of offices and positions of responsibility in the political and economic institutions of the basic structure.
4. Income and wealth.
5. The social bases of self-respect.[42]

However the above list of goods in Rawls's distributive justice does not rests solely on psychological, social or historical facts. "The list of goods rests in part on the general facts and requirement of social life, it does so only together a political conception of the persons as free and equal, endowed with the moral powers, and capable of being a fully cooperating member of society".[43] In "justice as fairness", one objective view that is relevant in the notion of distributive justice is the primary goods. These are essential institutional requirement for the development of each individual as a human being. According to Rawls,

> Primary goods are conceived as a scheme of equal basic liberties and fair opportunities, which, when guaranteed by the basic structure, ensures for all citizens the adequate development and full exercise of their two moral powers and a fair share of the allpurpose means essentials for the advancement of their conception of the good.[44]

For Rawls, primary social goods are distributed fairly so that each one will get fair share to lead a good life. There are two divisions of primary goods, namely, natural and social primary goods. The former consists in person's natural endowments of characteristics that are essential for achieving some specific ends such as health, intelligence and physical strength. The later, that is, social primary goods such as liberty, opportunity, income and wealth and human respect not at the disposal of the person's natural endowment but at the disposal of the society. Primary goods are one of the basic rights that every person wants because they use it to achieve rational plan in their life. In fact it is one of the means by which each individual can achieve their ends whatever those ends may be. Social primary goods are measurement of people's access to basic institutions because of the impossibility of redistribution of natural primary goods so that their ideas of good life irrespective of their interests would be fulfilled.

The foundational idea in Rawls distributive justice has to be seen in terms of the demand of fairness. Our society still suffers from a very unbalanced distribution of wealth which creates inequality between rich and poor. In that situation we need to construct a just society where each person would get equal opportunities in fair way. Moreover, the idea of fairness can be given shape in various ways: equity, equality, need, merit, veil of ignorance and so on. "The idea of Justice is often, though not always, roughly equivalent to the idea of fairness or equity. Equity is frequently contrasted with equality".[45] For instance, Rawls's justice is based on equity principle rather than equality principle which promotes social goods should be distributed equally as egalitarian believes. In other way, equity principle of fairness is a matter of proportionate distribution and that it does not include any principle of strict equality. Just like fair shares are not the same as equal shares. How they differ? Fair shares depend on merit, need and equality, which of course not equally distributed. For example, it is not fair that workers should not receive as much as an engineer and that those with greater need should give no more than those with less need, that opportunities should go to those who cannot benefit from them rather than to those who can.[46]

Everyone needs food to live but diabetic needs insulin as well. In the same way, every child needs education but disabled child cannot be educated by the means of normal provision meant for other children and has to be given special facilities. The needs of diabetic and disabled one are greater than those of the normal one. So, the provision for their needs is greater than the normal. Therefore justice has to be with equity and not equality. It allows discrimination by reference to morally relevant differences and forbids discrimination in the absence of such differences. It is fair to discriminate in favor of the needy, or the meritorious or able and it is unfair to discriminate between people who are equally needy. The rule is to treat cases alike unlike cases differently within a society.

In the contemporary times, Rawls's conception of justice, particularly distributive justice is based on equality which presupposes each and every individual are treated equally under the law. However the principle of equality in the notion of distributive justice in itself is unjust in particular situation. In the case of distributive justice, equality principle some time leads to inequality because people's requirement varies from one person to other person. Hence, "Rawls specification of demands of fairness is based on his constructive idea of the original position or hypothetical situation under the device of veil of ignorance which is central to his theory of justice". "The original position is considered to be an imagined situation of primordially equality when the parties involved have no knowledge of their personal identities, self-interest within the group as a whole". Rawls argues, "The idea of original position is to set up a fair procedure so that any principles agreed to will be just Now in order to do this I assume that the parties in are situated behind the veil of ignorance".[47]

> This strong impartiality conditions is the most operative feature of Rawls's social contract; the parties are required to put aside reliance on knowledge of all particular facts about themselves and their social and historical circumstances, including their particular conceptions of the good, and even including their comprehensive religious, philosophical, and moral convictions.[48]

Without the idea of veil of ignorance, fairness cannot be achieved because person's intelligence, skills, gender, religion race, wealth, health and so on do not serve as a good reason to justify the principle of distributive justice. Kristjansson has also pointed, "Being impartial means that they must be applied in a non arbitrary, unbiased and consistent manner to everyone in the relevant category. This condition rule outs favoritism".[49] It is clear that impartial principle underlies fairness, for instance, in a public exam; the answer of all students shall be marked in accordance with the impartial criterion while hiding their personal traits.

Rawls's justice as fairness evolved out of the original position behind veil of ignorance which underlies the fundamental notion of equality with the requirement that everyone could be *better off* so that inequality between rich and poor can be removed. Rawls used social contract theory to formulate the theory of distributive justice by saying that,

> Society is a system of cooperation for mutual advantage between individuals. As such, it is marked by both conflicts between differing individual interests and an identity of shared interests. Principle of justice should define the appropriate distribution of the benefits and burdens of social cooperation.[50]

As an egalitarian, he believed in equality among all individuals and the idea of equity in the distribution of social benefits and burdens. His contention is to distribute all social and economic goods and services equally except in those cases where an unequal distribution for the benefit of the worst off in society. Rawls's fair justice acknowledges all personal attributes as being morally arbitrary, and thus justice requires the sense of equality and fairness. In short, D. D. Raphael has pointed in his article entitled "Justice" that,

> Rawls adapts the idea to an agreement about justice. He suggests that we can best understand the notion of justice by thinking of it as

> a set of principles that would be agreed upon by everyone if they had to decide in a hypothetical position, what should be the rules for distributing benefits and burdens in society.[51]

As John Mandle has rightly pointed, "we need some principled way for choosing among the vanous social arrangements which determine this division of advantages and for underwriting an agreement on the proper distributive shares".[52] For this, Rawls's ignorance model in the hypothetical situation where,

> Participants are all faced with a device i.e. veil of ignorance about particular facts. They are supposed to have general knowledge of psychology and the social sciences, but they do not know the historical date or geographical location of their society, nor do they know anything about the individual capacities or social position of them selves or others. Rawls asks us to assume that they will form their judgment with an eye to self-interest. Since, nobody knows whether he will be lucky or unlucky, rich or poor, clever or stupid, everyone will think it prudent to provide adequately for the worst possible case, since it might tum out to be their lot. And that, Rawls concludes, is justice, a set of rules which everyone would accept as fair. The rules would be accepted by everyone, thinking only of their own self-interest, because the veil of ignorance puts everyone in the same boat when planning for the future. And the same time the planning would have regard to all possible positions in society because the veil of ignorance makes any such position equally possible for any individual.[53]

In distributive justice, ignorance model plays an important role to design the basic structure of the society where structural inequalities in the distribution of social goods would be vanishes. Rawls identifies basic structure of society with "the arrangement of major social institutions into One scheme of cooperation".[54] For Rawls principles for determining the basic institutions of a society as to what is just are:

> First: each person has the same indefensible claim to a fully adequate scheme of equal basic liberties, which scheme is compatible with the same scheme liberty for all.
>
> Second: Social and economic inequalities are to satisfied two condition: first, they are to attached to offices and positions open to all under conditions of fair equality of opportunity; and second, they are to be the greatest benefit of the least advantaged members of society (the difference principle).[55]

These two principles of justice are chosen under an innovative device i.e. veil of ignorance which ensures that no one is advantaged and disadvantaged in the choice of principles by the outcome of natural chances and social circumstances. Rawls has called, first principle as the principle of *equal liberty,* first part of the second principle as the principle of fair *equality of opportunities,* second part of the second principle is the *difference principle.* Moreover, the first principle embodies the notion of *liberty* on the one hand, and on the other the first part of the second principles along with first principle embodies the idea of equality and the second part of the second principle guarantees fraternity". These principles underlie social justice that how social goods are distributed on the one hand and the other some social good are more important than others which cannot be scarified for the sake of other goods. It emphasized that equal liberties take precedence over equal opportunity which take precedence over equal resources. Rawls's two principles arranged in lexical order where second principle cannot require even the slightest violation of the first principle.

The first priority rule is the principles of liberty are the principle of Justice arranged in such a manner so that it cannot be restricted by other principle so its priority asserts that liberty can be restricted for the sake of liberty.[56]

The second priority rule (the priority of justice over efficiency and welfare) - the second principle of justice is lexically prior to the principle of efficiency and to that of the maxmuzmg the sum of advantages; and fair opportunities is prior to the difference principle.[57]

Now equating with the two principle of justice, the representative in the original position under veil of ignorance would organize a well ordered society around the liberty principle and the difference principle. "These principles primarily apply to the basic structure of the society and they distinguish between those aspect of the social system that define and secure the equal liberties of citizenship and those that specify social and economic inequalities".[58] The former implies principle of "equal personal liberty which is given priority over the demands of the second principle which relates to the equality of opportunities and to equity in the distribution of resources. Because liberty that human being enjoy cannot be violated on the grounds of wealth or distribution of economic resources among the people". The liberty principle states that each members of a society as a human being has an equal basic liberties compatible with the similar liberty for all. It reminds us of Kantian notion of universal autonomy. Moreover, on Rawls view,

> The basic liberties of citizens are roughly speaking political liberty (the right to vote and to be eligible for public office) together with freedom of speech and assembly; liberty of conscience and freedom of thought; freedom of the person along with the right to hold (personal) property; and freedom from arbitrary arrest and seizure as defined by the concept of the rule of law. These liberties are all required to be equal by the first principle, since citizens of a just society are to have the same basic rights.[59]

The second principle applies to the distribution of income and wealth, the design of organizations that makes use of differences in authority, responsibility and chains of command.[60] In other words, its first condition implies social and economic inequalities are to be arranged so that people with the same talents and willingness to use them should have the same educational and economic opportunities regardless of whether they were born rich or poor. In this way, first part of the second principle is concerned with the institutional requirements of making sure that public opportunities open to all without anyone being excluded on the basis physically or mentally handicapped or impairment, race, caste or religion and region etc. For instance slavery in terms of anything is the violation of this principle.

Moreover, the second condition is *difference principle* which underlies social institutions arranged in such a manner so that the inequalities of wealth and income work to the advantage of those who considered to be *less well off* people. In other way, it is primarily concerned with distributive equity as well as overall efficiency and it takes the form making the less badly-off members of society as well-off possible. This can be possible through equity based distribution of primary goods where distribution of wealth and income need not be equal; it must be to everyone's advantage. In short, social and economic inequalities are allowed if they benefit the least well off without violating the first principle. Further, the second principle is lexically prior to the principle of efficiency and that of maximizing the sum of advantage. The positions of authority must be accessible to all. Rawls suggests one measure of determining the least advantaged, namely income and wealth and not the social position. All person with less than median income and wealth maybe taken as the least advantaged segment. Since the principles are to be applied to the basic structure it is to be arranged to maximize the worth of the least advantaged of the complete scheme of equality liberty shared by all.

However, Rawls's justice as fairness in terms of distribution of primary goods has come under lot of criticisms because the use of primary goods inadequately address individual differences to convert these primary goods into valuable functionings in terms of what people are able to be and to do in their lives. In other words, Sen's criticism on the fact that, "different people even when receiving the equal primary goods end up with the very different situations because of the very different abilities they have in converting these rights and liberties".[61] Even he has pointed out that, "the primary goods seems to take little note of the diversity of human beings".[62]

> "If people were basically very similar, then an index of primary goods might be quite a good way of judging advantage. But, in fact people seems to have very different needs varying with health, longevity, climatic conditions, location, work conditions, temperament and even body size...so what is being involved is not merely ignoring a few hard cases, but overlooking very widespread and real differencesv."63

It shows that the index of primary goods in distributive justice overlooks individual differences to convert these goods in their life. It is obvious that primary goods to some extent are the "means to pursue their life plan. However, the real opportunities that a person has to pursue in their life are not only determined by the primary goods".

Alasdair MacIntyre[64] criticizes Rawls on the notion of justice under veil of ignorance. MacIntyre criticizes about Rawls's liberal theory of justice by saying that liberals misunderstood the nature of justice and argues that original position under veil of ignorance is not at all going to give us justice because it attains to prevent us from getting the complete information of the subject matter of justice. Though ignorance model of fairness helps us to deliver justice without favor or revenge but it is also likely to detach or detract us from perpetuating injustices and suffering from injustices. As he says in, *Whose Justice? Which Rationality?*

> We all approach our own circumstances as the bearers of a particular social identity. I am someone's son or daughter, someone else's cousin or uncle. I am a citizen of this or that city, a member of this or that society or profession; I belong to this clan, that tribe, this nation.[65]

He believes that ignorance model separates individuals from their background, tradition and community which is an indispensible part of life. MacIntyre contrasts liberal individualism of Rawls and Kant. According to McIntyre, "I am what I myself choose to be. I can always if

I wish to put in question what are taken to be the merely contingent social features of my existence".[66] The communitarian critique like McIntyre believes that the original positions through veil of ignorance device are not sufficient to distribute the primary goods fairly on the basis of two institutional principles. Then the question arises what will happen in distribution when these principles would conflict and is it fair distribution in the social system? In spite of all criticism about veil of ignorance and fairness, the idea of ignorance model helps us to set up a fair procedure so that any institutional principle will be just. However restrictions on particular information in the original position are of fundamental importance because it gives fair institutional principle in the conception of justice.

Part- III

Liberty, Equality and Fraternity: The Tripartite Principle

Rawls's distributive justice comprises of institutional arrangement where liberty, equality and fraternity can be taken together as the condition of social justice. Historically, liberty, equality and fraternity are tripartite values since the French Revolution however; the least discussed concept is that of fraternity. "Equality and liberty are regarded as ideals or principles: something men aim at or by reference to which they guide their conduct".[67] The idea of freedom incorporates an ideal of equality and respect which implies that all men have the right to be free and ought to be treated equally. Moreover, Rawls has provided a general criterion for ordering liberty and equality in the idea of free and equal persons with two moral powers namely sense of justice and the conception of good. The former is the "capacity to apply and act from the institutional principle that specify the fair terms of social cooperation. The other moral power is conception of good aims to specify a person's conception of what is value in human life".[68] From the idea of free and equal persons with two moral powers the idea of fraternal attitude evolves in Rawls's distributive justices. However, the notion of fraternity has been originated since French Revolution but it is not substantiated like liberty and equality and this is because fraternity concerns our common humanity and therefore IS more difficult to integrate in a theoretical framework. Generally fraternity can be defined as feeling of brotherhood, community and mutual responsibility. According to Tobias Gombert,

> The sense of fraternity arises from a common set of interests and finds expression in behavior that benefits society in some cases even

against the individual's own short term interests and goes beyond the formal claim to reciprocal justice. It is a common 'social identity', which has its source in a similar mode of life and common values.[69]

Further, he says, "Fraternity is strong force that ties our society together, both in spontaneous and individual readiness to provide assistance with common rules and organizations, and in the welfare state, which is a form of politically guaranteed and organized solidarity".[70] It is clear that the values of fraternity has been played substantial role in social history of institutional reform.

Rawls's justice as fairness relied more on Kantian moral idea of freedom and equality of human being. For Kant, every human being is to be treated as an end in himself or herself and not as a means to the ends of others. Following this maxim of Kant, Rawls thinks that utilitarian institutional principle is unjust because it leads to human inequality and tries to focus on the moral principle on individual rights in the form of the freedom and equality of every person. For the utilitarian, the creation of justice in a society is the aggregate sum of utility or happiness or welfare it produces and not the well-being of each member of the society. As Rawls has pointed, "utilitarianism does not take seriously the distinction between persons".[71] He observes that utilitarianism ignores the distinction that exists between persons. In fact utilitarian principle created a sense of inequality in favor of people with merit because it relies on individual's desert or merit which produces general welfare.

Rawls believed that utilitarian theory is unfair and morally flawed which justifies the discrimination and sacrifices of some individuals for the sake of maximization of general welfare. Moreover, he presumes that utilitarianism idea of greatest happiness of the greatest number ignores the interest of least advantaged people. Here the basic question arises why the greater gain of some should not be compensated for the lesser losses of others? Here we can say that utilitarianism treats some persons as a means towards the end of others and it is not compatible with the basic rights of humanity that every human being must be treated as an end not as means. Rawls's justice focuses on individual liberty and equality so that each person would be treated as an end not as means which culminates in the idea of fraternity.

The notion of freedom is one of the ingredients in Rawls theory of justice because freedom is deeply rooted in human aspirations. For Rawls, "liberty can always be explained by a reference to a three items: first the agents who are free, the restrictions and limitations which they are free from and what it is that they are free to do or not to do".[72] Liberty as the essence of human being and justice demands that liberty ought to be fairly distributed to all members of the society irrespective of their race, gender, religion, class of origin, and so on. On Rawls view, liberty cannot be violated for the sake of other values. In order to maintain individual's liberty, the state should not impose any restraints on their activities in their sphere of life.

In Rawls's justice as fairness, freedom plays an important role because it has got priority over wealth and resources. Now the basic question arises what does freedom or liberty mean? Is both concepts are synonyms to each other? Generally freedom implies the absence of constraint. As Raphael says, "a man is free in so far as he is not restrained from doing what he wants to do or what he choose to do if he knew that he could. The idea of choice itself implies a kind of freedom".[71] It is clear that freedom is the essence of human being to choose their life without any constraint. However, the word freedom implied two sense, firstly freedom as *essence* of human being because human being is capable of free will to choose their life without any constraint. Secondly, freedom as the *condition* of human being implies realm of liberty. Liberty is conceived as the social condition in which everyone fallows their freedom to pursue their life without curtailing other's freedom. This ideal is sometimes paraphrased in the maxim "do as you please unless your pleasure interferes with that of others".[72] Liberty as the social condition in which everyone fallows his own inclination so long as it does not collide with that of anyone else's freedom.

Further liberty as 'absence of constraint or restraint' can be internal or external and it further called as positive liberty and negative liberty respectively. As Isaiah Berlin says in his essay - "Two Concepts of Liberty", liberty can be divided into negative as well as positive sense, "negative liberty as freedom from coercion while positive liberty means autonomy, that is, the power of selfdirection".[73] Further he says,

> I shall call the 'negative' sense, is involved in the answer to the question- 'what is the area within which the subject- a person or group of person- is or should be left to do or be what he is able to do or be without interference by other persons. The second, which I shall call the positive sense, is involved in the answer to the question 'what or who is the source of control or interference that can determine someone to do, or be, this rather than that?[74]

Isaiah Berlin has pointed out in his article entitled "Two concepts of Liberty", "By being free in negative sense, I mean not being interfered by others".[75] Then he says that, "The wider the area of no-interference the wider my freedom. The positive sense of the word liberty derives from the wish on the part of the individual to be his own master. I wish my life and decision to depend on myself, not on external forces of whatever kind".[76] It makes clear; when individual possess positive liberty, acts upon one's own free will and the role of agency plays an important role to act independently from inhibition of external forces and to make their own free choice. In other way, in the state of negative liberty, state has no interference which led to the doctrine of Laissez Faire. In this way, positive liberty is the possibility of acting in such a way as to take control of one's life while negative liberty is the absence of obstacles, barriers or constraints on the other.

Rawls's conception of 'well ordered society' is governed by fair institutional principle of liberty and equality. "The first is the idea of liberty is a certain pattern of social forms because rights and liberties referred by these principles are those by which are defined by the public rules of the basic structure".[77] The "first principle simply requires that certain sort of rules, those define basic liberties, apply to everyone equally and that they allow the most extensive liberty compatible with a like liberty for all".[78] To understand what basic liberties, Rawls has suggested a list of basic liberties and these are namely:

1. Political liberty (the right to vote and to be eligible for public office)"
2. Freedom of speech and assembly
3. Liberty of conscience and freedom of thought
4. Freedom of the person
5. Right to hold personal property
6. Freedom from arbitrary arrest and seizure as defined by the concept of the rule oflaw.[79]

Moreover, it is important to clarify that Rawls's notion of liberty is not understood as general principle of liberty rather he is giving special protection to what he calls the 'basic liberties', by which he means the standard civil and political rights recognized in liberal democracies- the right to vote, to run for office, due process, free speech, mobility etc. These dimensions of liberty: civil, political and economic liberty etc in the capacity of an individual as a person. Rawls principle of Justice underlies in above "list of basic liberties and its priority focuses on maximum liberty for each individual to all human being. Freedom of thought and liberty of conscience, freedom of the person and the civil liberties, ought not to be sacrificed to political liberty."[80] These liberties are the basic and most extensive liberties that can satisfy person's interests as an equal and free status. However, for equal liberty, we require an "institutional mechanism that restricts absolute liberty and ensure equal liberty for all irrespective of differences relating to caste, creed, gender and sex. Rawls suggests liberty in connection with constitutional and legal restrictions".[81] It is clear that to some extent liberties are restricted because if liberties would be unrestricted they collide with one another and loose its significance. "The constitutional process as the proper standard to restrict liberty because liberty is the certain structure of institutions, a certain system of public rules defining rights and duties".[82] It is therefore restriction by public rules such as constitution is not to restrict liberty but to ensure liberty by regulation and that's why Rawls discusses liberty in connection with constitutional and legal restrictions. In this case, liberty particularly basic political liberty can be restricted on the grounds restriction will lead to just legislation under the condition that such legislation ensures equal liberty.[83] As Hart interpreted Rawls basic liberties in his article - "Rawls on Liberty and its Priority", "the basic liberties to which Rawls's principle thus refers are identified by the parties as essential for the pursuit of their ends, whatever those ends tum out to be, and so as determining the form of their society".[84] Further he criticizes Rawls's position on extensive liberty by saying that the most 'equal liberty' may not be the most extensive basic liberty and says that,

> Basic liberties can be incompatible with each other, some cases of mediation among basic liberties can happen. For example, free discussion without rules can mean more extensive liberty because when most people want to speak, they can speak. But, it also means that they, in fact, do not enjoy their liberty extensively because they cannot communicate their opinion effectively. That is, their intention (or liberty) to communicate their opinion is limited.[85]

Rawls's justified his position on institutional principle of extensive liberty by the very idea of constitutional mechanism wherein each and every person would get equal liberty to the most extensive liberty for all. This can be explain through example of debate and discussion where we introduces certain rules and regulation of order which does not restrict the content of our speech but to regulate the order of speech which promotes greater liberty for all.

However, this position has been clarified by Rawls in his later work *Political Liberalism* where he argues, "Each person has an equal claim to a fully adequate scheme of equal basic rights and liberties, which scheme is compatible with the same scheme for all and in this scheme the equal political parties, and only those liberties are to be guaranteed their fair value".[86] Although, Rawls' own position of liberty principle with liberal values which demands that people should get fair value which assures adequate all-purpose means to make effective use of their liberties and opportunities.[87] This seems to be reasonable, because to secure fair value of equal political liberties guarantee effective extensive liberty for all. This can be possible through what Rawls says, citizen's basic needs as constitutional essentials[88] so that liberty can be realized in the constitutional stage. Thus, Rawls view relating to liberty principle in his later work is the modification which addresses a more practical and proper representation of liberty.

Having discussed liberty as the institutional principle of justice in detail, let us tum to the concept of equality which is the operative terms III Rawls's distributive justice. Equality is one of the foundational elements III Rawls's distributive justice which ensures that "all social primary goods - liberty and opportunity, income wealth, and the bases of self respect - are to be distributed equally unless an unequal distribution of any or all of these goods is to the advantage of the least favored".[89] On Rawls view, there cannot be absolute equality as it is impossible to distribute social and economic goods to everyone equally. The basic conception of Justice ties the idea of equality in the conception of distributive justice implies that a just distribution of benefits and responsibilities in accordance with people's requirement. However Rawls adds an important twist that "we treat people as equal not by removing all inequalities, but only those which disadvantaged someone".[90] Further, if certain inequalities benefit everyone, by drawing out socially useful talents and energies, then they will be acceptable to everyone.[91] It is clear that Rawls's notion of equality underlies in relative equality and the fact that there cannot be absolute equality. For instance, everyone needs food to live but diabetic needs insulin as well. In the same way, every child needs education but disabled child cannot be educated by the means of normal provision meant for other children and has to be given special facilities. The needs of diabetic and disabled one are greater than those of the normal one. So, the "provision of their needs is greater than the normal. Therefore, Rawls's institutional principle of equality allows discrimination by reference to morally relevant differences and forbids discrimination in the absence of such differences. It is fair to discriminate in favor of the needy, or the meritorious or able and it is unfair to discriminate between people who are equally needy. The rule is to treat cases alike unlike cases differently within a society.[92]

The purpose of Rawls's equality of opportunity is to introduce 'equal start' in the race for social position on the one hand and difference principle is 'evening out the result' of that race on the other. It can be argue that Rawls's principle of equality interoperated in the form as democratic equality which acknowledges institutional requirement which makes sure that public opportunities open to all on the one hand and distributive equity as well as overall efficiency on the other so that those who are less well off members of society as well off possible. The purpose of difference principle is to introduce equity based distribution of primary goods to achieve a good life for those people who are considered to be less well off. In reality, principle of equal opportunity cannot be completely realized. That's why Rawls introduce an innovative idea of difference principle of equality. Rawls's difference principle of equality can be explained through reasonable distribution of cake-piece. For instance, difference principle of equality is not simply to divide a cake into equal pieces but to distribute it reasonably so that each one will get their fair pieces and not equal pieces. This reasonable distribution of cake-pieces leads some inequalities may be inevitable and useful for those people who are less well off. For him, distribution of wealth and income need not be equal; it must be to everyone's advantage. The positions of authority must be accessible to all. Rawls suggests one measure of determining the least advantaged, namely income and wealth and not the social position. For instance, a person with less than median income and wealth considered as the least advantaged section of the society. Hence, the principles are to be applied to the basic structure it is to be arranged to maximize the worth of the least advantaged of the complete scheme of equality liberty shared by all. It applies to the distribution of income and wealth, the design of organizations that regulates difference in authority, responsibility and chains of command.

Further Rawls argues that social and economic "inequalities are allowed if they improve my initially equal share, but are not allowed if, as in utilitarianism, they invade my fair share".[93] Rawls's equality cum inequality institutional mechanism tries to justify economic and social inequality. This is called as the principle of fair equality as it justified inequality for the betterment of those who are least advantaged people. It regulates the distribution of offices and positions of responsibility, income and wealth and the social bases of self respect so that social and economic inequalities are to be arranged in such a way that they are to the greatest benefit to the least advantaged people. Martin Rex interpreted Rawls's second part of equality principle and says that, "each would want those positions to be open to all on some principle of equitable competition".[94] It primarily focused on economic opportunities and refers to hold a position that generates income and wealth. Further he says "they concur in the stipulation that the wealth generating positions to be open to all by some reasonable principle of equality of opportunity".[95] Therefore, Rawls develops the two principles of justice by distinction between the distributive or equality-related and the libertyrelated aspects in distributive justice which underlies in fair society wherein such institutional mechanism ensures each person are free, equal and have dignity. In such society every person treats other as a free, equal and sense of belongingness.

Rawls vision of Justice underlies the value of fraternity because a just society consists of fair institutional arrangements wherein liberty and equality principle ensures a sense of belongingness and brotherhood among individuals. Rawls just society underlies not only in the values of liberty and equality but the value of fraternity as well so that each individual would be treated as an end. It focuses on the maxim that "men are free, men are equal and men are brother".[96] The notion of fraternity emphasize on dignity of the individual so that each individual would get equal respect and treated others as brotherhood. It inculcates the habit of mutual assistance and readiness of people to stand up for each other and help one another. This attitude creates strength for change and revolution in a society.

Professor R.P. Singh says in "Justice and Secularism A Conceptual and Cross-Cultural Analysis", "fraternity assuring the dignity of the individual and unity and integrity of the nation".[97] It is clear that the vision of fraternity underlies justice because our society consists of diverse nature and manifested in various ethnic identities, community structure, linguistic identities, different nationalities, language and so on. Because of these pluralistic natures of Indian society we require such an institutional arrangement which inculcates the virtue of fraternity to protect and promote individual's dignity irrespective of their diversity. According to

Annie Besant, "Fraternity binds us together, each to each; fraternity is the strong cord which shall give to one the power of the whole. Liberty and equality can only be won by combined effort, and combination is only possible as brotherhood is recognized and felt".[98] Fraternity is the only value that unites all human being irrespective of differences between caste, creed, sex and religion. It plays an important role while treating humanity and demand that each individual ought to inculcate the feeling of brotherhood by loyalty, by working hand-in-hand with others for the betterment at individual and social level.

Fallowing general conception about fraternity, I will substantiate how Rawls's notion of justice as fairness underlies the vision of fraternity. Indeveloping fraternal sentiments in justice as fairness, I will substantiate if there is a connection between the values of fraternity and equality? GeoffreyCupit argues,

> Fraternity is concerned with what we owe to each other on account of there being relationships between us - relationships of brotherhood, sisterhood, and fellowship. Fraternity requires benevolence: it requires us to want, and where appropriate to promote, the good of those who are our brothers, sisters, or fellows.[99]

It can be argue that the act of benevolence and fraternity is understood as distinctive from fraternity since the act of benevolence presupposes kindness and good will and other virtue aside from fraternity. Take for example what Geoffrey Cupit writes in Fraternityand Equality,

> We owe to others in virtue of fraternity is to be different from what we owe on account of kind of beings those others are., or in virtue of the qualities that others have or as what others have done good for us. However one should make clear that fraternal obligation in the society is not the act of benevolence. Fraternal obligations are distinctive in being based on a specific type of relation or connectedness.[100]

Fraternal obligation implies that we ought to treat each and every individual on the assumption that "people are by nature equal and free".[101] This assumption is an ideal which is going to be fully realized only in a well ordered society. Therefore, in this aspect human nature is not something granted, but something which needs to be realized in the form of institutionalizing fraternity with the help of equality principle particularly difference principle.

The values of fraternity and equality are considered as a complementary to each other. We often perceive the values of fraternity and equality together because a people who believe in fraternity also believe in equality and vice versa. Both are the two sides of the same coin and the denial of equality corrodes the fraternal sentiments. When inequality and discrimination occur in our society then the sense of fellowship and brotherhood is less likely to flourish. Inequality may strain our sense of being 'all in it together', our sense of being members of one 'family'. It creates sense of gap between people who are better off and worse off and less fraternal feelings to treat others as our brother and sisters. It might that those who are well off people can treated those who are less well off out of sympathy or pity rather than from a sense of solidarity and brotherhood. In Rawls's just society, the sense of inequality undermines fraternal sentiments of brotherhood. However, Rawls's difference principle does not undermine fraternal sentiments because it plays an important role in institutionalizing the values of liberty, equality and fraternity.

Rawls's difference principle focuses that social and economic inequalities are justified only when these inequalities are beneficial for the sake of the least advantaged people of the society. According to Geoffrey,

> Difference principle is the way of institutionalizing fraternity. The difference principle, however, does seem to correspond to a natural meaning of fraternity: namely to the idea of not wanting to have greater advantages unless this is to be the benefit of others who are less well off. The family, in its ideal conception and often in practice, is one place where the principle of maximizing the sum of advantages is rejected. Members of family commonly do not wish to gain unless they can do in ways that further the interest ofthe rest.[102]

Rawls's equality principle of justice particularly difference principle can be seen as capturing a plausible understanding of what fraternity requires. The difference principle justified inequality so long as the degree of social and economic situation of the worst off would be improved. Its purpose is to make those who are less well off to well off so that their improvement reduces the inequality. While minimizing their social and political inequality of those who are worst off is way to promotes fraternal feeling. Therefore, tripartite principle of liberty, equality and fraternity comprise of institutional arrangement Rawls's perfect society wherein each person would be fairly treated as free and equal. The idea of freedom incorporates an ideal of equality and fraternity which implies each individual have the right to be free and ought to be treated equally. It ensures that every individual by nature are free and equal and justice demands that individual's freedom and their respect is to be realized in a well ordered society. However no two individual alike justice demands that each individual by nature differ in respect of their capacities and abilities to develop their talents. So the idea of equality and difference principle guarantees equal start on the one hand and individual's achievements depend on their effort and merit and not on any kind of privileges of the society.

To bring this chapter an end, I can say that, Rawls use of social contract under veil of ignorance has immense effect that concern for what makes for a just society. Rawls notion of distributive justice is the most influential one as he criticizes utilitarian conception of justice while developing a contractual liberal conception of justice. He combines several criteria of justice under the idea of contract which exemplifies consent and voluntarism by trying to show how self-interested persons, with legitimate competing claims arrive at naturally acceptable social arrangements. In Rawls's distributive justice citizens can best understand the notion of Justice by thinking of it as a 'set of principles' that would be agreed upon by everyone if they had to decide in a hypothetical or original position. This position is one in which the participants are all faced with veil of ignorance which denies all knowledge of personality's social status, moral characters, wealth, talents, life plans. It enables the contracting parties to choose principles of justice without prejudice. It is assumed that persons in the original position are rational, capable of 'conception of good' and have a 'sense of justice'. They are rational with capacity for intelligent pursuit of one's own interests to enter into an agreement that they adhere and fulfill. Therefore he adopts an idea of an agreement about justice and formulates an institutional principle in a well ordered society wherein wealth and opportunity should be distributed fairly. These institutional arrangement plays an important role to address the problem of Justice directly and not via social welfare. Rawls distributive justice plays an important role to build an egalitarian society wherein each individual's aspiration would be taken care by not liberty and equality of opportunities but through institutional mechanism of fraternity.

In formulating Rawls's perfect justice with reference to distributive justice, natural liberty and liberal equality of opportunity unable to develop a just society because society consists in diversity of natural, social and economic inequality etc. In such diversity, justice demands that, liberal equality does not institutionalize the idea of fraternity. It can be possible through 'democratic equality'[103] which promotes not only the idea of fair equality of opportunity but the idea of 'difference principle' so that any social inequalities can be taken by institutional arrangement in favor of those who are naturally, socially, economically deprived. Moreover such impartial institutional principle fills the gap between privileged and underprivileged and reduces discrimination, inequality and conflict in society. In this way, the justice occurs in democratic equality with tripartite principle of liberty, equality and fraternity can be taken together as the basic requirement of Rawls's 'well-ordered society'.

References

Rawls, John. *A Theory of Justice.* Cambridge: Harvard University Press, 1971.

Rawls, John. *Justice as Fairness A Restatement.* Edited by Erin Kelly. USA: Harvard University Press, 2001.

Aristotle. *Nichomachean Ethics,* Translated by J. A. K. Thompson. London: Penguin Books, 2004.

James P. Sterba. *Justice: Alternative Political Perspectives.* Canada: Wodswort/ Thomson Learning, 2003.

Freeman, Samuel. *Introduction: John Rawls- An Overview.* Cambridge: Cambridge University Press, 2003.

Johnston, David. *A Brief History of Justice.* Edited by David Johnston. 143-165. United Kingdom: Willy Blackwell, 2011.

Singh, R. P. "Justice and Secularism A Conceptual and Cross-Cultural Analysis". *Morality and Social Justice.* Edited by Abha Singh. Decent BOOK: New Delhi, 2010.

Posner, A. Richard. *The Economic of Justice.* Cambridge: Harvard University Press, 1981.

Sen, Amartya. *The Idea of Justice.* London: Penguin Books, 2009.

Rawls, John. *Political Liberalism.* New York: Columbia University Press, 1996.

Raphael, D. D. *Problem of Political Philosophy.* London: Macmillan Press Ltd, 1990.

Kristjansson, Kristjan. *Justice and Desert - Based Emotions* . England: Ashgate Publishing Limited, 2006.

Mandle. Jon. *Rawls's A Theory of Justice: An Introduction.* UK: Cambridge University Press, 2009.

Kymlicka, Will. "Liberal Equality". *Contemporary Political Philosophy An Introduction.* New York: Oxford University Press, 2002.

Macintyre, A1asdair. *Whose Justice? Which Rationality?* London: Duckworth, 1988.

Rees, John. *Equality.* New York: Praeger Publishers, 1971.

Gombert Tobias, "Foundations of Social Democracy". Berlin: Friedrich-EbertStiftung, 2009.

Raphael, D.D. "Liberty and Authority". *Problems of Political Philosophy.* Britain: Macmillan Press Ltd, 1990.

Gilman, Ives Benjamin. "What is Liberty When Two or More Persons are concerned?" *International Journal of Ethics* 32. No. 2.1922: 124-128.

Berlin, Isaiah. "Two concepts of Liberty," *Four Essays on Liberty.* Oxford: Oxford University Press, 1970.

Pogge, Thomas. *Realizing Rawls.* Ithaca: Cornell University Press, 1989.

Hart, H.L.A. "Rawls on Liberty and its Priority," In Norman Daniels (Ed.), *Reading Rawls.* New York: Basic Books, 1975.

Martin, Rex. *Rawls and Rights.* Kansas: University of Kansas Press, 1985.

Besant, Annie. "Liberty, equality, fraternity", *Bristol Selected Pamphlets, 1880.* URL: http://www.jstor.org/stab1e/

Cupit, Geoffrey. "Fraternity and Equality". *Philosophy* 88, No. 2, 2013: 300-305.

Notes

1. Rawls. *A Theory of Justice.* p. 3.
2. *Ibid,* p. 3.
3. Rawls. *Justice as Fairness A Restatement.* p. 5.
4. *Ibid.* p. 136.
5. *Ibid,* p. 303.
6. Aristotle, *Nichomachean Ethics.* p. 115.
7. *Ibid.* p. 120.
8. James P. Sterba. *Justice: Alternative Political Perspectives.* p. 32.
9. Rawls. *A Theory of Justice.* p. 11.
10. Freeman, Samuel. *Introduction: John Rawls- An Overview.* p. 142.
11. Rawls. *A Theory of Justice.* p. 212.
12. Rawls. *Justice as Fairness: A Restatement.* p. 107.
13. Rawls. *A Theory of Justice.* p. 3.
14. *Ibid,* p. 30.
15. Rawl s. *A Theory of Justice* p. 184.
16. Johnston, David. *"A Brief History of Justice.* p. 197.
17. Freeman, Samuel. *Introduction: John Rawls- An Overview.* p. 146.
18. R.P. Singh. *Morality and Social Justice.* p. 54.
19. Posner, A. Richard. *The Economic of Justice.* p. 76.
20. Rawls. *A Theory of Justice.* p. 27.
21. *Ibid.* p. 119.
22. Freeman, Samuel. *Introduction: John Rawls- An Overview.* p. 148.
23. Rawls. *A Theory of Justice.* p. 119.
24. *Ibid.* p. 142.
25. *Ibid.* p. 472.
26. *Ibid.* p. 472.
27. Freeman, Samuel. *Introduction: John Rawls- An Overview.* p. 143.
28. Rawls. *A Theory of Justice.* p. 7.
29. Rawls. *A Theory of Justice.* p. 7.
30. *Ibid.* p. 454.

31. *Ibid.* p. 56.
32. Sen. *Idea of Justice.* p. 7.
33. Rawls. *Political Liberalism.* p. 20.
34. Sen. *Idea of Justice,* p. 7.
35. *Ibid.* p. 7.
36. *Ibid.* p. 7.
37. Rawls, *Justice as Fairness A Restatement.* pp. 41-43.
38. Rawls, *A Theory of Justice.* p. 142.
39. *Ibid,* p. 119.
40. *Ibid,* p. 136.
41. Rawls. *Justice as Fairness: A Restatement.* p. 57.
42. Rawls. A *Theory of Justice.* p. 92.
43. Rawls. *Justice as Fairness: A Restatement.* p. 58.
44. *Ibid.* p. 258.
45. Raphael, *Problem of Political Philosophy.* p. 119.
46. *Ibid,* pp. 113-145.
47. Rawls, *A Theory of Justice* . p. 136.
48. Freeman, Samuel. *Introduction: John Rawls- An Overview.* p. 154.
49. Kristjansson, Kristjan. "Justice and Desert - Based Emotions". p. 44.
50. Rawls. *A Theory of Justice.* p. 4.
51. Raphael, "Justice". *Problems ofPolitical Philosophy.* p. 146.
52. Mandle. *Rawls's A Theory of Justice: An Introduction.* p. 36.
53. Raphael, *Problems ofPolitical Philosophy.* pp. 146-147.
54. Rawls. *Justice As Fairness A Restatement.* p. 43.
55. *Ibid.,* p. 56.
56. Rawls. *A Theory of Justice.* p. 61.
57. *Ibid.*, p. 61.
58. *Ibid.*
59. Sen. *Idea of Justice.* p. 78.
60. Sen. *Idea of Justice* . p. 78.
61. *Ibid.*, p. 78.
62. MacIntyre. *Whose Justice? Which Rationality?* p. 207.
63. *Ibid.,* p. 207.
64. Rawls, *Theory of Justice.* p. 208.
65. Rees, John. *Equality.* p. 11.
66. Rawls. *Justice as Fairness: A Restatement.* pp. 18-19.
67. Gombert Tobias, "Foundations of Social Democracy". p. 36.
68. *Ibid.,* p. 36.
69. Rawls. *A Theory of Justice.* p. 27.
70. *Ibid.*, p. 202.

71. Raphael, D.D. "Liberty and Authority". *Problems of Political Philosophy.* p. 56.
72. Gilman, Ives Benjamin. "What is Liberty When Two or More Persons are concerned". pp. 124-128
73. Berlin, Isaiah. "Two concepts of Liberty". *Four Essays on Liberty.* p. 121.
74. *Ibid.,* p. 122.
75. *Ibid.,* p. 131.
76. *Ibid.,* p. 131.
77. Rawls. *A Theory ofJustice.* p. 63.
78. *Ibid.,* p. 64.
79. *Ibid.,* p. 65.
80. Rawls, *A Theory of Justice,* p. 201.
81. Rawls. *A Theory of Justice.* p. 202.
82. Pogge, Thomas. *Realizing Rawls.* p. 159.
83. *Ibid.,* p. 159.
84. Hart. "Rawls on Liberty and its Priority". *Reading Rawls.* p. 235.
85. Martin, Rex. *Rawls and Rights.* p. 240.
86. Rawls. *Political Liberalism.* pp. 5-6.
87. *Ibid.,* p. 6.
88. *Ibid.,* p. 230.
89. Rawls, *A Theory of Justice.* p. 29.
90. Kymlicka, "Liberal Equality". *Contemporary Political Philosophy An Introduction.* p. 55.
91. *Ibid.,* p. 55.
92. Raphael, "Justice". *Problem of Political Philosophy.* p. 125.
93. *Ibid.,* p. 55.
94. Rex, Martin. *Rawls and Rights.* p. 67.
95. *Ibid.,* pp. 66-67.
96. Besant, Annie. "Liberty, Equality, Fraternity". p. 3.
97. Singh, R.P. "Justice and Secularism A Conceptual and Cross-Cultural Analysis". *Morality and Social Justice.* p. 54.
98. Besant, Annie. "Liberty, Equality, Fraternity". p. 7.
99. Cupit, Geoffrey. "Fraternity and Equality". pp. 300-305.
100. *Ibid.,* p. 300.
101. Rawls. *A Theory of Justice.* p. 12.
102. Cupit, Geoffrey. "Fraternity and Equality". p. 305.
103. Rawls. *A Theory of Justice,* pp. 65-70.

Chapter - 3

Amartya Sen on Justice as Welfare

This chapter focuses on the notion of justice as welfare in Amartya Sen's philosophy which deals with minimizing injustices at individual and social level becomes the foundational element in notion of justice as welfare. In justice as welfare, Sen's capability approach is an attempt to address the issues of injustices by removing obstacles in actual opportunities and highlighting that human being has a dignity with their ability to pursue their own ends. It ensures a new conception of justice as welfare in terms of human functioning and capabilities which enable people to pursue their wellbeing. For Sen, the notion of minimizing injustice is very necessary wherein less people are capable to use their freedom, rights and toleration. More importantly, the search for perfect justice could distract us from tackling real-life, immediate injustices such as discrimination relating to education, skill, health, environment, etc. for women, tribal people and marginalized community who are deprived of all these. The perfect justice focuses on "ideal institutional choices and arrangements such as right behaviour as well as right institutions where everyone is expected to act fairly to do his or her part in upholding just institutions."[1] In this way, ideal institutional choice and arrangement focused approaches to justice are not sufficient conditions because society consists of human beings who are outside of the institutions and the each individual gets affected by the institutional arrangement.

Sen's minimizing injustice is an alternative and dynamic departure from perfect justice of Kant and Rawls's idea of justice. It can be argued that, instead of institutional mechanism which governs collective choices; Sen's minimizing injustices make each and every individual to "act on his/her own preferences".[2] Sen's justice as welfare does not concentrate on the means of primary goods and just institutions but minimizing injustices by removing obstacles in actual opportunities in day to day life. On Sen's view, one must start from the question of what makes a good life and build up from this to a theory of the social good. The opportunity to live a 'good life' matters most for well-being rather than the accumulation of resources, and that opportunities result from the capabilities that people have. The 'capability approach' focuses more on person's more on wellbeing and less on the possessions of goods. According to capability approach, resources do not have an intrinsic value; instead their value derives from the opportunity that it provides to people. It concentrates on human functioning and capability. The former corresponds anything that a person succeeds in doing or being like engaging in any activity and being well nourished. The latter consists in people's opportunity to achieve particular functioning if one chooses to do or to be.

In justice as welfare, capability approach constitutes an important contribution to enable people to enable them to live long life, healthy life, being educated and more important the having a voice to participate in decision which affects their life. It underlies in the provision which ensures that the minimum level such as health, education, nutrition and political participation. Its purpose is to promote human well-being and development which is not assesed by income and about what people have but about what each individual are able to do and to be with what they have. There are various ways Sen's capability approach contributes to human wellbeing in justice as welfare. Firstly, capability approach concerns for human beings and their quality of life to be the central focus and does not entails on the means (opulence or economic growth in terms of GDP rather wellbeing)[3] to promote the quality of life as an ends in themselves. Secondly, it focuses on human freedom and the ability to make decisions that affect their life. Thirdly capability approach is central to people's agency and their dignity.

For the sake of clarity and precision", I shall divide the present chapter into three parts. In Part I, I will develop critical exposition of perfect justice which amounts to the lack of genuine information concerning injustices. However, it fails to address society's real problems that manifest injustices in the form of poverty and malnutrition, slavery, hunger and deprivation, subjugation of women, lack of education, health facilities and other injustices. It can be argue that Kant and Rawls's perfect justice concentrate "primarily on getting the institutions right with transcendental institutionalism and it is not directly focused on the actual societies that would ultimately emerge"[4]. Sen's minimizing injustice is deeply concern for the assessment of how to reduce injustices from the society rather to identify what perfect society would look like. In Part II, I'll substantiate Sen's freedom and capability for the enhancement of individual and collective quality of life so that each individual has to enjoy valuable activities and states of being. It tries to seek capability approach is an innovative approach for the assessment of human development and does not concentrates for the assessment people's wellbeing through accumulation primary goods like commodities, liberty and self respect. In Part III, I will develop public enlightenment and well-being as the operative terms for justice as welfare. Sen's incorporates people's capability and their wellbeing as an alternative which emphasizes that people, instead of resources, are the real wealth and the purpose of justice is to create an enabling society. Public enlightenment entails enabling society wherein individual's wellbeing is understood by person's capability to do things he or she has reason to value. Sen's minimizing injustice promotes human quality of life at the stage of public enlightenment where each individual becomes enlighten and capable to make decision about issues that affect their lives and minimize injustice to that extent. The core element of public enlightenment is to focus on people's agency as the realization of goals and values he or she has reason to pursue, whether or not they are concerned with her own well-being, emphasizes that people must seen simply as passive patients of social patterning but rather as active agents of their own well-being.

Coming to the basic issues which I am discussing in the above three parts, I would like to point out that, Sen criticizes the original position, i.e. "veil of ignorance' of Rawls theory of justice" which amounts to the lack of genuine information concernmg injustice. Sen has also criticized the utilitarianism of Bentham and Mill on the ground that act utilitarianism and rule utilitarianism along with hedonistic calculus cannot help us much either in minimizing injustices or enhancing happiness. Instead of transcendental institutionalism in Rawls, Sen proposes *realization - focused comparison* which is concerned in removing the manifest injustice from the world and hence he goes to 'retreat of justice.' On minimizing injustices, Sen distinguishes between *niti* and *nyaya* both concepts give the vision of justice but the notion of *nyaya* which underlies comprehensive idea of realized justice in terms of individual's suffering and with this, I will formulae and understand justice in broader sense for the sake of entire humanity. I will bring out the discrepancies and the implications between wellbeing (collective) and happiness (individualistic) to substantiate minimizing injustice in Sen. With this brief remark regarding

Sen's minimizing injustice and formulating the notion of justice as welfare; I shall come to the Part I of the chapter.

Part - I

Forms Of Injustices: Unfreedom, Poverty, Lack of Education and Health

Sen is primarily interested in removing various types of injustices form the world and hence he goes on to 'retreat of justice'. Often, when we are concerned for justice, we understand that justice is to being treated fairly, just desert, just society and its fair institutional arrangement in the matter of resource allocation. Justice is a complex and contested concept because of the discrepancies that arises out of debates on moral, legal, religious, human rights issues. There are systematic types of injustices comes in various forms, wherever the institutional principle of distributive justice, procedural justice, or human rights relating to political, economic and social rights are violated. It can be argue that an institutional principle does not address society's real problems that manifest injustices in the form of lack of freedom, poverty and malnutrition, slavery, hunger and deprivation, subjugation of women, lack of education, health facilities etc. To remove various forms of injustices, Sen relies on welfare mechanism that plays an important role to enhance people's standard of living. For Sen, "there is no law against dying of hunger".[5] For the elimination of such type of injustice requires attention to not only employment and food entitlement but also the promotion of health care, elementary education as well as clean water, environment and sanitation etc.

There are numbers of important questions surrounding justices have been fiercely debated over the course of human history like what is justice? What is a perfectly just society? Is justice has much to do with being treated fairly, equally etc.? How can the form of injustices relating to the discrimination between rich and poor, caste system, racism and sexism of the present state of affairs be removed? There are number of ways where systematic forms of invisible injustice persist in a society which can be difficult to recognize. These are discrimination between privileged class of people and underprivileged class who are less well off in society. In comparison to 'well off' people the 'less well off lacks freedom and gets lesser opportunities. As a result, many of them are deprived of basic necessities such as food, education, housing, and employment. Their access to resources is limited and most of the time, they feel helpless as there is nothing much they can do about it. Ultimately, the 'well-off' are getting richer and the 'worst off' are getting poorer. The unequal distribution of wealth between the rich and the poor is a major concern. For example, the caste discrimination in India is one of the important forms of injustices that has been there in our society since a long time. The caste system based on different caste hierarchies has fragmented the society among various sections. The upper caste dominates on lower caste's people. They do not provide them with an opportunity to grow. This kind of caste based discrimination creates a huge gap between the economic condition of the rich and the poor which leads to injustices at individual and social level in the case of India. Racism is one of the other forms of invisible injustice. The superiority complex of one race against other races often imparts hatred in the minds of people, taking numerous lives. It acts as a big obstacle in minimizing injustices in general and development of society in particular. There is another form of social injustice underlies in the form of gender discrimination based on sex. Women have been considered as an inferior sex for centuries now. In comparison to men, women own very less property, not only in the developing countries, but in the developed countries as well. Such discriminations related to man and woman is considered to be a major issue in the process of imparting justice that can translate into welfare. Apart from gender discrimination, there is example of impaired or physically disadvantaged people who are discriminated at every sphere of life including their workplaces which is one of the most alarming issues and it turns out to be a major cause of social injustice.

In justice as welfare, Amartya Sen is not looking for a perfectly just society rather tries to remove various "forms of social injustices"[6] that are occurring in our society. He argues that, "we do need to know what perfect justice is to know that a particular state of affairs is unjust and comparatively more unjust than some other state of affairs".[7] Instead of looking a perfectly just society, Sen tries to remove various form of social injustices to make 'less unjust society' wherein each and every individual can develop the capacity of self-determination so that so that they realize their full potential. In the search of less unjust society, he propounded the realization focused approach to justice which is not concern for fair institutional arrangement and its process rather tries to seek social outcomes through a comparative evaluation of social injustice relating to unfreedom, poverty and malnutrition, slavery, hunger and deprivation, subjugation of women, lack of education, health facilities on the one hand and invisible injustices relating to social discrimination between rich and poor, caste, races, and gender etc on the other. These forms of injustices have been occurring in the society since long time and the only way to tackle this menace through Sen's realization focused approach to justice.

Sen has propounded the 'idea of Justice' as a departure from both "transcendental institutionalism and 'realization-focused comparative' approaches, and he inclined towards latter i.e. *realization focused*"[8] approach to justice which tries to remove various form of injustices that are occurring in our society. The realization focused approach to justice is not concern for perfectly just institutions rather tries to seek 'least unjust society'. For Sen, the search for 'least unjust society' can be possible through comparative evaluation of social alternatives based on plurality of reasons and a principle of democracy is the central concern of Justice. Moreover, the concern for Sen's advancement of Justice makes to move beyond comparative focused to realization understanding wherein actual realization of justice in the society is more important than the institutional arrangements *per se.* According to Sen,

> It is some time claimed that justice is not a matter of reasoning at all; it is one of being appropriately sensitive and having the right nose for injustice. It is easy enough to be tempted to think along these lines. When we find, for example, a ranging famine, it seems natural to protest rather than reason elaborately about justice and injustice. And yet a calamity would be a cause of injustice only if it could have been prevented, and particularly if those who could have undertaken preventive action had failed to try. Reasoning in some form cannot but be involved in moving from the observation of a tragedy to the diagnosis of injustice. Furthermore, cases of injustice may be much more complex and subtle than the assessment of an observable calamity. There could be different arguments suggesting disparate conclusions, and evaluations of justice may be anything but straight forward.[9]

An eternal law of justice demands that one should be sensitive towards injustices that emerges which deeply concerned about how to minimizes injustices from the society. The idea of perfectly just society seeks to identify just or fair institutional arrangement. However, it ignores society's real problems that manifests in the form of injustices such as slavery, suppression of women, hunger and deprivation, lack of health and educational facilities, and most importantly, inability to use social opportunities in valuable activities and states of being. It primarily concentrates on right institutions and does not concern for the identification of injustices in the form of capability deficiency.

Sen tries to construct an inclusive society wherein each individual can pursue their wellbeing and minimizes various form of injustices at individual and social level. In formulating the notion of minimizing injustice, Sen has revisited the two traditions of reasoning about justice and injustices during European Enlightenment of 18th and 19th century. For him, "identification of perfect justice is neither necessary nor sufficient and more incline towards comparative justice". "Its aim is to clarify how we can proceed to address question of enhancing justice and removing injustices".[10] It does not based on compliance with fair institutional principles formulated by social contract theory which limits itself to comparing social states with respect to degrees of injustices. Sen's alternative approach to justice is based on social choice theory that identifies welfare society wherein all possible injustices would be removed.

> Social choice theory as a discipline is concerned with arriving at over all judgments for social choice based on a diversity of perspectives and priorities. The outcomes of the social choice procedure take the form of ranking different states of affairs from a social choice procedure take the form of ranking different states of affair from a social point of view in the light of assessment of the people involved.[11]

Justice based on social choice theory underlies comparative justice IS very different form transcendental institutionalism which is looking for a perfectly just society.

Historically, the enlightenment movement of the eighteenth and nineteenth centuries in Europe produced two intellectual traditions. These are, firstly, contracterian propounded by Hobbes, Locke, Rousseau, Kant, Rawls, and other philosophers of social contract school. Secondly, social realization focused comparative approach led by Smith, Condorcet, Wollstonecraft, Marx, Bentham, and Mill. The former concern for 'transcendental institutionalism' underlies 'perfect justice' and latter on the ground that its main concern is about 'social realization' underlies 'relative justice'. "This departure has the dual effect, first, of taking the comparative rather than the transcendental route, and second, of focusing on actual realizations in the societies involved, rather than only on institutions and rules".[12] In these two traditions of reasoning about justice, Sen calls the former is "transcendental institutionalism which concentrates its attention on what identifies as a perfect justice, rather than on relative comparison of justice and injustice".[13] Its enquiry is "aimed at identifying the nature of 'the just', rather, than finding some criteria for an alternative being 'less unjust' than another".[14] Further, the contracreian approach "concentrated on identifying just institutional arrangement for a society".[15] Moreover, the contracterian approach has two distinct features:

1. The contracterian approach tries only to identify social characteristics that cannot be transcended in terms of justice and its focus is thus not on comparing feasible societies, all of which may fall short of the ideals of perfection.[16]
2. In searching for perfection, transcendental institutionalism concentrates primarily on getting the institution right and not directly focused on the actual societies that would ultimately emerge. The nature of the society that would result from any given set of institutions must, of course depend also on non-institutional features, such as actual behaviors of people and their social interactions.[17] On the other hand, the followers of social realization focused approach remain in engaged in arriving at the least unjust society through "comparisons of societies that already existed or could feasibly emerge, rather than confining their analyses to transcendental searches for a perfectly just society".[18]

Fallowing two traditions of justice namely contractarian approach and social realization approach to justice, Sen proposes his idea of justice as welfare in terms of 'minimizing injustice' as a departure from both enlightenment traditions. However, in contrast to transcendental institutionalism, Sen advocates what he calls *a realization-focused approach* to justice. Now it is necessary to see what makes him to move beyond comparative focused to realization focused understanding wherein actual realization of justice in the society is more important than transcendental institutional arrangements in the conception of justice. Sen has two fundamental problems with "transcendental institutionalism' and he calls it the problem of (a) 'infeasibility' and (b) redundancy".[19] It can be argue that there are two problems,

> First, there may be no reasoned agreement at all, even under strict conditions of impartiality and open minded scrutiny on the nature of the just society: this is the issue of the feasibility of finding an agreed transcendental solution.
>
> Second, an exercise of practical reason that involves an actual choice demands a framework for comparison of justice for choosing among

the feasible alternatives and not an identification of a possibly unavailable perfect situation that could not be transcended: this is issue of the redundancy of the search for a transcendental solution.[20]

The problem of 'transcendental institutionalism' and its arrangements are surrounded with two flaws i.e. infeasibility and redundancy. It is infeasibility because 'transcendental institutionalism' tries to search for perfectly just institutions which are based on the assumption that there is a mutual consensus arrived through public reason on the perfectly just or fair institutions and society. However the plurality of argument based on public reason does not reach the stage of mutual consensus to what constitute fair or just society or institution. To Sen, contracterians are unable to realize this problem of infeasibility. for instance utilitarian, egalitarian and libertarian approach to justice argues for their own institutional principle and their logical ground for their claim to be just. Take for example in the debate on the conception of justice, Sen provides a practical illustration- which he calls "Three Children and a Flute"[21]. Imagine which of the three children Anne, Bob and Carla should get a flute about which they are quarrelling. Anne says, the flute should be given to her because she is the only one who knows how to play it. Bob, on the other, claims the flute should be handed to him as he is so poor that he has no toys to play with. Carla then intervenes and says that it was she who made the flute. How do we decide between these three legitimate claims? Who gets the flute depends on institutional arrangement, for instance, utilitarian will argue for Anne because she can actually play and she will get maximum pleasure. Bob, the poorest, will have the support of the egalitarian. The libertarian would opt for Carla. However, for Sen, there is no such institutional arrangements can help to resolve this dispute in a universally acceptable manner. However, their position would not arrive at mutual agreement and therefore does not solve the problem of arriving on a perfectly transcendental solution. The second problems is the problem of redundancy in transcendental institutionalism and it states that if the exercise of reason for the actual choice of perfectly just institutions demands comparisons of existing situation, then there is no need to search for transcendental perfect institutions.

Sen, says, "If a theory of justice is to guide reasoned choice of policies, strategies or institutions, then the identification of fully just social arrangements is neither necessary nor sufficient".[22] For example, Sen has illustrated the problem of redundancy in accordance with the choice between *Picasso* and *Dali*. It is obvious that the ideal picture in the world is the *Mona Lisa* and it is not essential to talk about what may be the greatest picture in the world, to choose between the two alternatives that we are facing. When the choice is between *Dali* and *Picasso* only then it is neither sufficient nor any help to know that the *Mona Lisa* is the most perfect picture in the world and in this way if the choice has to be made out of possible alternatives then the search for ideal one is unnecessary.

While the search for a 'least unjust society', where "justice cannot be indifferent to the lives that people can actually live"[23]. In advocating realizationfocused approach to justice, Sen is leaning towards philosophers such as Adam Smith, Condorcet, Mary Wollstonecraft, Bentham, Mill, Marx and others.

> Even though these authors, with their very different ideas of the demand of justice, proposed quite distinct ways of making social comparisons, it can be said, at the risk of only a slight exaggeration, that they were all involved in comparisons of societies that already existed or could feasibly emerge, rather than confining their analyses to transcendental searches for a perfectly just society. Those focusing on realization-focused comparisons were often interested primarily in the removal of manifest injustice from the world that they saw".[24]

Moreover, Sen is more inclined towards social realization approaches to justice on the ground that its main concern is to identify the desirability of particular social realizations rather than looking for fair institutional principles in an ideal society. Sen has focused on actual realization in the societies rather to concentrates just institutional rules as it may not possible to have mutual consensus on ideal institutions . The comparative approach to justice helps us to arrive at a widespread consensus on the injustice of certain practices or outcomes relative to others. Sen's comparative approach to justice closely aligns with his social choice theory.

However, Sen is leaning towards philosophers who do not believe in perfect justice rather comparative kind of justice. It is important to see their attempt towards minimizing injustices in one way or another way. On Sen's view, enlightenment tradition thinkers such as Marry Wollstonecraft, Condorcet, Adam Smith, Karl Marx held the same view of comparative justice. Bentham and Mill have also tried to maximize the welfare through social utility in one way or another. For Adam Smith, the idea of justice is not understood simply as a protection of person's property rights but also a protection from a violation of their human dignity that can provide equal opportunity for human flourishing. As an expert of social choice perspective is the intellectual giant in enlightenment tradition. Smith's conception of justice underlies in protection of property rights as well as human dignity as a moral worth. "By considering Smith's idea on education and human development, protecting person's dignity turns out not simply to be a matter of protecting a person from insult and personal injury but rather a matter of protecting their material livelihood and the opportunities to develop their mental and moral capacities".[25] So the virtue of avoiding injury is justice and justice is the foundation of law and the subject ofjurisprudence. Smith is considered as a 'moral egalitarian' and believed that, each person is of equal moral worth. This claim that departs radically from the received view - generally found among economists, at least - that the soul of Smith's thought was unconcerned with matters that have major implications for social justice.[26] Smith's conception of justice is not simply the liberal account of justice but an account of the removal of obstacle in the way of human flourishing.

Moreover, Smith's conception of justice has both negative and positive effects. On the one hand it can be understood negatively as the reduction or minimization of these obstacles such as material deprivation, domination, oppression, lack of individual autonomy, on the other hand, it can also be taken positively in terms of the provision of opportunities to develop themselves in accordance with their conscience. Sen has adopted social choice theory for the preference of social realization over institutional arrangements. It is social choice theory tries to focus on society's problems rather concentrates on fair institutional arrangement. Sen has rightly addresses question like why does social choice theory has been satisfactory than social contract in *Idea of Justice,*

> How would justice be advanced? Rather than others, for example, 'what would be perfectly just institutions? This departure has the dual effect, first, of taking the comparative rather than the transcendental route, and second, of focusing on actual realizations in the societies involved, rather than only on institutions and rules?[27]

Fallowing Adam Smith, Condorcet is an inspired proponent of human rights and particularly rights of women. Through educational and constitutional reforms, he created a liberal, rational and democratic society. In Condorcet's social choice theory, the concept of collective reason plays a central role in his analysis of public life. In fact, in public life he campaigned for economic freedom, religious toleration, legal reforms, the abolition of slavery and the removal of the privileged of the nobility. For him, "It is not enough for society to be governed by the law; that law must be just. It is not enough for individuals to obey the law; the law must conform what is required to maintain the rights of each individuals".[28] For Condorcet, collective reason must necessarily lead to a fundamental principle of justice. And any form of just social decisions must focus on the protection of the equality and human rights. Further, when people in a particular community set aside their own interests they feel that all members of the community, as human beings, share the same moral faculties: in particular, reason and sensitivity. As a result, people must share the same fundamental rights which can be justified through reflection on the moral nature of humanity. The social choice theory is revived by Kenneth Arrow are generally considered as the basis of the modem social choice theory.

> Arrow put the discipline of social choice in a structured and analytical form, with explicitly stated and examined axioms, demanding that social decisions satisfy certain minimal conditions of reasonableness, from which the appropriate social thinking and choice of social states would emerge.[29]

Further, Mill and Bentham have attempted towards minimizing injustices on the basis of maximizing utility on the ground that act utilitarianism and rule utilitarianism along with hedonistic calculus attempt to seek welfare society. However in utilitarian arrangement, people who are deprived can distort their own apprehension of utility prospects when utility information is poor and lead to the stage of poverty. So utility principle is unable to justify severe deprivation and inequality and such social realization can be evaluated through capability that people have rather their utilities or happiness. According to Sen, "utility, happiness and desire implies twin characteristics: firstly, of being fully grounded on the mental attitude of the person and secondly avoiding any direct reference to the person's own valuation exercise. The former he calls as 'physical condition neglect and latter valuation neglect".[30]

There are two major problems with utilitarianism; firstly, it concentrates entirely on individual's utility or happiness as the adequate measure of well-being and secondly, it ignores individual's agency which is an indispensible part of being human. "A person who is ill-fed, undernourished, unsheltered and ill can still be high up in the scale of happiness or desire-fulfillment if he or she has learned to have realistic desires and to take pleasure in small mercies".[31] It shows that despite of person's ill situation one can have "adapted preferences so utility can easily be affected by mental conditioning and adaptive preferences".[32]

Further he says, "The deprivations are suppressed and muffled in the scale of utilities by the necessity of endurance in uneventful survival".[33] Sen criticizes utilitarian approach for its fully dependence on personal satisfaction and its exclusion of other sources such as physical and social conditions in assessing welfare which ultimately leads to various kinds of injustices in society.

After a brief critical assessment of utilitarianism that focuses on minimizing injustices and enhancing happiness, now I tum to resource-based approach of Rawls. Rawls approach is unsatisfactory in removing injustices. Noman Daniels says in his book *Equality of What: Welfare, Resources, or Capability,* "individuals vary in their ability to convert primary goods into what is really important to them, namely, the freedom or capability to do or to be (to function) what they choose".[34] It is the moral concern that individual's variability in the ability to convert primary goods with equal efficiency. This kind of variability among individuals implies that the 'primary goods' are an inflexible measure because it ignores people's variability in converting goods with equal efficiency.

> Resources are only the means to enhance people's well-being and advantage, whereas the concern should be with what matters intrinsically, namely people's functionings and capabilities. Resources-based theories do not acknowledge that people differ in their abilities to convert these resources into capabilities, due to personal, social or environmental factors, such as physical and mental handicaps, talents, traditions, social norms and customs, legal rules, a country's public infrastructure, public goods, climate and so on.[35]

Resource based approach, ultimately overlooks fundamental moral concern for equality of capabilities which leads to various injustices at individual and social level. Further Sen, who develops this line of criticism suggests, "There is an element of 'fetishism' in Rawls' use of primary goods".[36] For Sen, ultimate concern is not about the "index of primary goods" but capabilities, which are the result of a "relationship between persons and goods".[37] This approach is an innovative approach where welfare has to be measured by assessing people's freedom to use these resources.

> In contrast with the resource-based lines of thinking, individual advantage is judged in the capability approach by a person's capability to do things he or she has reason to value. A person's advantage in terms of opportunities is judged to be lower than that of another if

> she has less capability - less real opportunity - to achieve those things that she has reason to value. The focus here is on the freedom that a person actually has to do this or be that - things that he or she mayvalue doingor being.[38]

Moreover, Sen is critical of comparative approach as well and proposes the argument for 'accomplishment based understanding of Justice' which focuses that the actual realization of justice in the society is more important than the fair institutional arrangements per se because real life of people and their problems matters more. It is true that an institutional arrangement and its rules are very important in influencing what happens in society but existing society and its form of injustices created not out of institutional arrangement rather includes the lives that people manage or do not manage to live.

To minimize various forms of injustices in a society, Senhas notrevived enlightenment movement of west but revisited argumentative tradition of the East as well. In formulating accomplishment based understanding of Justice, Sen, proposes a distinction between arrangement focused and realization focused understanding of Justice in terms of *niti* and *nyaya* in Indian tradition. Its purpose is to move beyond comparative focused to realization focused understanding wherein *nyaya* or actual realization of justice in the society is more important than *niti* or institutional arrangement. It is the *nyaya* underlies comprehensive outcome of justice. Sen writes in *Idea of Justice* by saying that both concepts: *"niti* and *Nyaya*"[39] underlies the vision of justice but the notion of nyayaunderlies comprehensive idea of realized justice in terms of individual's suffering and with this, justice has to be understood in broader sense for the sake of entire humanity. However, Sen has distinguishes between *niti* and *Nyaya,* one important distinction between two different concepts of justice in early Indian jurisprudence between *niti* and *nyaya.* The former idea, that of *niti,* relates to organizational propriety as well as behavioral correctness, whereas the latter, *nyaya,* is concerned with what emerges and how, and in particular the lives that people are actually able to lead, both stands for justice but *"niti* is an arrangement focused and *nyaya* is concept of realized notion of justice"[40].

Moreover in "Indian jurisprudence, *Niti* and *Nyaya"* are related to the notion of justice but the notion of *nyaya* gives the vision of comprehensive idea of justice. With the vision of *nyaya,* forms of injustice have to be reduces at individual and social level and with this justice has to be understood for the sake of entire humanity. Sen believes that *nyaya-*

based perspective is necessary while dealing with niti and other institutional arrangement which affects present situation as well. That's why he more relies realization focused approach rather transcendental institutional approaches. The former focus on the idea of individual's capability-building rather on accessibility of social goods for individual and social wellbeing.

Therefore, the kind of institutional approach to justices in one way or another way contributes serious problems relating to social, political and economic sphere. For Sen, there is nothing more immediate than the question of people's injustices and their welfare. In this way injustices can be minimized through welfare mechanism in the form of people's substantive freedom and capabilities to enhance their well-being.

Part - II

Freedom and Capability as the Key Terms for Minimising Injustices

To minimize various forms of injustices requires the "removal of major sources unfreedom: poverty, as well as tyranny, poor economic opportunities as well as systematic social deprivation, neglect of public facilities as well as intolerance or over activity of repressive states".[41] There are varieties of unfreedom which restricts people's substantive freedoms that they enjoy for instance, lack of nutritional food, health care, basic education and other social and economic security etc. deprives their basic freedom to survive a good life. In this way, people's substantive freedom plays an important role which focuses on people's development in terms of their freedom and capabilities "that a person actually has to do this or be that- things that he or she may value doing or being".[42] The wellbeing and freedom is person's freedom to achieve those things that are valuable for them. According to the capability approach, an individual's achieved well-being is evaluated by considering the level of her valued functionings...., or the 'beings and doings' that she can attain. potentialfunctionings are her capabilities.

Sen's freedom based capability approach seeks minimization of injustices at individual and social level. Sen's freedom based capability approach concentrates on the well being of each and every individual. Itsmain concern is on minimizing injusticess by removing obstacles in actual opportunities in day to day life rather focusing only on the means of primary goods and just institutions Its purpose is to create an enabling society wherein each individual becomes capable to make decision about issues that affect their lives and minimizes injustices to that extent.

Sen's justice as welfare focuses on removal of major sources of unfreedom: poverty as well as tyranny, poor economic opportunities as well as systematic social deprivation, neglect of public facilities as well as intolerance or over activity of repressive states.[43] It can be realized when each individual would get substantive freedom and eliminates various sources that brings injustices such as poverty, lack of educational and health facilities, sense of intolerance etc. Sen argues that lack of freedom or unfreedom sometimes closely links to the "lack of public facilities and social care, such as the absence of epidemiological programs, or of the organized arrangements for healthcare or educational facilities, or effective institutions for the maintenance of local peace and order".[44] "The violation of freedom results directly from the denial of political and civil liberties by authoritarian regimes and from imposed restrictions on the freedom to participate in the social, political and economic life of the community".[45] Moreover, the expansion of human freedom is not undertaken only as the primary end of development but also its principle means. It is fact that, "many people across the world suffers from varieties of unfreedom. Famines continue to occur in particular regions, denying to millions the basic freedom to survive".[46] By focusing on freedom, justice can be seen in terms of human welfare where,

> Freedom to choose gives us the opportunity to decide what we should do, but with that opportunity comes the responsibility for what we doto the extent that they are chosen actions. Since a capability is the power to do something, the accountability that emanates from that ability - the power - is a part of the capability perspective, and this can make room for demands of duty- what can be broadly called deontological demands.[47]

In assessing the quality of lives, it is argued that life can only be lived well when people are free, and can make real choices. For Sen, human welfare can be defined, "as the process of expanding the real freedoms that people enjoy".[48] Here the question is- what does imply by real choice? Real choice is something that possesses a transformative effect in the quality of human life, for instance, person's quality oflife is grounded on his/her freedom to choose that he/she finds truly worth living. Lack of people's substantive freedom creates injustices at individual and social level because they are deprived of their substantive freedom to transform their lives. On Sen's view, human welfare should be founded on their development as a process of expanding the real freedom that they enjoy as a substantive freedom in society.

Justice in the form of human development argued here, as a process of expanding the real freedoms that people enjoy and its concern is not to focus on material welfare (people's well off) rather on human welfare (people's wellbeing). "In the field of development, many other approaches have been moving away from the income-led definition of poverty by including people's perceptions and accepting the multiple facets of poverty".[49] Its purpose is to make a shift from the income-led evaluation method to assess people's ability to achieve those things that they value. It ensures that people's wellbeing cannot be measure by their income rather their freedom and choices that they have. It is not concern for development as economic growth rather maintains that the main purpose of justice is to provide freedoms to human beings. According to Sen,

> Development can be seen; it is argued here, as a process of expanding the real freedoms that people enjoy. Focusing on human freedoms contrasts with narrower views of development, such as identifying development with the growth of gross national product, or with the rise in personal incomes, or with industrialization, or with technological advance, or with social modernization. Growth of GNP or of individual incomes can, of course, be very important as a means to expanding the freedoms enjoyed by the members of the society.[50]

For him, focus on development in terms of resources has been misleading us because justice is not sum total of commodities but what and how people use these resources to be what they want. According to Sen,

> In contrast with the resource-based lines of thinking, individual advantage is judged in the capability approach by a person's capability to do things he or she has reason to value. A person's advantage in terms of opportunities is judged to be lower than that of another if she has less capability - less real opportunity - to achieve those things that she has reason to value. The focus here is on the freedom that a person actually has to do this or be that - things that he or she may value doing or being.[51]

This approach moves away from the income-led evaluation to people's ability to achieve the things that they value. It can be argued that justice should not be seen on the expansion of people's income rather as a process of expanding people's freedoms that they enjoy. So, justice can be measured by assessmg people's substantive freedom and their choice rather than resources.

In justice as welfare, freedom as employed in human development discourse which emphasis that people must have freedom of opportunity and choice. It is not maximization of choices without regard to people's quality and their values. Rather freedom includes the capabilities to perform activities that people's value to develop themselves in ways of their own choosing. It makes clear that justice in terms of human development tries to focuses on person's wellbeing and their substantive freedom. It is argues that individual incomes is very essential means to expanding the freedoms. However, individual's substantive freedoms does not entirely on their income but dependent on social and economic arrangements which provides educational facilities, health care, and other facilities so that each and every individual can pursue their well being in the society. For Sen, "sometimes the lack of substantive freedom underlies poverty which hurts people of the freedom to satisfy hunger, or to achieve sufficient nutrition, or to obtain remedies for treatable illnesses, or the opportunity to be adequately clothed or sheltered, or to enjoy clean water and sanitary facilities".[52] It is argued that each individual holds some capacity to choose what is best for his/her and freedom is that capacity of persons to do those things that they themselves choose. Freedoms enhance human capabilities to live as they wish and to do what they desire.

In Sen's view, freedom is the process of human welfare for two reasons namely the evaluative and effectiveness. "The evaluative reason: assessment of progress has to be done primarily in terms of whether the freedoms that people have are enhanced. The effectiveness reason: achievement of development thoroughly dependent on the free agency of people".[53] The former type of freedom implies that a just society would be evaluated in the form of substantive freedom that the members of that society enjoy. In evaluative side, justice involves the need to assess the requirements of development in terms of removing the unfreedom from which the members of the society may suffer. For Sen, "this evaluative position differs from the informational focus of more traditional normative approaches, which focus on other variables, such as utility, or procedural liberty, or real income".[54] Justice demands that each individual should have substantive freedom to do the things that one has reason to value. For Sen, development in terms of human beings makes each person not merely a tool rather core focus of development and this is called as a human development. Its objective is to enhance human well-being and to improve the quality of lives. It is argue that person's income is necessary to lead a good life but not something leading to the ultimate goal of development.

There are varieties of unfreedom which restricts people's wellbeing that they enjoy for instance, lack of nutritional food, health care, basic education and other social and economic security etc. Besides, lack of basic freedom in leading their lives, people is even deprived of important freedom i.e. civil and political freedoms as an opportunity to take part in crucial decisions making in public affairs.[55]

These unfreedom has been depriving the basic freedom which makes them people to survive a good life. In this way, people's substantive freedom plays an important role in terms of individualistic (intrinsic) and social role of freedom (instrumental) injustice as welfare. For Sen,

> The substantive freedom includes elementary capabilities like being able to avoid such deprivations as starvation, undernourishment, escapable morbidity and premature morality, as well as the freedom being associated with being literate and enjoying political participation and uncensored speech and so on.[56]

Intrinsic idea of freedom ensures welfare at individual level in terms well nourished, gets provisions for health care, enjoys good education and also given the chance to participate in the affairs of governance. In such condition, there is no reason for individuals to live a life of misery. In other way, in absence of people's intrinsic freedom, there would be degradation of human life, suffering and their injustice etc. For Sen, freedom is pursued as an end in human development because it enables the individual to improve the quality of his or her human life. However, freedom is not valued as intrinsic but valued for instrumental reasons which concerned about the way different kinds of rights, opportunities, and entitlements contributes the expansion of human development as a whole. It is important to note that instrumental substantive freedoms make the possibility in the attainment of well-being. Sen has enumerated five forms of substantive instrumental freedoms in *Development as Freedom* and these are:

1. Political freedoms, broadly conceived (including what are called civil rights), refer to the opportunities that people have to determine who should govern and on what principles, and also include the possibility to scrutinize and criticize authorities, to have freedom of political expression and an uncensored press, to enjoy the freedom to choose between different political parties and so on.[57]

2. Economic facilities refer to the opportunities that individuals respectively enjoy to utilize economic resources for the purpose of consumption, or produuccttiion, or exchange.[58]
3. Social opportunities refer to the arrangements that society makes for education, health care, and so on, which influence the individual's substantive freedom to live better.[59]
4. Transparency guarantees deal with the need for openness that people can expect the freedom to deal with one another under guarantees of discourse and lucidity. These guarantees have a clear instrumental role in preventing corruption, financial irresponsibility etc.[60]
6. Protective security provides a social safety net for preventing the affected population from being reduced to abject misery, and in some cases even starvation and death. This is necessary because no matter how well an economic system operates, some people can be typically on the verge of vulnerability and can actually succumb to great deprivation as a result of material changes that adversely affect their lives.[61]

These instrumental substantive freedoms contribute in the expansion of human development. It concerns for development with several rights, opportunities, and entitlements which enhances human welfare as a whole in any society. Further, instrumental substantive freedom is one of the important keystones in minimizing injustice at individual and social level. Then the question is that what kind of freedom minimizes injustices: positive and negative freedom? Here it is necessary to see distinction between positive and negative freedom and what kind of freedom promotes welfare? "This distinction between the conceptions of liberty as freedom from coercion, on the one hand, and freedom to achieve valued outcomes, on the other, has been captured by the terms of negative and positive freedom".[62] The concept of negative freedom implies absence of interference and commonly goes back to Hobbes. It corresponds as non-interference rights which are called as freedom from oppression.

The positive freedom consists in person's ability to achieve desired goals. It underlies in people's positive power or capacity of doing or enjoying something worth in terms of their autonomy and self-mastery which regulates by rational and reflecting selves and not passions and impulses. It is a fact that positive freedom has been associated with Rousseau, Kant, and recently Sen who has emphasized on the "real freedoms that people enjoy. It is the positive freedom refers as a real opportunity that can be given to people in terms of the extent of their capabilities. Take for example, a 'rickshaw puller' who is 'less well-off' and he feels secure at home. However, his financial condition does not affect on his security because his negative freedom is not curtailed by others and he feels secure at home. In such situation rickshaw puller's negative freedom has little or no value to him. It is a fact that due to 'less income' he is unable to fulfill basic requirement on given his condition of life that is not well-lived. In such a situation, welfare arrangement should be in such a manner where positive freedom enhances individual's capability or ability to be the person she desires herself to be.

Further, Sen's conception on substantive freedom incorporates in the idea of real opportunity that people enjoy and try to actualize what they value. Sen argues that,

> Freedom is valuable for at least two different reasons. First, more freedom gives us more *opportunity* to pursue our objectives - those things that we value. It helps, for example, in our ability to decide to live as we would like and to promote the ends that we may want to advance. This aspect of freedom is concerned with our ability to achieve what we value, no matter what the process is through which that achievement comes about. Second, we may attach importance to the *process* of choice itself. We may, for example, want to make sure that we are not being forced into some state because of constraints imposed by others.[63]

The process aspect of freedom implies that each and every individual is free to make choices and social arrangement must represent their choices. The opportunity aspect of freedom promotes person's freedom to choose what he/she value and this freedom should not be restricted and curtailed by others.

> The opportunity aspect of freedom, involve the ability to fulfill all the vital human capabilities, from the capability of a child to drink clean water or have elementary medical care, and the capability of a young woman to have the education which will enable her to hold a job and attain independence, to the capability of a scientist or an artist to carry out their work.[64]

It is clear that person's substantive freedom is utmost important to pursue their life plan which is valuable for them. For instance, Sen often distinguishes between a starving child and fasting monk, both have same level of functioning because both are kept away from food. Though starving child does not have freedom to eat while monk has, but does not eat. In one case starving child does not have freedom of opportunity as well as agency freedom to choose what he wants.

The idea of freedom particularly opportunity aspect and agency aspect of freedom is one of the important keystones in minimizing injustices at individual and social level. It argues that, Sen has conceived substantive freedom into two forms namely opportunities and processes freedom. The processes freedoms allow freedom of actions and decisions, and the actual opportunities that people have, given their personal and social circumstances. According to Sen, unfreedom can arise either through inadequate process such as the violation of voting privileges or other political and civil rights which are important freedoms in people's lives. In justices in the form of unfreedom can occur through inadequate opportunities that some people have for achieving what they minimally would like to achieve including the "absence of such elementary opportunities as the capability to escape premature mortality, disease, and starvation".[65]

Sen distinguishes "opportunity aspect of freedom from the process aspect which is the freedom involved in the process itself".[66] This relates to the concept of agency which for Sen is the ability to pursue goals that one has reason to value. Freedom as an opportunity and process understood as a concept comprising components of both wellbeing and agency. "Wellbeing freedom is concerned with objectives that a person values for his/her wellbeing. Agency is concerned with the individual's freedom to choose and bring about the things that he/she values"[67]. Further he says, Agency freedom is affected by three conversion factors:

1. Personal characteristics ((such as metabolism, physical condition, sex, reading skills, intelligence)
2. Social characteristics (such as public policies, social norms, discriminating practices, gender roles, societal hierarchies, power relations),
3. Environmental characteristics (such as climate, infrastructure, institutions, public goods).[68]

People's freedom in the form of agency aspect is primarily includes a states of affairs that a person chooses the things that they value. Moreover, people's freedom particularly agency freedom is affected by their personal and social conditions such as personal, social, environment and other structural factors. These factors affecting on individual's capability to choose what he/she values and the way that choices become achievements. The notion of capability is closely related with Sen's conception of freedom, which he defines as the real opportunity that we have to accomplish what we value. According to Sen,

> The concept of capability is thus linked closely linked with the opportunity aspect of freedom, seen m terms of comprehensive opportunity. It points to an informational focus in judging and comparing over all individual advantages and does not propose any formula about how that information may be used.[69]

Sen's capability approach underlies justice that focuses on individuals' command over goods and opportunities to achieve the kind of lives he/she has reason to value. It makes interpersonal comparisons by focuses on person's functioning of what he/she wants to do and be what they want to be which includes being physically fit, being well nourished, being healthy, being confident, etc.

Freedom based Sen's capability approach tries to seek individual's advantages by capability to do things that he/she has reason to value. It is conceived as a normative framework for the assessment of person's capacity to do or to be with the extent of freedom that they have to achieve what they value. Sen argues in *Idea of justice,*

> person's advantage in terms of opportunities is judged to be lower than that of another if she has less capability- less real opportunityto achieve those things that she has reason to value. The focus here is on the freedom that a person actually has to do this or be that things that he or she may value doing or being. Obviously, the things we value most are particularly important for us to be able to achieve. But the idea of freedom also respects our being free to determine what we want, what we value and ultimately what we decide to choose.[70]

Capability is thus a kind of freedom: the substantive freedom to achieve alternative functioning. On the other hand, it is the freedom to achieve various life styles. For example, an affluent person who fasts may have the same functioning achievements in terms of eating or nourishment as a destitute person who is forced to starve, but the first person does have a different capability set than the second (the first can choose to eat well and be well nourished in a way the second cannot)"[71] Capability approach can be understood as the various combinations of functioning i.e. beings and doings that a person can achieve. So it is a set of vectors of functionings, reflecting the person's freedom to lead one type of life or another to choose from possible livings.

Capability approaches to justice IS distinct from utilitarianism, and Rawlsian theory of justice. On Sen's view, capability approach focuses on the effect of goods on human rather than the mental reaction to that effect one hand and people's basic capabilities' shifted attention from the goods of themselves to what goods do to human beings on the other. According to Sen, "in the context of utilitarian calculus, its major demerits is that it does not lead immediately to any way of making interpersonal comparisons, Since it concentrates on each individual's choice separately".[72] Moreover, utilitarian perspective overlooks individual values and focuses on individual's utility which leads substantial loss of information in interpersonal comparisons. Hence, these are the limitations of utilitarian approach:

1. Distributional indifference: the utilitarian calculus tends to ignore inequalities in the distribution of happiness (only the sum total matters - no matter how unequally distributed). We may be interested in general happiness, and yet want to pay attention not just to "aggregate" magnitudes, but also to extents of inequalities in happiness.[73]
2. Neglect of rights, freedoms and other non-utility concerns: the utilitarian approach attaches no intrinsic importance to claims of rights and freedoms (they are valued only indirectly and only to the extent they influence utilities). It is sensible enough to take note of happiness, but we do not necessarily want to be happy slaves or delirious vassals.[74]
3. Adaptation and mental conditioning: even the View the utilitarian approach takes of individual well-being is not very robust, since it can be easily swayed by mental conditioning and adaptive attitudes.[75]

Moreover utilitarian institutional arrangement ignores individual's capability to live a good life in terms of the set of valuable 'beings and doings. Sen has criticized utilitarian principle of consequentialism, welfarism, and sum ranking in his book *Resources, Values and Development,*

> Consequentialism focuses that the rightness and wrongness of actions should be judged by the goodness of the consequent state of affairs. Welfarism states that goodness of states of affairs should be judged by the goodness of the state of individual utilities in the respective

state of affairs. The sum ranking implies the goodness of any set of individual utilities must be judged by their sum total[76]

It can be argue, despite of person's achievement in terms of happiness, satisfaction and desire fulfillment, utilitarianism unable to minimize injustice at individual and social level. Sen has rightly says,

> Utilitarianism loses a wealth of information when it comes to interpersonal comparisons. For example, it is usually unable to differentiate between 'values' and 'utilities' and where it does- it puts 'utilities' ahead of 'values'. That is, an individual is assumed to value something because he/she desires it instead of saying that an individual desires something because he/she values it.[77]

It neglects individual values on the one hand and fails to address social injustice on the other. Subodh has rightly criticizes about the lacuna of utilitarian principle where the utility of 'desire fulfilled/ happy/ satisfied' individual that is well endowed with resources is rated the same as another individual's that is resources deprived but equally 'desire fulfilled/happy/ satisfied' because the latter may desire small pleasures.[78] Utilitarianism, thus, focuses on psychological wellbeing and does not give broad information concerning injustice. It ignores social and economic factors such as basic education, elementary health care, and secure employment and others to secure a good life in terms of set of valuable beings and doings.

Carrying utilitarianism and its limitation, Rawls's approach to justice is unsatisfactory in minimizing injustices at individual and social level. Sen criticizes the original position, i.e. 'veil of ignorance' of Rawls's distributive justice which amounts to the lack of genuine information concerning injustice. Sen argue that index of primary goods cannot adequately account for inter individual differences in people's capacities to convert these primary goods into what people are able to be and to do in their lives. According to Sen,

> The primary goods approach seems to take little note of the diversity of human beings. If people were basically very similar, then an index or primary goods might be quite a good way of judging advantage. But, in fact, people seem to have very different needs varying with health, longevity, climatic conditions, locations, work conditions, temperament, and even body size. So what is being involved is not merely ignoring a few hard cases, but overlooking very widespread and real differences.[79]

It makes clear that each individual capacity is different from others. It is important to focus directly on people's beings and doing, i.e. on their capabilities to function rather on accessibility of primary goods. However, Rawls' primary goods are considered to be the means and not end to pursue one's own life plan. It is a fact that person's life plan is not only determined by the primary goods that he/she has at his/ her disposal, but there are various factors that determine to what extent he/ she can utilize these primary goods into valuable states of being and doing. It ensures that individual advantage is judged by an index of primary goods however, its inflexibility does not recognize inter-individual differences between people. For instance, Rawlsian strategy of difference principle provides primary goods to the worst off people and does not explain why differences in individual needs exist. It determines how person can become well off in terms of income and wealth only and not on their well-being. It does not recognize people's need and their requirement. Take an example, a person who is severely disabled and his disability is not address by the conceptualization of index of primary goods. Moreover, it does not justify any redistribution to the disabled on the ground of their disability.

The resource based approach to justice primarily focuses on the fair distribution of resources and what Rawls believed that, "primary resources are the things every rational individual is supposed to want".[80] It is clear that resources are considered to be a means for people's basic functioning. It is important and valued only instrumentally towards individual freedom to do what he/ she values. Adam Smith has rightly says, "primary resources are closely related to the notion of necessity that includes resources that are not only indispensable for the support of life but whatever the custom.... renders it indecent for creditable people to be without.[81] It makes clear that primary resources have been used in very different manner according to customs and tradition of that society. For instance, 'necessities' in 'society-X' can be considered 'luxuries' in 'society-Y' and individual in former society may need this luxury to function at about the same basic level as an individual in latter society (i.e. society-X) that possess necessities. That's why Sen argues that, relative deprivation of resources can lead to absolute deprivation of a person's ability to function properly.[82]

Sen's capability approach tries to improve the quality of human life in terms of set of 'doings and beings'. It does not focus on people's mental satisfaction and income and wealth rather on people's substantive freedom i.e. on their capabilities. In assessing the quality of life, utility-based assessment is unsatisfactory because it overlooks people's substantive freedom which includes both processes and opportunities on the one and recognition of the heterogeneity of distinct components of freedom in terms of functioning's and the capability to function. Injustice cannot be minimizes while focus on simply utilitarian calculus that helps those doings and beings in accounting of the quality of life. A person's quality of life cannot be assessed on the basis of psychological well-being or utility in terms of mental condition, such as pleasure, happiness, and desire fulfilment.

This subjective perspective of utilitarian calculus fails to reflect a person's real deprivation on the one and it leads substantial loss of information in interpersonal comparisons. For instance, a person who is suffering from longstanding deprivation may not appear to be badly off in terms of the mental metric of utility. In such situation deprived person do not go on weeping all the time and he/she knows how to reduce personal desires to get pleasure. So it is not possible to show person's deprivation in the metrics of pleasure, desire fulfillment, etc. even though he/she may quite unable to be adequately nourished, decently clothed, and minimally educated and so on.

> When Sen first introduced the concept of basic capability, his emphasis was on the provision of an objective basis for interpersonal compansons of well-being which were essential for an adequate welfare. Another shortcoming of the utility approach was that a person who was is easily pleased might feel no worse off than others in utility terms but still be greatly disadvantaged in terms of his/her ability to do things.[83]

The equalization of objective basic capabilities is an objective basis for interpersonal comparison in minimizing injustices in terms of welfare mechanism. The purpose of basic capabilities is to acknowledge people's right to make their own decisions about matters affecting their well-being that are potentially within their own control. In other way, basic capabilities admit that people's well-being may be affected by matters which individual have no control and thus they would require extra consideration. For instance someone who is being handicapped or crippled would require extra resources to enable them to achieve the same capability in terms of mobility as an able-bodied person.

Sen's capability approach can be understood in terms of people-centric rather resources centric because capability approach primarily concerns for people's real opportunities to do what they want to do and be what they want to be. Instead of focusing on social primary goods and its distribution for people's advantages, capability approach surrounded with their agency and functioning is called as people-centric approach.

> A person's capability set can be defined as the set of functioning vectors within his or her reach. In examining the wellbeing aspect of a person, attention can legitimately be paid to the capability set of the person and not just to the chosen functioning vector. This has the effect of taking note of the positive freedom in a general sense (the freedom "to do this" or "to be that") that a person has?[84]

Sen says in *Inequality Reexamined,* "Capability is primarily a reflection of the freedom to achieve valuable functioning. It concentrates directly on freedom as such rather than on the means to achieve freedom, and it identifies the real alternatives we have. It can be read as a reflection of substantive freedom".[85] It shows that capability approach tries to reflect person's substantial freedom so that people can freely choose to realize their basic functioning. For instance, Mr. 'A' has a capability of being nourished but he might choose to fast for religious purpose because he/she has substantive freedom to choose either being nourished or being deprived of food in the form of fast.

Sen's formulation of capability approach holds the expansion of individual's freedom as the central objective of development. The central objective of capability approach is to see either in the form of *realized functionings* (i.e. what a person is actually able to do) and the *capability set* of alternatives she has (her real opportunities). It gives two different types of information such as realized functioning implies about the things a person does and capability set holds about the things a person is substantively free to do. It states about wellbeing of a person which can be assessed in the space of various vector of functioning. According to Sen, "Capability is primarily a reflection of the freedom to achieve valuable functioning. It concentrates directly on freedom as such rather than on the means to achieve freedom, and it identifies the real alternatives we have....It can be read as a reflection of substantive freedom".[86] It underlies in the concept of functionings which are valuable activities and states that become a person's wellbeing such as a healthy body, being safe, being educated, having a good job, being able to move and visit people. Sen defines functionings as the "various things a person may value doing or being".[87] The concept of capabilities refers to the freedoms one has to do these valuable activities or reach these valuable states. Take for example, Mr. A and Mr. B is considered as starving and fasting person and both performs their functioning, however functioning of Mr. A is differs significantly from that of Mr. B because A's starving unlike B's fasting involves a choice to have fast for religious, political and other purpose despite the presence of other alternatives.

Further Sen's capability approach can be contextualized in terms of various combinations of functionings (beings and doings) that the person can achieve. "Capabilities are, thus, a set of vectors of functionings, reflecting the person's freedom to lead one type of life or another to choose from possible livings".[88] Sen's capability approach relates to the idea of agency as an ability to pursue goals that one has reason to value. It entails a key normative argument that social arrangements should aim to expand people's capabilities, that is, their freedom to achieve valuable doings and beings, and in doing so those arrangements should respect people's agency. In other words, agency aspect of capability approach includes 'the substantive freedoms' a person enjoy to lead the kind of life he or she has reason to value.[89] Capability in the form of functioning emphasis on human wellbeing which includes various states of activities that people can undertake in their day to day life.

According to Sen, "functioning are the achievement of functioning refers to a person's wellbeing or the quality of a person's being".[90] Consider a person has raw materials for food such as rice, millet and vegetable etc. and he knows (functioning) to convert these resources into its characteristics i.e. nutritional meal. Functioning reflects how efficient a person can succeed in converting bare resources into its valuable characteristics according to their purposes. So with the help of functioning, for instance, a carpenter with his skill can convert bare wood into valuable item such as chair, table and other wooden items. It minimizes injustices through normative framework of valuable state of affairs and activities that inculcates various aspects of functioning of person's wellbeing.

In other words, individual's functioning is the subject of the capabilities which assess their opportunities in terms of what and how people are capable in various things of doing and being. It underlies in human capability that implies a person can be recognized either as a doing and being which incorporates in terms of 'doing' includes travelling, caring for a child, voting in an election, taking part in a debate, paying tax, and donating money to charity etc. Functioning in terms of 'being' implies being educated, being well nourished, being employed, being safe, being happy, being calm and having dignity and so on so forth.

Therefore, capability approach to justice has been the foundational elements in the assessment of people's well-being in the fallowing way:

1. Sen's capabilities approach to justice concern for human beings and their quality of life to be the central focus of welfare mechanism. Its concern is not to focus on material welfare (people's well off) rather on human welfare (people's well being).
2. Justice as welfare concerves human freedom and the ability to make decisions that affect one's life as central to human agency and their dignity. Sen has given a very fascinating example, where he often distinguishes between a starving child and fasting monk". Since both of them are kept away from food so they have the same level of functioning. However, the starving child does not have freedom (freedom can be seen in terms of choices and opportunities) to eat while monk has, but does not choose to eat. In such case the starving child does not have freedom of opportunity as well as agency freedom to choose what he has reason to value.
3. Capability approach to justice as welfare evolved out of ethical consideration of human welfare in terms of human functioning and a capability that highlights human being has a dignity with their ability to pursue their own ends.
4. Finally, capability approach to welfare fosters an enabling environment and allow for flexibility in way of reframing many of the social issues concerning injustices.

Part - III

Public Enlightenment and Well-being as the Foundation for Minimising Injustices

In Sen's welfare mechanism, people's enlightenment and their well-being is on top priority which ensures that people, instead of resources, are the utmost important and real wealth. Its purpose is to assess individual and collective quality of life through enabling society wherein each and every person becomes enlighten in terms of capability. This enabling society in the form of functioning and capabilities promotes public enlightenment wherein individual's well being is understood by "person's capability to do things he or she has reason to value".[91] The idea of behind people's capabilities recognizes that each and every individual differ in their capacity to convert enlighten opportunities into valuable achievements due to personal and social factors. It broadens informational space for making evaluative judgments by acknowledging the multidimensional nature of human wellbeing. Marianne T. Hill has pointed out in "Development as Empowerment" about Amartya Sen's capability approach to human welfare which is an alternative to traditional welfare theory. "The capability space - that is, the matrix of all attainable functionings- in tum is the proper evaluative framework for measuring a person's advantage, or the capability to achieve wellbeing. It can also used in evaluating social arrangements".[92]

> The capability approach takes into account the uniqueness of each person. A young child, for example, needs fewer calories than an adult, a disabled person may require more than usual economic resources to attain a given level of mobility. Since each individual has different needs and abilities, a given set of goods and services will result in a different outcome relative to the set of functionings attainable by each person. What Sen stresses is the outcome in terms of valued functionings, including the ability to choose. Only valued functionings contribute to well-beingi[93].

Hence, public enlightenment concerned about human welfare in terms of their capabilities to do certain things that are valuable for them. It incorporates that justice is going beyond a mere consideration of the material aspect of well-off and taking into account a sphere more intrinsically related to the people's well-being in the concept of basic needs, command over resources, ability to achieve a functioning, and capabilities etc. It focuses on people's enlightenment and their capabilities to become autonomous and self-sufficient to get their well-being. It is argued that, the idea of 'being well' implies for the betterment of each and every person for their social, economic, psychological, spiritual or medical state. A people's well-being ensures how well a person's life goes not in terms of their material pursuit or well-off but their freedom to undertake valuable doings and beings. Public enlightenment underlies people's well-well-being,

> Development consists of the expansion of substantive freedoms; Sen recognizes the importance of institutions to development: 'A variety of social institutions…contribute to the process of development precisely through their effects on enhancing and sustaining individual freedoms. He mention in the particular the role of democratic institutions, civil liberties and free press in the formation of social norms, ethics, and goals, and the importance of public deliberation

> in addressing problems ranging from corruption to the neglect and oppression of women and the poor. Although democratic institutions alone don not ensure that injustices affecting those with lesser power will be addressed, there are strong arguments that democratic institutions do increase equity.[94]

Social institutions and the capability approach plays brings out people's enlightenment to become capable to make decision about issues that affect their lives and minimizes injustice to that extent. Moreover, capability based social institutions guarantees not only basic need relating to freedom and autonomy, human right, toleration, and public and private reason but their basic capabilities so that each one can attain their physical and psychological well-being. It can be argue that a just society promotes people's enlightenment and their wellbeing so that gender, class, caste, religion, status, and all other divisions created by man do not exist, and everyone has access to basic capabilities. If these requirements are not met, the society is termed as unjust, and injustice prevails in such societies. The reason for focusing on public enlightenment in terms of people's capabilities is to respect the choices of people in determining their well-being. It is the capability approach underlies public enlightenment which makes "each and every individual to act on their own preferences".[95] It highlights the value of people's agency while promoting public enlightenment.

The concept of public enlightenment and well-being is a foundational element in Sen's justice as welfare which represents an important parameter in assessing people's quality of life. However, to substantiate public enlightenment in Sen's view, it is imperative to revisit enlightenment in general and Kant's enlightenment rationality in particular. The insight of enlightenment in eighteenth century claims that progress is possible only through the use of reason. During this time there is remarkable great changes occurred in scientific thought and invention. New ideas filled the horizon and man was eager to explore these ideas freely. In other words, the process of enlightenment was still unfolding. In this process, individual and society were battling on a daily basis to get rid from selfincurred tutelage".[96] However such type of tutelage is surrounded with complex web and gets rid from this is not easy as may seem. Kant's intellectual autonomy focuses that each men has to be his own guardian in thinking, feeling and willing. It is no doubt these are the contextual factors within which the enlightenment has to take place. However, Kant's intellectual autonomy unable to culminate in the form of public enlightenment because "rationality in terms of some formulated conditions that have been proposed in the literature such as satisfying some prespecified axioms of internal consistency of choice, or being in conformity with intelligent pursuit of self-interest," or being some variant of maximizing behavior".[97] According to Amartya Sen, "Rationality is interpreted here, broadly, as the discipline of subjecting one's choices - of actions as well as objectives, values and priorities - to reasoned scrutiny different values.[98] Furthermore, rationality conceived in general terms as the need to subject one's choices to the demands of reason. Freedom is central to rationality in the same way rationality is important in assessing individual's freedom.

Kant's intellectual autonomy is unable to culminate in the form of people's capabilities which make them enlighten. It is the people's capability has played an important role to reach at the stage of public enlightenment because it does not recognize only basic needs approach which concern for the assessment of poverty and deprivation only. "The concept of basic needs approach concerned with providing all human beings, but particularly the poor and deprived, with the opportunities for a fulllife"[99], however, capability approach extends beyond the analysis of people's rights and duties, and basic needs. It focuses on poverty and deprivation in the one hand and their well-being on the other. It recognize not only people's diversity but drawing attention on individual disparities based on gender, race, class, caste or age. It is people's capability embracing human agency and participation to promote public enlightenment by emphasizing the role of practical reason, deliberate democracy and public action in forging goals, making choices.

In the notion of justice as welfare, Sen's idea of freedom and capabilities enhances people's collective quality oflife to promote public enlightenment in the form of enabling society wherein each individual becomes capable to make decision about issues that affect their lives and minimize injustice to that extent. As Jonathan writes,

> four fundamental elements that foster an enabling environment: Awareness of the problems poor people face and ways of mitigating them; access to all the resources required to enhance the quality of their lives; affordability of the resources required for people to improve their welfare; and, accountability of those in positions of power, and who claim to represent the interests and welfare of ordinary people.[100]

This enabling environment promotes an attitude that facilitates public enlightenment for all people. Public enlightenment refers to the enhancement of human capabilities which involves process of decision making as well as opportunities to achieve valued outcomes.

In justice as welfare, it tries to seek each and every individual becomes capable to get enlighten. It is argue that capabilities are people's potential functioning but it is insufficient in the way of enlightenment rather capability becomes the foundational tool for the enlightenment. It is the capabilities rather than functioning of individual indicates the habit of autonomous and self-sufficient to reach at the stage of enlightenment. Therefore, public enlightenment tries to seek an enabling attitude in the form of capability to make decision about issues that affect their lives and minimize injustice to that that extent. This enabling society ensures public enlightenment with the vision of people's substantive freedom and their capabilities promotes not only individual wellbeing but social well-being as well

In formulating justice as welfare, the notion of public enlightenment becomes the foundational element because it encourages each individual to become enlighten. It ensures that justice is going beyond a mere consideration of the material aspect of 'well-off' and taking into account a sphere more intrinsically related to the individual's enlightenment and their personal dimension such as freedom, rights and opportunities, etc. It focuses on people's freedom, rights, opportunities and their capabilities to become autonomous and self-sufficient to reach at the stage of enlightenment. Now the basic question is that how one can become enlightened?

This is possible through assessing freedom particularly opportunity aspect of freedom. In assessment of opportunities that a person has would require some understanding of what the person would want to have and have reason to value having. In public enlightenment, capability approach can be used to assess individual advantage in a range of different spaces, for instance, the assessment of poverty might involve concentrating on a relatively small sub set of basic capabilities on the one hand and evaluating well-being on the other hand requires diverse lists of capabilities. Public enlightenment promotes people's capabilities which refer their freedom to function in certain ways and ability to do certain things that are deemed valuable. A person's capability concerns ways of functioning that someone can choose and achieve while the ways of functioning concern the actual choosing and doing of the valued things. The reason for focusing on public capability rather on their functioning is to respect people's choices in determining meaningful lives, highlighting the value of individual agency. The idea is that there are certain functions people should be empowered to achieve which, where a life developed and shaped by such opportunities constitutes a dignified life. Instead, aiming to empower a life by ensuring that it meets or exceeds some capability threshold is how we respect the dignity of life. What matters is having the capability to do a variety of things and then choosing for ourselves whether to exercise our capability to function. Fasting when we have access to plenty of food, for example, highlights the importance of focusing on capability rather than functioning as the purpose of justice.

Public enlightenment focuses on people's substantive freedom so that people are able to do and to be, that is on their capability. It is the public enlightenment which promotes people's well-being. It is important to note that the approach to well-being developed here is consistent with the concept of public enlightenment. This concept of rationality is consistent with "internal consistency of choice"[101] which incorporates that each enlightened person acts accordance with their rationality. This intellectual stimulation must be non-native which asserts: "we want to think and act wisely and judiciously, rather than stupidly or impulsively".[102] A rational persons, according to Sen, is one who, acquired "rationality of choice respectively with: (1) internal consistency of choice; (2) self-interest maximization; and (3) maximization in general"[103] makes right choices, a choices that contributes to one's well-being. It can be argued that this 'rationality of choice' would minimize people's injustices and promotes their well-being not at individual level but social level as well.

To properly understand Sen's view of well-being, it is important to have a comprehensive conception of 'being well' which implies for the betterment of human being in their social, economic, psychological, spiritual or medical state. It ensures people's well-being and how well a person's life goes, not in terms of their material pursuit or well-off but their freedom to undertake valuable doings and beings. However, human well-being underlies not in subjective sphere but objective aspect as well. The subjective aspect concern for people's mental, emotional, spiritual, etc. factors which affect well-being. The objective aspect implies that there are external observable conditions that affect people's functionings, and thus, one's well-being[104]. People's well-being depends on both objective and subjective consideration, the objective factors are necessary but not sufficient for well-being, and the same goes for the subjective factor.

There are wide variety of concepts and ways of seeing the quality of living such as "pleasure, happiness, the satisfaction of desires or preferences, the fulfillment of needs, the achievement of aims or objectives, the development of capacities or potentialities, virtue or excellence, the maintenance of normal functioning, living a form of life appropriate to one's nature, and doubtless many others besides".[105] In assessing the quality of life, the objects of value such as pleasure, happiness, excellence, functioning and etc. can sensibly be taken to be aspects of the life that he or she succeeds in living. For instance, pleasure, happiness and doings and beings a person achieves are potentially relevant to the evaluation of that person's standard oflife. The quest for human well-being is not primarily concern for people's material well-being, but psychological, as well spiritual well-being. For instance, economic well-being has little importance unless it is translated into falling child mortality and greater life expectancies. That's why Sen distinguishes between the idea of well-being from being well-off and the former is not based on the concept of opulence while the latter is based on material pursuits. According to Sen, "well-being is not something outside her that she commands, but something in her that she achieves. What kind of a life is she leading? What does she succeeds in doing and in being?"[106]. Further, the concept of 'being well-off is "really a concept of opulence - how rich is she? What goods and services can she buy? and what offices are open to her? and so on. This refers to a person's command over things outside".[107] It may help other things given to have well-being but does not incorporates personal capabilities to succeeds 'in doings' and 'in beings'.

Further Sen says about standard of living in *The Tanner Lectures on Human Values,* "opulence in the form of commodity possession is undoubtedly important in enhancing the standard of living, but is the standard of living best seen as opulence itself'.[108] In other way, having well- off refers to a people's command over things. Moreover, an opulent person can command over things but unable to pursue his/her well-being. Take for example, 'Mr. A' and 'Mr. B' both are quite poor in terms of opulence. In comparison to 'Mr. B' 'Mr. A' is better-off in terms of higher income and able to buy more food and consumes more of it. However, 'Mr. A' is suffering from some parasitic disease so that despite of his higher food consumption, unable to pursue higher standard of living because he is more undernourished in comparison to 'Mr. B'. 'Mr. A' may be more opulent but it is not justified that he has higher standard of living since he quite clearly more undernourished because of parasitic disease. So people's well-being or standard of living is not a standard of opulence, even their well-being is *inter alia* influenced by opulence.

In other way, having well-off refers to a people's command over things outside of person's capabilities in them that they she achieve such as being healthy, being educated, etc. It must be directly a matter of the life one leads rather than of the opulence and means one has to lead a life. For Sen, "The primary feature of a person's well-being is the functioning vector that he or she achieves".[109] This well-being is consistent with Sen's capability approach which focuses on various functioning and capabilities. It plays an important role in the assessment of people's quality of life. It tries to seek people's well-being which includes variety of functioning related to nourishment, safety, security, health, longevity, literacy, recreation, entertainment, sexual relations, comfort, housing, transportation, social relationships, etc.

Historically, the concept of well-being has been developed since Greek times and its nature are as old as philosophy itself. It is important to acknowledge that traditionally on the subject of well-being, Aristotle is the preeminent philosopher. For him, human well-being is a life of well-lived and it emerges from what we do and what we become, not from what we have. According to Aristotle, "The good life is one in which a person most fully, and at the highest level of excellence, fulfills his deepest nature. It is a life in which there is a flourishing of one's truest self. This kind of life is an end in itself and not as a means to some other ends.[110] To the Greeks, *eudaemonia* means something like living a good life and this is the reason Aristotle believes *eudaemonia* is the *telos* of human life which affect all our choices and decisions. In modem time the concept of 'well-being' described about 'living well' and 'doing well' which is the ultimate end of human life. Further, Aristotle's concept of well-being in the philosophy of *Eudaemonia,* Amartya Sen has introduced the concept of human capabilities in the assessment of their well-being that departed from the narrow utilitarian approach and Rawls's approach of social goods. The former approach based on utility principle and latter is based on commodities or index of primary goods.

To assess well-being at individual and social level, Sen, sees neither commodities nor utility as a measure of well-being but their capacity to achieve valuable functionings.[111] "The content of utility is often seen differently not as pleasure, satisfaction or happiness, but as the fulfillment of desire, or as the some kind of representation of a person's choice behavior. It is not hard to see that this redefinition of utility does not in itself eliminate the indifference to freedoms, rights and liberties that is a characteristic feature of utilitarianism in general".[112] Sen criticizes utilitarianism in general and the most criticism is that of utility principle namely pattern of choice, happiness and desire fulfillment in the assessment of people's well-being.

Firstly Sen says pattern of choice is non-starter since it provides no basis for interpersonal comparisons.

Secondly happiness and desire fulfillment conception of utility are inadequate because people's desire and their capacity for happiness adapt too easily to their expectations. For instance a person who is resigned from office to extreme poverty may be no less happy than someone who is well-off so it does not provide a basis for interpersonal comparison in the assessment of person's well-being.

Further utilitarian principle that aim to measure well-being, one such approach to measure individual real income that is the market value of commodities he consumes. Such measures, Sen argues, are too crude to take account of differences between individual's capacities to make use of commodities. More generally people vary in their capacity to convert commodities or primary goods in to well-being. As a result if we take the primary goods as the appropriate measure well-being for purpose of justice, we may treat people unfairly.[113] It argues that, commodity or 'index of primary goods' is inflexible measure of well-being because it ignores variability among individuals. For instance, some person is inefficient converters of commodities or primary goods into his/her well-being because he/she is ill or handicapped. In other way, there are could be variability in the nutritional needs of individual such as between those with low or high metabolic rates or between pregnant women and others. So the index of primary social goods ignores this variability in the assessment people's well-being.

It can be argue that, human well-being is not emerge from what they achieve in terms their pattern of choice, happiness, desire fulfillment, and commodity but what can they do or achieve in terms of various functioning. It can be argue that, the idea of people's well-being occurs in their opportunities and capabilities to achieve a certain level of functionings by virtue of the alternative combination of functionings available to them. For Sen well-being can be actualize through valuable functionings which implies what the person is succeeding in 'doing' or 'being'. It can be seen as consisting of set of interrelated 'functionings' consisting of beings and doings.[114] Functionings range from the fairly specific, such as being well-dressed, being well-nourished, and ability to obtain pleasure from food or music, to the broad and/or vague, such as having self respect, acting freely, keeping track of what's going on, appreciating beauty, being psychologically well-adjusted, and being wise and contented.[115] According to Sen,

> A functioning is an achievement of a person: what he or she manages to do or to be. It reflects, as it were, as a part of the state of that person. It has to be distinguished also from the happiness generated by functioning. A functioning is different from both from having goods and the corresponding characteristics to which it is posterior and having utility in the form of happiness resulting from that functioning to which it is, in an important way prior.[116]

It is important to focus on people's functioning that what he/she can or cannot do can or cannot be to lead a valuable life. Therefore, the purpose of well-being is to achieve "well lived" where life would not be evaluated in terms of material pursuit but rich in valuable life. This valuable life could acquire through people's functioning and their capabilities so that they can pursue their well-being.

To bring this chapter an end, I can say that, Sen's justice as welfare tries to promote people's capability and their wellbeing so that each one can pursue their quality of life not in terms of 'being well- off but 'being well'. It is not captured by income and about what people have but about what each individual are "able to do and to be" with what they have. It does not concentrate on just institutions and the means of primary goods but to minimize injustices by removing obstacles in "people's actual opportunities in day to day life. It concerned about minimum level of welfare in terms health, education, nutrition and political participation so that each person can minimize injustices to some extent. It promotes public enlightenment which makes them "capable to live long life, healthy life, being educated and more being well fed, taking part in the community, being sheltered, relating to other people, working on the labor market, caring for others, and being healthy important the having a voice to participate in public life which affects their life".[117] It constitutes a welfare mechanism where institutional choice and arrangement focused approaches to justice is not sufficient because it unable to acknowledges immediate injustices such as discrimination relating to basic education, skill, health, etc. Moreover, such kind procedural justice in one way or another contributes to serious problems concerning injustices at social, political and economic level. In such situation injustices can be minimize through welfare mechanism in the form of people's capabilities and enlightenment to construct an "enabling society" where each individual "recognize the value of democratization, of seeking out the voices of the underrepresented, and of building channels through which they can more effectively enter the social choice process and shape social institutions to advance their welfare".[118]

Thus, instead of institutional arrangement to welfare which governs collective choices, capability approach to justice as welfare capable each and every individual to act on his/her own choices or value. It promotes an enabling society wherein each individual becomes capable to make decision about issues that affect their lives to minimize injustice to that extent. Last but not least justice as welfare does not concern for people's happiness, desire fulfillment, and commodity but what can they do or achieve in terms of various functioning. It can be argue that, human welfare occurs in their opportunities and capabilities to achieve a certain level of functionings by virtue of the alternative combination of functionings relating to their nourishment, safety, security, health, longevity, literacy, recreation, comfort, housing, transportation and social relationship etc. For instance, being happy, being well-dressed, being well-nourished, being educated, being employed, being safe, being calm, having dignity and other activities that inculcates various aspects of functioning of person's wellbeing.

References

Sen, Amartya. *The Idea of Justice.* London: Penguin Books, 2009.

Anand, Paul. Hunter, Graham. Smith, Ron. "Capabilities and Well-Being: Evidence Based on the Sen-Nussbaum Approach to Welfare". *Social Indicators Research* 74, no. 1. 2005: 9-55.

Sen, Amartya and Dreze, Jean. *Hunger and Public Action.* Oxford: Clarendon Press, 1989.

Boot, Martijn. "The Aim of a Theory of Justice". *Ethical Theory and Moral Practice* 15, no. 1. 2012: 15 100.

Pankaj K Ashok. "Review of Idea of justice". *Social Scientist.* Vol. 39. No. 112. 2011: 74-77.

Fleischacker, S. *On Adam Smith's Wealth of Nations: A Philosophical Companion.* Princeton: Princeton University Press. 2004.

Smith, Adam. *Theory of Moral Sentiments,* ed. D. D. Raphael, A. L. Macfie. Oxford: Oxford University Press, 1976.

Williams, David. *Condorcet and Modernity.* Cambridge: Cambridge University Press, 2004.

Sen, Amartya. *Commodities and Capabilities.* Amsterdam: North Hol- land, 1985.

Daniels, Norman. "Equality of What: Welfare, Resources, or Capabilities?" *Philosophy and Phenomenological Research* 50, 1990: 273-296.

Ingrid Robeyns. "Sen's Capability Approach and Gender Inequality Selecting Relevant Capabilities". *Capabilities, Freedom, and Equality Amartya Sen's Work from a Gender Perspective.* Edited by Bina Agarwal, Jane Humphries & Ingrid Robeyns. UK: Oxford University Press, 2006.

Sen. "Equality of What?". In *Tanner Lectures on Human Values.* edited by

S.M.McMurrin. Salt Lake City: University of Utah Press. 1980. pp. 215- 216.

Sen, Amartya. *Development as Freedom.* Oxford: Oxford University Press, 1999.

Frediani Apsan, Alexandre. "Sen's Capability Approach as a framework to the practice of development". *Development in Practice* 20, no. 2. 2010: 173-187.

Prendergast, Renee. "The concept of freedom and its relation to economic development- a critical appreciation of the work of Amartya Sen". *Cambridge Journal ofEconomics* 29. no.6. accessed on 21-01-2016.

Walsh, Vivian. "Amartya Sen on Rationality and Freedom". *Science &Society* 7l, no. l. 2007. pp. 59-83.

Sen, Amartya. *Resources, Values and Development.* Cambridge, MA: Harvard University Press, 1984.

Kulkarni P, Subodh. "Justice as Freedom": Do We Have a New Approach to a Firm's Enterprise Strategy?" *Business &Professional Ethics Journal,* Vol. 28, No. 1/4 (2009), pp. 3-26.

Sen, Amartya. "Equality of What?" m S. McMurrin, ed. *Tanner Lecture on Human Values, Volume}.* Cambridge: Cambridge University Press, 1980.

Sen, Amartya. "Well-Being, Agency and Freedom: The Dewey Lectures 1984". *The Journal ofPhilosophy* 82, no. 4. 1985), pp. 169-221.

Sen, Amartya. *Inequality Reexamined.* Oxford: Clarendon Press, 1992.

Marianne T. Hill. "Development as Empowerment". *Capabilities, Freedom, and Equality Amartya Sen's Workfrom a Gender Perspective.* Edited by Bina Agarwal, Jane Humphries & Ingrid Robeyns. UK: Oxford University Press, 2006.

Kant, Immanuel. "An Answer to the Question: What Is Enlightenment? (1784)", What is Enlightenment Eighteenth-Century Answers and Twentieth-Century *Questions.* Edited by James Schmidt. 58-64. London: University of California Press. 1996.

Clark, A David. "The capability approach: its development, critiques and recent Advances". Global Poverty Research Group. Website: http://www.gprg.org/

Makuwira, Jonathan. "Development? Freedom? Whose Development and Freedom?". *Development in Practice.* Vol. 16. 2006. pp. 193-200.

John F. Tomer. "Human Well-Being: A New Approach Based on Overall and Ordinary Functionings". *Review ofSocial Economy* 60, no. 1. 2002. pp. 23-45.

L. W. Sumner ."The Subjectivity of *Welfare".Ethics.* 105, no. 4. 1995. pp. 764-790.

Sen. "Standard of Living". *The Tanner Lectures on Human Values,* Delivered at Clare Hall, Cambridge University. March 11 and 12, 1785.

Aristotle. *The Ethics of Aristotle.* Translated by J. A. K. Thompson. London: Penguin Books, 1958.

Sen, Amartya. "Capability and Well-being" in A K Sen & M. Nussbaum, *The Quality of Life.* Oxford: Clarendon Press, 1993.

Daniels, Norman. "Equality of What: Welfare, Resources, or Capabilities?" *Philosophy and Phenomenological Research* 50, 1990: 273-296.

Sen, Amartya. *On Ethics and Economics.* Edited by John M. Letiche. Oxford: Oxford University Press, 1990.

John F. Tomer. "Human Well-Being: A New Approach Based on Overall and Ordinary Functionings". *Review ofSocial Economy* 60, no. 1. 2002. pp. 23-45.

Ingrid Robeyns. Sen's capability Approach and Gender Inequality: Selecting Relevant Capabilities. *Capabilities, Freedom, and Equality Amartya Sen's Work from a Gender Perspective.* Edited by Bina Agarwal, Jane Humphries & Ingrid Robeyns. UK: Oxford University Press, 2006.

Notes

1. Sen. *The Idea of Justice.* p. 7.
2. Paul Anand, Graham Hunter, Ron Smith. "Capabilities and Well-Being: Evidence Based on the Sen-Nussbaum Approach to Welfare". pp. 9-55.
3. Sen. *The Idea of Justice.* p. 4.
4. *Ibid.,* p. 6.
5. Sen and *Dreze. Hunger and Public Action.* p. 20.
6. Sen, *Idea of Justice.* p. 5.
7. *Ibid.,* pp. 5-7.
8. *Ibid.,* p. 10.
9. *Ibid.,* p. 4.
10. Boot. Martijn. "The Aim of a Theory of Justice". p. 8.
11. *Ibid.,* pp. 16-17.
12. Sen. *Idea of Justice.* p. 9.
13. Sen. *Idea of Justice.* p. 6.
14. *Ibid.,* p. 6.
15. *Ibid.,* p. 5.
16. *Ibid.,* p. 6.
17. *Ibid.,* p. 6.
18. *Ibid.,* p. 7.
19. Pankaj K Ashok. "Review of Idea of justice". pp. 74-77.
20. Sen. *Idea of Justice.* p. 9.
21. *Ibid.,* p. 12.
22. *Sen. Idea of Justice.* p. 15.
23. *Ibid.,* p. 18.
24. *Ibid.,* p. 7.
25. Fleischacker, *S. On Wealth of Nation: A Philosophical Companion.* p. 5.

26. Smith, Adam. *Theory of Moral Sentiments.* pp. 9-10.
27. *Ibid.,* p. 9.
28. Williams, David. *Condorcet and Modernity.* p. 173.
29. Sen. *Idea of Justice.* p. 92.
30. Sen. Commodities and Capabilities. p. 14.
31. *Ibid.,* p. 14.
32. *Ibid.,* p. 62.
33. *Ibid.,* p. 15.
34. Daniels, Norman. "Equality of What: Welfare, Resources, or Capabilities?". pp. 273-296.
35. Ingrid Robeyns. "Sen's Capability Approach and Gender Inequality Selecting Relevant Capabilities". p. 72.
36. Sen. "Equality of What?" p. 363.
37. *Ibid.,* p. 366.
38. Sen. *The Idea of Justice.* pp. 232-33.
39. *Ibid.,* pp. 14-20.
40. *Ibid.,* pp. 15-20.
41. Sen. *Development as Freedom.* p. 3.
42. Sen, *Idea of Justice.* p. 233.
43. Sen. *Development as Freedom.* p. 3.
44. *Ibid.,* p. 4.
45. *Ibid.,* p. 36.
46. *Ibid.,* p. 15.
47. *Ibid.,* p. 19.
48. *Ibid.,* p. 3.
49. Frediani, AAlexandre. "Sen's Capability Approach as a framework to the practice of devel opment". pp. 173-187.
50. Sen. *Development as Freedom,* p. 3.
51. Sen. *The Idea of Justice.* pp. 232-33.
52. Sen. *Development as Freedom.* p. 4.
53. *Ibid.,* p. 4.
54. *Ibid.,* p. 18.
55. *Ibid.,* p. 16.
56. *Ibid.,* p. 36.
57. *Ibid.,* p. 38.
58. *Ibid.,* pp. 38-39.
59. *Ibid.,* p. 39.
60. *Ibid.,* pp. 39-40.
61. *Ibid.,* p. 40.
62. Prendergast, Renee. "The Concept of Freedom and its Relation to Economic Development A Critical Appreciation of the Work of AmartyaSen". pp. 44-45.

63. *Ibid.,* p. 228.
64. Walsh, Vivian. "Amartya Sen on Rationality and Freedom". pp. 59-83.
65. Sen. *Rationality and Freedom.* p. 17.
66. *Ibid.,* p. 10.
67. Frediani, A Alexandre. "Sen's Capability Approach as a framework to the practice of development". pp. 173-187.
68. *Ibid.,* p. 176.
69. Sen. *Idea of Justice.* p. 232.
70. *Ibid.*, pp. 231-232
71. Sen. *Development as Freedom.* p. 75.
72. Sen. *Development as Freedom.* p. 61.
73. *Ibid.*, p. 62.
74. *Ibid.*, p. 62.
75. *Ibid.*, p. 62.
76. Sen. *Resources, Values and Development.* p. 278.
77. Sen. *Commodities and Capabilities.* p. 32.
78. Kulkami P. Subodh. "Justice as Freedom: Do We Have a New Approach to a Firm's Enterprise Strategy?". pp. 3-26.
79. Sen. "Equality of What?". *Tanner Lecture on Human Values, Volumel.* pp. 215-216.
80. Rawls. A *Theory of Justice.* p. 92.
81. Adam Smith, *Theory of Moral Sentiments.* pp. 869-870.
82. Sen. *Development as Freedom.* p. 89.
83. Prendergast, Renee. "The Concept of Freedom and its Relation to Economic Development- A Critical Appreciation of the Work of AmartyaSen". pp. 11-55.
84. Sen. "Well-Being, Agency and Freedom: The Dewey Lectures 1984". pp. 169-221
85. Sen. *Inequality Reexamined.* p. 49.
86. *Ibid.,* p. 49.
87. Sen. *Development as Freedom.* p. 75.
88. Sen. *Inequality Re-examined.* p. 40.
89. Sen. *Development as Freedom.* p. 87.
90. Sen. *Inequality Reexamined.* p. 39.
91. Sen. *Idea of Justice.* p. 231.
92. Marianne T. Hill. "Development as Empowerment". p. 132.
93. *Ibid.,* p. 113.
94. *Ibid.*, p. 135.
95. Paul Anand, Graham Hunter and Ron Smith, "Capabilities and Well-Being: Evidence Based on the Sen-Nussbaum Approach to Welfare". pp. 9-55.
96. Kant. "An Answer to the Question: What is Enlightenment?" p. 58.
97. Sen. *Rationality and Freedom.* p. 4.

98. *Ibid.,* p. 4.
99. Clark, A David. "The capability approach: its development, critiques and recent Advances". pp. 23-24.
100. Makuwira, Jonathan. "Development? Freedom? Whose Development and Freedom?". pp. 193-200.
101. Sen. *Rationality and Freedom.* p. 19.
102. *Ibid.,* p. 42.
103. *Ibid.,* p. 19.
104. John F. Tomer. "Human Well-Being: A New Approach Based on Overall and Ordinary Functioning". p. 40.
105. L.W. Sumner. "The Subjectivity *of Welfare". Ethics.* pp. 764-790.
106. Sen. "Well-Being, Agency and Freedom: The Dewey Lectures 1984". p. 195.
107. *Ibid.,* p. 195.
108. Sen. "Standard of Living". *The Tanner Lectures on Human Value.* p. 15.
109. Sen. "Well-Being, Agency and Freedom: The Dewey Lectures 1984". p. 198.
110. Aristotle. *The Ethics of Aristotle.* p. 51.
111. Sen. "Capability and Well-being". *The Quality of Life.* p. 31.
112. Sen, *Development as Freedom.* p. 57.
113. Daniel, Norman. "Equality of What: Welfare, Resources, or Capabilities?" p. 276.
114. Sen, *Inequality Reexamined.* p. 39.
115. John F. Tomer. "Human Well-Being: A New Approach Based on Overall and Ordinary Functionings". pp. 23-45.
116. Sen. o*n Ethics and Economics.* p. 7.
117. Ingrid Robeyns. Sen's capability Approach and Gender Inequality: Selecting Relevant Capabilities. p. 70.
118. Marianne T. Hill. "Development as Empowerment". p. 146.

Chapter - 4

Martha Nussbaum on Gender Justice

The concept of gender justice with reference to Martha Nussbaum's capability approaches is not as a procedural justice but as an outcome-oriented approach that gives an impartial account of justice. It attempt to bring out the close relationship between the institutional and constitutional design in Martha Nussbaum with the quest for justice and equality of opportunities between genders. It addresses the questions concerning minimizing injustice in terms of discrimination, particularly gender discrimination in the cultural practices of different people on the one hand and legal, political, social and economic status of women on the other. The discrimination and the deprived situation of women are due to the cultural traditions and practices that mould their lives. It also tries to interrogate the conflict between cultural practices and women's rights. The question arises - are we going to minimize women's injustice and bring gender equality under the purview of human rights or let the culture or tradition decide their lives? In other words Martha Nussbaum's conception of gender justice addresses the ongoing gender-based injustices from which women suffer. With feminist perspective, Martha Nussbaum attempts to establish an inclusive society which not only incorporates the basic philosophic visions of Kant, Rawls and Sen, but also transcends it.

As a matter of fact gender justice tries to eliminate all forms of violence against women and achieve gender equality under the purview of human rights. Its purpose is to addresses various forms of injustice relating to women's rights violation at national and global level. It can however be pointed out that gender is a common term where as gender based discrimination is meant only for women. In other words, women are the only victims of gender based violence and discrimination. It can be argue that from the cradle to grave, women are under the clutches of various forms of injustices like discrimination, oppressions, violence within the family, at the work places and in the society. The root causes of gender injustices and its practices faced by the women are illiteracy, economic dependence, caste restrictions, religious prohibition, lack of agency and lack of leadership qualities and more importantly patriarchal attitude of men towards women in the society. Nussbaum has pointed in her article entitled Women's Bodies: Violence, Security, Capabilities,

> Throughout the world, women's bodies are vulnerable to a range of violent assaults that include domestic violence, rape within marriage, rape by acquaintances or dates, rape by strangers, rape in wars and communal conflicts, honor killing, trafficking and forced prostitution, child sexual abuse, female infanticide, female genital mutilation, and sex-selective abortion.[1]

It is a harsh reality that women all over the world have been ill treated in every society and India is no exception. Indeed some practices that are not seems to be violent but also contribute to the atmosphere of threat in which all women live the entirety of their lives: sexual harassment, stalking, threats of violence, deprivation of bodily liberty, the undernutrition of girls. Women are deprived of economic resources and are dependent on men for their living. Women works are often confined to domestic sphere, she had to do all house hold works, which are not recognized and unpaid. In modem times many women are coming out to work but has to shoulder the double responsibility; one she has to work where she is employed and secondly she also has to do all the house hold works, moreover, she is last to be considered and first to be fired as she is considered to be less productive than her counterpart. Her general status in the family and in the society has been low and unrecognized. In number, females are nearly 50 percent of the total population but their representation in public life is very low. The issue of gender based violence has been a concern in many nations including India for centuries.

For the sake of clarity and precision, I shall divide the present chapter into three parts. In Part I, I will discuss women and human rights with reference to Martha Nussbaum's conception of gender justice. Its attempt is to discuss women injustices in the form of their violation of human rights at global and national level. I'll argue with Martha Nussbaum that the majority of women across the world are deprived of legal, political, social and economic status enjoyed by men. This discrimination and their deprived situation are due to their cultural traditions and practices moulding their lives. I'll go into the details of the conflict between cultural practices and women's rights which have been prevailing since the society has evolved. In Part II, I will aaddress poverty and gender inequalities for empowering women are very important in the notion of gender justice. Its purpose is to meet the challenge of improving food and nutrition security and enabling poor rural people to overcome poverty. In Part III, I will develop capability and gender justice with reference Martha Nussbaum. Nussbaum uses capability approach to minimize poverty and gender inequality from feminist perspective because women have been facing discrimination and unequal treatment at every stage. She has tried to bring equal opportunities of all human being through human capability irrespective of their gender and brought feminist notion of justice.

Coming to the basic issues which I am discussing in the above three parts, I would like to point out that even after so many years of modernisation and its principles of liberty, equality and fraternity, gender justice, still appears to be an unresolved agenda. Martha Nussbaum considers the quest for justice and equality of opportunities between genders. She tried to establish an inclusive society and the possibility of feminist perspective on justice. Nussbaum's conception of gender justice begins from the real lives of women and the

> Lives of women are highly varied. It is myopic to focus only on conditions and problems that are shared by local or national groups while neglecting the very different gender related problems that may be faced by women in very different political and economic circumstances.[2]

She considers that the need to recognize that the lives ofwomen are highly varied, that women live within a variety of traditions, and that the "best account of Justice not one that merely projects western values onto groups with different concerns".3 Her main concern is to pay attention to the actual experiences and circumstances of individual women. For instance the experience of white class women in the United States is different form black women in the South Africa.

Moreover, without recognising the experience of women from their cultural and religious practices that are moulding their lives, gender injustice cannot be minimised. She has pointed out,

> "The isolationist habits of nation lead us to focus inward rather than on urgent needs at a distance. Thus by now there is a rich feminist literature on the question such as rape and sexual harassment, which are common concerns of women all over the world. Much less is known and said about women's hunger, about sex-selective

> infanticides and abortion, about the denial of the right to work, about sex discriminationin religious courts of family law".[4]

In order to minimize injustice against women, we must incorporate historical and cultural circumstances of different women. It is a fact that no woman in the world is free from injustices such as rape and sexual harassment only but hunger, infanticides, and their bodily is a cause of concern. India is no exception of gender discrimination in religious court of family law. In India, nearly, half of the population consists of women and suffered from patriarchy which is supported by tradition, religion and culture.

> Gender inequality, too, is exceptionally high in India, particularly in large parts of the northern and western regions, where the subjugation of women is fairly comprehensive. It is the mutual reinforcement of severe inequalities of different kinds that creates an extremely oppressive social system, where those at the bottom of these multiple layers of disadvantage live in conditions of extreme disempowerment.[5]

Tradition, religion and the culture of Indian society subordinated women and deprived their rights which are equal to men. Women had to struggle for equality, liberty and justice. Women suffered from gender based prejudices and therefore they are marginalized. Women are often victimized, ignored, traditions, have however proved to be a formidable barrier to recognize the rights of women within the religious courts of family law. Nussbaum pointed out that "India has a uniform criminal code; although it does not have uniform civil code, civil matters are handled by many distinct religious system of law".[6] It may be pointed out that all the Indian personal laws have been originated from ancient religious texts which discriminate against woman vis-a-vis the men within each religion.

Broadly speaking injustice against women may be found in the political, economic and cultural sphere vis-a-vis men. Firstly, feminists argue that women have been discriminating since a society has evolved and justice demand that they should get equal rights under the purview of human rights. It can be argue that the advanced nations of Europe and America withheld women's right to vote for a very long time. However women won their political rights but their actual participation in political power is far behind that of men. For instance in America, women won the right to vote but their share in the House of Representative is less than 20 percent. In the Senate women's representation is less than 10 percent.

Since nine decades women got political rights in the United States but no women has become President in the history of America. Due to such discrimination Hillary Clinton could not become first women president of America. Secondly, feminist have also identified problems concerning women's economic rights. It is a fact that women's contribution to economic life has been largely ignored. For instance, national income accounting ignores the unpaid work done by women for the benefit of family and community. Their domestic work towards child bearing does not constitute in countries GDP. Women are also involving in various domestic works including cooking, house-keeping, sewing, weaving, etc apart from child rearing. In fact, the market value of these services is not taken into account. Moreover, women's unpaid labour benefits not only their family but to make significant contribution to society. Thirdly, women are facing gender discrimination and they become victims in cultural sphere as well. Nussbaum argues, "Men did not have to fight against cultural opprobrium and political opposition to get jobs; men did not have to struggle to get an educationf[7]", Many social practices reflect a cultural climate of masculine dominance in which women regularly experience shame, embarrassment and vulnerability.

Moreover, the status of women in India has been subject to many changes over the past few millennia. S. Vats and Shakuntla Mudgal has pointed the status ofwomen in ancient Indian society in *Women and Society in Ancient India,*

> In the Vedic age, women enjoyed a higher status in home as well outside. The Rigveda shows abundant evidence pointing to the fact that women were fully the equals of men as regards access to and capacity for the highest knowledge, even the knowledge of the Absolute or Brahma.[8]

> Jayapalan has also argues in *Indian Society and Social Institutions,* Women enjoyed equal status and rights during the early Vedic period. However, later the status of women began to decline with the Smiritis and with the Islamic invasion of Babur and the Mughal Empire and later Christianity curtailing women's freedom and rights.[9]

From equal status with men in ancient times through the low points of the medieval period, to the promotion of equal rights by many reformers, the history of women in India has been eventful. In modem India, women have adorned high offices in India including that of the Prime Minister, President, Speaker of the Lok Sabha, Leader of Opposition, etc. In spite of women's contribution in all spheres of life to enjoy a unique position in every society and country of the world, but they suffer in silence and belong to a class which is in a disadvantaged position on account of several barriers and impediments. India, being a country of paradoxes, is no exception. Here too, women, a personification of Shakti, once given a dignified status, are in need of empowerment. Women's empowerment in legal, social, political and economic requires to be enhanced. With this brief remark regarding the status of women's injustice in every sphere; I shall corne to the Part I of the chapter i.e. women and human rights.

Part - I

Women and Human Rights

In order to minimize gender injustice, we must recognise the violation of women's rights and to address all forms of violence against women. As Martha Nussbaum has pointed out in her book *Frontiers of Justice: Disability, Nationality, Species Membership* that, "The world contains inequalities that are morally alarming, and we need to know about how the most deprived people in the world are doing. Women, for example notoriously lag behind men in education, employment opportunities, and even in basic life chances".[10] The majority of women across the world are deprived of legal, political, social and economic rights and status enjoyed by men. This discrimination and their deprived situation is due to their cultural traditions and practices that mould their lives. "Although there is no doubt that the apartheid of gender is considerably more pervasive than the apartheid of race; it has never provoked the same degree of international concern or opprobrium".[11] Inother words women's rights should be protected in the society because women are considered as the fundamental pillars of civilization. It is a fact that women constitute an important role in transforming the family and society at large. So their role in shaping the family and molding the society cannot be ignored. Moreover, Kofi Annan, the former Secretary General of United Nations Organisations has stated about women's rights and their empowerment is the need of an hour, "Women's rights are the responsibility of all humankind; combating all forms of violence against women is duty of all human kind and achieving the empowerment of women is the advancement of all humankind".[12] It seems clear that, without preserving and protecting women's basic rights, no society can claim to have an established a just social order.

Martha Nussbaum argues in her recent book-Sex *and Social Justice* that how our society appeals to cultural traditions and practices that are moulding women's lives in its own way. Moreover it seems impossible to deny that cultural traditions, "Both Western and non-Western perpetuate injustices against women in many fundamental ways, touching on some of the most central elements of a human being's quality oflife-health, education, political liberty and participation, employment, self-respect, and the life itself[13]. Martha Nussbaum argues,

> "Throughout the world, cultural traditions pose obstacles to women's health and flourishing. Depressingly, many traditions portray women as less important than men, less deserving of basic life support or of fundamental rights that are strongly correlated with quality of life, such as the right to work and the right to political participation. Sometimes, the traditions have become so deeply internalised that they seems to record what is "right" and "natural and women themselves endorse their own second-class status".[14]

It is clear that our society appeals to cultural traditions in its own way to justify women's unequal treatment. These cultural traditions perpetuate injustices against women in varied ways. Then question arises - are we going to minimize women's injustices and bring gender equality under the purview of human rights or let the culture or tradition decide their lives? Regarding the cultural traditions that perpetuate injustice, Nussbaum looks a matter of survival of a young widow in Rajasthan state that how Metha Bai along with two children are forced to die because her customs treat women as people who cannot go out for employment. Women are traditionally or culturally prohibited from working outside the home even though her survival itself as an issue. "I may die, but still I cannot go out. If there's something in the house, we eat. Otherwise, we go to sleep. If she stays at home, she and her children may shortly die".[15] It is a fact that women's human rights are violated in a variety of ways. Of course, women sometimes suffer abuses because of religious and cultural repression that are not similar to abuse suffered by men. However, the conflict between cultural practices and the violations of women's rights has been prevalent as a social phenomena and it has to be interrogated.

To minimise women's injustice, gendered nature of the human rights system is very necessary because women's fundamental rights are violating in all spheres of life. The rights and dignity of a woman is often violated by the family, society and the state. Discriminatory practices towards girls start in the family. Gender classification of tasks, behavior, dress, food, toys, games, space and time utilization start at home. In the family, the woman is treated not as an end in herself, but as an adjunct or instrument of the needs of others, as a mere reproducer, cook, cleaner, sexual outlet, caretaker, rather than as a source of agency and worth in her own right. Limitations of women's activities in domestic functions result in the improper development of the personality of women and complete submission to the male members of the family. Violence committed against women in private domain has also become a matter of serious concern. Family is the basic institution which preserves to continue the unequal social relations. It can be argue that women are most discriminated against by those with whom they are most intimate and whom they trust most. Moreover Charlotte Bunch has also pointed out that,

> Significant numbers of the world's population are routinely subject to torture, starvation, terrorism, humiliation, mutilation, and even murder simply because they are female. Crimes such as these against any group other than women would be recognised as a civil and political emergency as well as gross violation of the victims' humanity. Yet, despite a clear record of deaths and demonstrable abuse, women's rights are not commonly classified as human rights. This is problematic both theoretically and practically, because it has grave consequences for the way society views and treats the fundamental issue of women's lives.[16]

It is a fact that women's human rights are violated in a variety of ways such as torture, starvation, humiliation, mutilation, even rape and murder and more importantly inequality of opportunities in every sphere of lives. "Achieving equality between women and men requires a comprehensive understanding of the ways in which women experiences discrimination and are denied equality so as to develop appropriate strategies to eliminate such discrimination."[17] To eliminate all forms of discrimination and attain equality between women and men are the fundamental values of United Nations. However, both the International law and national law on human rights prohibit discrimination on the basis of sex and guarantee women and men equality in the enjoyment. Hence, non-discrimination and equality between women and men are central principles of human rights law. Moreover, women around the world suffer violation of human rights throughout their lives.

The concept of human rights is conceptually dynamic so it is difficult to define. Martha Nussbaum argues,

> The idea of human rights is by no means a crystal clear idea. Rights have been understood in many different ways, and difficult theoretical questions are frequently obscuredby the use of rights language, which can give the illusion of agreement where there is deep philosophical disagreement.[18]

It is difficult to find out about the basis of a rights claim. She has pointed in her book *Frontiers of Justice,* "People differ about the basis of a rights claim is: rationality, sentience, and mere life have all had their defenders. They differ, too about whether rights are pre political or artifacts of laws and institutions".[19] It is a fact that people have differences about whether rights belong only to individual person, or to group. However, historically, human right is considered to be the natural and moral right which implies that every person is entitled to certain fundamental rights, simply by the fact of being human. United Nations Report on Human Rights categorically stated that, "Human rights are those rights that are inherent in our nature and without which we cannot live as human being"[20] Further it also stated, "Human rights and fundamental freedoms allow us to develop fully and use our human qualities, our intelligence, our talents and our conscience and to satisfy our spiritual and other needs".[21] It may be pointed human rights have emerged out of the idea of natural rights which are inherent in our nature and without which a person cannot satisfy his/her basic needs.

In short, human rights implies for those fundamental rights i.e. right to life, liberty, equality, security and equal protection under law and most importantly free from all forms of discrimination etc as human beings. These rights considered to be basic condition for the survival of human beings which are embedded formally at the "United Nations through Universal Declaration of Human Rights".[22]

> "Indeed the need for the Declaration of HumanRights has arisen from the sense of insecurity faced by human beings after World War II. Moreover, it raises the question of human dignity, self-respect, right to live, and work in the world that has become the driving force and furtherance of humanrights".[23]

As a matter of fact the concept of human rights has moral visions which aim at the protection of the human dignity and elimination of inhuman treatment to any person under any circumstances. It is therefore that international agreements like the United Nations Universal Declaration of Human Rights of 1948 become important to uphold human rights. "Human right was unanimously adopted by the General Assembly on

10th December, 1948 since then 1 Oth December is celebrated as the Human Rights Day".[24] It is the first document on human rights which brought about international cooperation and consensus regarding the inherent rights of all human beings. It concern about the lives of people globally to protect their basic rights as a human being. However Charlotte Bunch argues in "Women's Rights as Human Rights: Toward a Re-Vision of Human Rights", "The 'Universal Declaration of Human Rights' adopted in 1948 symbolizes this world vision and defines human rights broadly while not much is said about women, Article 2 entitles all to "the rights and freedoms set forth in this Declaration, without distinction of any kind, such as race, colour, sex, language, religion, political or other opinion, national or social origin, property, birth or other status".[25] It is a fact that Article 2 of the Universal declaration of human rights stated every individual is equal in dignity and rights and entitled to freedoms and does not addressed the question of gender per se.

As Blanch Wiesen Cook has pointed in an article entitled "Eleanor Roosevelt and Human Rights: The Battle for Peace and Planetary Decency", "Eleanor Roosevelt and Latin American women who fought for the inclusion of sex in the Declaration and for its passage clearly intended that it would address the problem of women's subordination".[26] It is a fact that since 1948 the world community has continuously debating about the violation of human rights, however, little has addressed about women's rights and experiences at global and national level to uphold certain basic rights. Such international agreements oblige governments to uphold certain basic rights enshrined in the declaration. The declaration consists of a preamble and 30 Articles. The preamble of Universal Declaration of Human Rights recognizes inherent dignity and of the equal and inalienable rights of all members of the human family is the foundation of freedom, justice and peace in the world. The Universal Declaration of Human Rights made it clear that every human being, irrespective of race, color, sex, language, religion is entitled to all the rights and freedoms. It recognized as a historic document articulating a common definition of human dignity and values. The declaration has thirty articles which can be elaborated in the following manner:

1. Articles 1 and 2: implies that every human being is equal in dignity and rights and everyone is entitled to all human rights and freedoms.
2. Articles 3 to 21: include civil and political rights, such as right to life, liberty and security of person, equality before the law, right to nationality etc.

3. Articles 22 to 27: provide for economic, social and cultural rights. They include among others, right to social security, right to work and right to education.
4. Articles 28 to 30: enunciate that everyone is entitled to an international order for realization of all the freedoms, everyone has responsibility to the community and that the Declaration cannot be interpreted in a way for the destruction of any right and freedom".

It can be interpreted that, firstly, the rights incorporated in "article 1-2 of the Universal Declaration of Human Rights" stated moral vision that how every individual is treated equally in terms of their freedom and dignity, basic rights and security etc. For instance article 1 of the universal declaration of human rights adopted by the UN in 1948 stated that: all human beings are born free and equal in dignity and rights. While article 2 states that everyone is entitled to all the rights and freedoms set forth in this declaration without distinction of any kind, such as race, colour, sex and language. Moreover it does not mention the question of gender based violence *per se.* Secondly, the rights incorporated in "article 221" implies human rights i.e. civil and political rights of a person as a human being. It is considered to be the *'first generation rights'*[27]. Such type of human rights conceives in negative terms because it favors the abstention rather than the intervention of government in the quest for human dignity. In other words, the rights included in Articles 2-21 of it stated equality and non-discrimination. It regards the enjoyment of human rights and fundamental freedoms i.e. right to "life, liberty and security of person, freedom from slavery and servitude, freedom from torture and cruel, inhuman or degrading treatment or punishment".[28] Traditionally, primacy has been given to civil and political rights toward protection for men within public life, i.e., in their relationship with the government. Hilary Charlesworth argues in "Human Rights as Men's Rights" that,

> The primacy traditionally given to civil and political rights by developed nations is directly toward protection of men within public life, in their relationship with government. But this is not the arena in which women most need protection. The operation of a public / private distinction at a gendered level is seen most clearly in the definition of those civil and political rights concerned with the protection of the individual from violence.[29]

The International Covenant on Civil and Political Rights" are inherently biased against women because it operates primarily in the public sphere which is within the walls of institutions. In other way public sphere that is government, politics, economics and the workplace areas traditionally associated with men on the one hand, private sphere of home that is associated with women on the other is the exclusion of human rights discourse and its implementation. It is often regarded as the 'right to life' is the most important rights of civil and political rights. Hillary argues,

> The most important of all human rights, is the right to life set out in Article 6 of the *International Covenant on Civil and Political Rights.* The right is concerned with the arbitrary deprivation of life through public action. But the protection from arbitrary deprivation of life or liberty through public action, important as it is, does not address the ways in which being a woman is in itself life threatening and the special ways in which women need legal protection to be able to enjoy their rights to life.[30]

It can be argue that, life of women is full of violence, because they are facing injustices throughout their lives relating to human rights such as political, economic and cultural rights at global and national level. For instance, these violence threats to women are right to life from birth to old age. Their womanhood is full of risks i.e. of abortion and infanticides because of social and economic pressure in some cultures to have son's preference. The other risks of malnutrition that women have been facing because of social practices give men and boys priority with respect to food. It can be argue that, our society discriminates between men and women in the matter of allocation of benefits and burdens. For instance, society failed to realize unpaid labor and even failed to acknowledge constraints under which women work and not to speak of reward for these contribution. Moreover women having less access to health care than men and of endemic violence against women in all spheres of lives, yet the right to life is not regarded as extending to these threats to women's lives. In other words the traditional construction of first generation rights i.e. civil and political rights obscure the most consistent harm done to women. However recent developments such as the United Nation's *Declaration on the Elimination of Violence Against Women*[31] indicate international concern on this women's issue, they do not directly challenge the inability of human rights law generally to respond to injuries sustained constantly by women worldwide. However this declaration does not define violence against women as a human rights violation, but present it implicitly as a discrete category of harm, on a different plane than serious human rights violation.

Carrying further, thirdly "Articles 22 to 27 of Universal Declaration of Human Rights" is regarded as the *second generation rights*[32] includes *social, economic and cultural rights* in positive terms. Unlike *first generation rights* that are civil and political rights, the *second generation rights* require state intervention to protect people's social, economic and cultural rights. Hilary Charlesworth argues,

> The covenant does not touch on economic, social and cultural contexts in which most women live, since the crucial economic, social and cultural power relationship for most women is not one directly with the state but with men-fathers, husband, or brothers-whose authority is supported by patn.archa1state structure.[33]

It can be explained through example that 'right to just and favorable condition of work is meant only for the within the public sphere and does not include the private sphere where women lives within the four walls of home. Hilary Charlesworth has pointed, "Article 7' s guarantee to women of "conditions of work not inferior to those enjoyed by men, with equal pay for equal work" thus sound rather hollow in light of the international myopia with respect to the extent and economic value of women's work".[34] Moreover, economic, social and cultural rights are considered as an indispensible for human dignity but it does not consider women's lives and their varied experiences within the private sphere. It is a fact that most of women lives within the four walls of home and their economic activities are invisible because it is performed without pay. Moreover, economic, social and cultural rights are considered as an indispensible for human dignity but it does not address women's experiences. Therefore it is necessary to ensure women's experiences in the definition of economic, social and cultural rights under the purview of human rights norms.

Lastly, "Articles 28 to 30 of *Universal Declaration of Human Rights"* is regarded as the *Third generation rights*[35] is beyond *first* and *second generations* of human rights that are not political, civil, economic, social or cultural in nature. It is considered to be a group rights that are based on the principle of fraternity to bring out collective welfare of the community beyond the interests of individual's rights. As Hilary Charlesworth argues,

> The philosophical basis of group rights rests on a pnmary commitment to the welfare of the community over and above the interests of particular individuals. It might seem that such rights would hold

> particular promise for women, whose lives typically centre more on the family, the group, and the community than the individual. There has been much controversy over the legal status of such rights, but, from a women's perspectives, they are, III fundamental ways, little different from the first and second generations of rights, since they too have developed in an androcentric way.[36]

However, third generation covers right to development which has both theoretically and practically delivered very little to women's development. For instance, right to development is both defined and implemented internationally to support male economic dominance. Moreover, the subordination of women to men does not enter the traditional development calculus: development conceived as economic growth is not concerned with the lack of benefits or disadvantageous effects this growth may have on half of the society it purports to benefit. Indeed, the position of many women in developing countries has deteriorated over the last two decades: women's access to economic resources has been reduced, their health and educational status has declined and their work burdens have increased.

The universal applicability of the right to development as formulated in the UN Declaration on the Right to Development is undermined by androcentric nature of the international economic system which accords far greater value to work conducted in the public (male) sphere than to women's work in the private sphere. The problematic nature, for Third World women, of current development practice cannot of course be attributed solely to the international legal formulation of the right to development. "More recent UN deliberations on development have paid greater attention to the role of women"[37]. However these concerns are usually presented as quite distinct and by the application of special protective measures rather than as crucial to the notion of development itself.

The concept of human rights emphasizes the universality of all human rights which connotes both males and female.

> The international community usually couches discussion of the advancement of women in terms of the acquisition and implementation of rights particular to women. While this is certainly an important and valuable project, it can also obscure some basic elements contributing to the oppression of women.[38]

Since the foundation of United Nations Organization, promotion of human rights has become a widely accepted universal goal. It provides a useful framework for seeking redress of human rights violation for all human being irrespective of caste, creed, sex and gender. Moreover, for a long period, gender based violations were not considered as human rights violation. As Peggy Antrobus says in the World Women's Congress,

> Although we are divided by race, class, culture, and geography, our hope lies in our commonalities. All women's unremunerated household work is exploited, we all have conflicts in our multiple roles, our sexuality is exploited by men, media, and the economy, we struggle for survival and dignity, and rich or poor, we are vulnerable to violence. We share our otherness, our exclusion from decision making at alllevels.[39]

It has been found that the rights and dignity of a woman is often violated at global and national level. However, it can be argued that there are problems in speaking about women and their experiences in a global context. "Sex discrimination kills women daily. When combined with race, class, and other forms of oppression, it constitute a deadly denial of women's right to life and liberty on a larger scale throughout the world"[40] Even women have been facing many disadvantageous situations due to the existence of gender difference and bias differently within different societies. Obviously, differences in class, wealth, race, and nationality will lead to differing power relationship among women. However patriarchy and the devaluing ofwomen, although manifested differently within different societies are almost universal. "Women's right as human rights has been used to explore, asserts and redress the gap between the international commitment to equality for women and the actual experience of women"[41]. It constitutes an integral part as it address women's issues from the human rights perspectives. It emerged as a consequence of exclusion of women's issues from the human rights issues. Thus, the failure to respect and recognize women as human led to the claim of 'Women's Rights as Human Rights'.

The concept of women's rights refers to legal norms on gender based non-discrimination and to promote equal rights, equal treatment and equal opportunities for both men and women being a human being. The need for the protection of and the respect for women's human rights occurs as a result of an ugly fact that substantial numbers of women regularly experience torture, murder, humiliation, beating, mutilation and rape simply because of being female. For instance crimes like torture have been recognized as a violation of human rights in the public realm.

> A central feature of the international legal definition of torture is that it takes place in the public realm: it must be inflicted by or at the instigation of or with the consent or acquiescence of a public official other person acting in an official capacity. Although many women are victims of torture in this public sense by far the greatest violence against women occurs in the "private", nongovernmental sphere. This is left untouched by the international definition of torture.[42]

It can be argue that many international human rights principles are inherently biased against women. An important example of international human rights law is the definition of tortures which primarily operates in the public sphere and excludes the experience of women in their private lives where the victim is a woman were regularly ignored quite a long time. As a result of discrimination, degradation and violation of women, a new concept i.e. women's human rights has emerged. "The specific experiences of women must be added to traditional approaches to human rights in order to make women more visible and to transform the concept and practices of human rights in our culture so that it takes better account of women's lives"[43]. Moreover United Nations Human Rights tries to address women's problem,

> United Nations has a long history of addressing women's human rights and much progress has been made in securing women's rights across the world in recent decades. However important gaps remain and women's realities are constantly changing, with new manifestations of discrimination against them regularly emerging. Some groups of women face additional forms of discrimination based on their age, ethnicity, nationality, religion, health status, marital status, education, disability and socio economic status, among other grounds. These intersecting forms of discrimination must be taken into account when developing measures against women and responses to combat discrimination against women.[44]

It can be argue that until the gendered nature of human rights system is recognized and transformed women's progress cannot be achieved. Women's right under the purview of human rights has been a paradigm shift for the protection women's rights and their empowerment. It is considered to be an integral and indivisible part of universal human rights. It tries to eradicate forms of discrimination on the grounds of gender identity and seek women's rights as political, civil, social, economic and cultural rights vis-vis men.

Women at global level and India in particular, have been facing genderbased discriminations and injustices in every sphere of life. Globally, the Universal Declaration of Human Rights (1948) and many subsequent declarations, including the two United Nations International Covenants, that on Economic, Social and Cultural Rights (UNICESCR) and that on Civil and Political Rights (UNICCPR) proclaim the equal rights of human beings without regard to their sex. Moreover the provisions of Universal Declaration of Human Rights were incorporated in the preamble of the Indian constitution. "India's constitution is a very women-friendly document. The right of non discrimination on the basis of sex is guaranteed in the list of justifiable fundamental rights, as is the right to the equal protection of the laws."[45] For instance, Constitution ofIndia guarantees equality to all under Article 14, no discrimination by the State by Article 15(1), equality of opportunity by Article 16, equal pay for equal work under Article 39(d). In addition to the above constitutional guarantee for gender equality and justice even then the condition of women in India is miserable. Moreover, Indian constitution allows special provisions to be made by the State in favor of women and children under Article 15(3), renounces practices derogatory to the dignity of women under Article 51 (A) (e). It also allows for provisions to be made by the State for securing just and humane conditions of work and for maternity relief (Article 42).

United Nations plays a significant role in safeguarding and promoting human rights in general and women's rights in particular. It may be pointed out that the most important and comprehensive international treaty for promoting women's rights is the CEDAW i.e. Conventions on the Elimination of All Forms of Discrimination against Women. It represents a milestone on the road to gender equality and empowerment of women. It is the most important convention of UN in general and Indian Constitution in particular have a long history of addressing women's human rights and much progress has been made in securing women's rights across the world in recent decades.

> However, important gaps remam and women's realities are constantly changing, with new manifestations of discrimination against them regularly emerging. Some groups of women face additional forms of discrimination based on their age, ethnicity, nationality, religion, health status, marital status, education, disability and socioeconomic status, among other grounds. These intersecting forms of discrimination must be taken into account when developing measures and responses to combat discrimination against women.[46]

Due to wide variety of women's issues relevant to their basic rights, it is very necessary to introduce the concept of women and human rights with reference to women's capabilities rather on human rights perspectives. Women's rights and varied forms of violence like rape, domestic violence, dowry-related deaths, honor killings, sexual harassment, female infanticides and other discrimination against women are the threat on women's capabilities. In other way, unless gendered nature of human rights is recognized, no real progress of women and society can be achieved. Hence, transforming human rights concept from a feminist perspective as a part of already recognized *first, second* and *third* generation of human rights is very necessary.

There are four ways to connect women rights to human rights and these are, namely:

1. Women's Rights as Political and Civil Rights"[47]: It considers "women's specific needs into consideration as part of the already recognized 'first generation rights' is the first approach". It considers both "raising the visibility of women who suffer general human rights violations as well as calling attention to particular abuses women encounter because they are female."[48] This approach is very useful to consider women's experiences and raises contradictions that reveal the limits of a narrow civil liberties view. One contradistinction is to define rape as a human rights abuse only when it occurs in state custody but not on the streets or in the home.[49]
2. Women's Rights as Socioeconomic Rights": It includes "the particular plight of women with regard to "second generation" human rights such as the rights to food, shelter, health care, and employment."[50] It tries to eradicate women's economic subordination as the key to other issues including women's vulnerability to violence. Looking at women's rights in the context of socioeconomic development is another example this approach. The focus of this approach is to highlight on "feminization of poverty" because "female comprise of higher percentage of poor.
3. Women's Rights and the Law": "The creation of new mechanisms to counter sex discrimination characterizes the third approach to women's rights as human rights. These efforts seek to make existing legal and political institutions work for women and to expand the state's responsibility for the violation of women's

rights"[51]. For instance, several institutional laws have made to address sex discrimination and violence against women is the exemplification of this approach.

Therefore, in order to minimize social injustices, we must incorporate the violation of human rights in particular and women's rights in particular. Although, women constitute an important role in transforming the family and society so their rights should be protected yet women have been facing many disadvantageous situations due to the existence of gender differences and biases. Hence, without protecting and preserving women's basic rights, no society can claim to have an established and just social order. Since the foundation of United Nations Organization, the concept of human rights has provided a normative framework to address human rights violation for all human being irrespective of caste, creed, sex and gender.

However, the majority of women across the world are deprived of legal, political, social and economic rights that are enjoyed by men. Moreover, for a long period, gender based violations were not considered as human rights violation because crimes against any person other than women would be recognized as a gross violation of the victims' humanity. There are many international human rights law and national human rights law is inherently biased against women. Such law operates primarily in the public spheres which is traditionally associated with men's life. On the other hand it does not operate in the private sphere of home and family which is generally regarded as the province of women. Thus, the failure to respect and recognize women as human led to the claim of 'Women's Rights as Human Rights'. The concept of women's rights refers to legal norms on gender based non-discrimination and includes women's rights into traditional approach to human rights to achieve equal rights, equal treatment and equal opportunities for both men and women being a human.

Part - II

Poverty and Gender Inequality

To minimise injustice, requires the removal of women's poverty and inequality in every sphere of their lives. According to Martha Nussbaum, "Women are unequal in many respects all over the world, and this is an enormous problem of justice. It is also a development problem, because denial of opportunity to women holds back the productivity of many nations".[52] Poverty and gender inequality has been one of the major problems that our society is facing since a long time. In general, poverty occurs due to the imbalance of economic, political and social opportunities that are essential to meet the basic necessities of life. When poverty comes to women's lives, its impact can be seen at large. Women's poverty represents the absence of some basic capabilities to function in terms of being well nourished, being adequately clothed, being sheltered, avoiding preventable morbidity etc. The impact of poverty makes women more likely to be vulnerable and poor than men. It is clear that the status of women is causes for concern as compared to men women have no reasonable income, no health care and no security which leads them to face extreme poverty. More than half a billion women in developing countries have no reasonable income, no health care and no security. Extreme poverty is female and means hunger, disease, no education, no ownership and no secure access to water and energy. Women also have limited opportunities owing to isolation, exclusion from decision-making processes, low mobility, overwork and violence.

Nussbaum holds that utility and resource approach fails to confront with poverty and gender inequalities. It is well known fact that utility is inadequate to capture women's poverty and inequality between men and women. Basically it fails to encounter for adaptive preferences for marginalized class, for example women. However, Nussbaum argues III "Capabilities as Fundamental Entitlements: Sen and Social Justice" that, "the utilitarian framework, which ask people what they currently prefer and how satisfied they are, proves inadequate to confront the most pressing issues of gender justice."[53] Further she has pointed out that, "utility suggests that the goal of development is a state or condition of persons (e.g. a state of satisfaction), and thus, undervalue the importance of agency and freedom in the development process"[54]

It makes clear that why feminist thinker criticizes about utilitarianism because it fails to encounter women's preferences and who often treated as passive members of the society. On the hand, it fails to take account of the fact that women's satisfaction consists in various elements of well-being relating to health, education, mobility, political participation, and others. Hillary Charlesworth says in "Martha Nussbaum's Feminist Internationalism",

> From evidence of the second-class status of women across the developing and developed country divide and their consistently lower quality of life when measured by access to health, education, political liberty and participation, employment, self respect, and life itself.[55]

Gender inequality deprives women's rights are depriving day by day and it is due to utilitarian and liberal conception of justice which overlooks their potentialities and problems as well. Women integrity for instance may be threatened with violence. In other words, resource approach to welfare is bad indicator of measuring gender inequality. Moreover it fails to account for individual's variability in general and women's ability in particular to convert social resources into actual functionings. In other way, poverty and gender inequality can be understood by comparing people's functionings and capabilities that what she can do and be to get away from vulnerable lives rather than resources or utility that he/she achieve. Nussbaum argues in her article entitled "Poverty and Human Functionings" that each person has different capabilities to convert resources into valuable functionings in their lives. "Some of these differences are straightforwardly, physical: a child needs more protein than an adult to achieve a similar level of healthy functioning, and a pregnant woman more nutrients than a non pregnant woman".[56] Nussbaum holds that utility and resource approach fails to confront with inequalities based on sex. For example, in a nation where women are traditionally discouraged from pursuing an education, it will usually take more resources to produce female literacy than male literacy. Amartya Sen also cited an example that a person in a wheelchair will require more resources connected with mobility than will the person with normal mobility, if the two are attain to attain a similar level of ability to get around. On the other hand Nussbaum cited an example that the wheelchair contestant in marathon finish quickly than normal contestants. She believes, what impedes their mobility in life generally is the lack of social provisions like ramps, wheelchair access and other social opportunities. It is the capability approach tells us how and what precisely do we measure in the matter of poverty and inequality?

Nussbaum's conception of gender justice tries to explore feminisation of poverty that is gender based poverty and how inequality between men and women are manifested in the reproduction of poverty? Nussbaum argues about the status of women in her article "Capabilities as Fundamental Entitlements: Sen and Social Justice",

> Many traditional conceptions of social justice and fundamental entitlements have made women second-class citizens, if citizens at all. Women's liberties, opportunities, property rights, and political rights have been construed as unequal to men, and this has been taken to be a just state of affairs. Nor have traditional accounts of justice

attended at all to issues that are particularly urgent for women, such as issues of bodily integrity and sexual harassment.[57]

It may be pointed out that majority of women suffers capability deprivation because of lack of social opportunities to access education, healthcare, employment and other public services which led them the victims of inequalities and social exclusion. Indeed, Martha Nussbaum has pointed out at the very beginning of her book *Sex and Social Justice,* "Women still face all kinds of inequality and discrimination in every sphere of life. Gender inequalities result from tradition, custom and prejudice which results from the traditional and stereotyped attitude towards women".[58] It can be argue that the disproportionate impact of poverty on women is not an accident but the product of systematic discrimination and inequalities between men and women by the society.

To minimize poverty and gender inequality is an imperative and the need of hour to gamer the support for gender justice. In general, poverty means hunger and insufficient resource for the satisfaction of basic needs i.e. food, clean water, shelter and other facilities etc. Poverty is a global phenomenon and India is not exception of it. It is considered to be a social malaise which deprives human dignity and agency to pursue a better life. Poverty is a multidimensional in its symptoms, multivariate in its causes, dynamics in its trajectory, and quite complex in its relation to people's lives. The basic questions arise - what is poverty? How do we measure poverty? Do people fall into the trap of poverty because of lack of income, opportunities and capabilities? Is poverty due to inequalities of opportunities and benefits in the society? How women's poverty is created and reproduced? What is meant to be a poor woman? How gender differentiates the social processes leading to poverty? What are the measures to move out of poverty? Most importantly what is the link between poverty and gender inequality? How to minimizes women's injustices and bring gender justice under the purview of equality and their empowerment? How poverty affects on women's lives? There are numbers of possible answers to these questions from divergent perspectives on the philosophical, political and economic spectrum relating to poverty.

The concept of poverty is too complex to be reduced to a single dimension of human life. Poverty is a deprivation of essential assets and opportunities to which every human being is entitled. In other words, poverty is a form of deprivation and it manifests itself in deprivation of the lives of people. It is an urgent concern of humanity, because intensification of poverty diminishes the dignity of humanity. It has been considerable discussion on the question whether poverty line should reveal either on economic aspect of 'absolute'/'relative' or human aspect.

> The first published poverty studies did not use an empirical definition of poverty but rather estimated poverty in relative terms by evaluating overall conditions of income, food, clothing, shelter, and the like. In subsequent decades, central debates regarding the definition of basic needs, the role of income compared with human deprivations in the persistence of poverty.[59]

The concept of poverty has a very long history in the conceptualization of poverty where people's deprivation can be seen not in terms of economic, rather 'basic needs' and 'capability-deprivation' as well. It can be argue that the emergence of multidimensional conceptions of poverty relating to people's basic needs and their capability deprivation within the long established discourse of material deprivation. Bhanushali argues III his book *Poverty Scenario in Indian Subcontinent,*

> Around 1.3 Billion people that is nearly a quarter of the world's population, live in extreme poverty. They survive on less than US $1 a day a person to satisfy all their needs. Seventy percent of these people are women. They have no access to health, service or schools. They feel isolated, powerless and have little say in how their lives are run. They are often victims of domestic violence, crime and conflict.[60]

Poverty essentially refers to material deprivation of a person to maintain a minimum standard of living to survive a decent life. For many years, poverty is explained through the perspective of material shortcomings and especially from the perspective of income. However, poverty in terms of people's income gives a narrow definition of poverty. "Poverty, in general economic reasoning, can be defined as social deprivation from a decent quality of life. Poverty has qualitative and quantitative dimensions. In literature, poverty is interpreted as income based, consumption based, or, alternatively, entitlement based".[61] Ingeneral, poverty was measured and discussed in terms of income of the people, society and country. Martha Nussbaum argues in her article entitled "Poverty and Human Functioning: Capabilities as Fundamental Entitlements",

> From many years, approaches to poverty in the international development and policy-making world were obtuse in human terms. They focused on economic growth as the primary goal of development and measured quality of life simply by looking at GNP per capita.

> That crude measure, of course, did not even take distribution into account, and thus was utterly useless in confronting nations with a lot of poverty and high rates of inequality.[62]

It can be argue, poverty is one of the most critical issues being faced by human being in global and national level. However, income aspect of poverty unable to address the complex nature of poverty and raises a number of issues related to poverty in terms of people's health, education, and life expectancy etc. Poverty creates high rate inequality because GNP focuses on people's economic improvement and failed to acknowledge other aspects of people's lives that are indispensible part of life i.e. health, education, gender related to human rights violation. Amartya Sen argues, "Poverty can be sensibly identified in terms of capability deprivation; the approach concentrates on deprivations that are intrinsically important (unlike low income, which is only instrumentally significant)".[63] Poverty can be seen as the deprivation of person's basic capabilities rather than merely as lack of incomes. Sen further argues, "The perspective of capability-poverty does not involve any denial of the sensible view that low income is clearly one of the major causes of poverty, since lack of income can be a principle reason for person's capability deprivation".[64] The capability approach to poverty extends poverty in terms of human deprivation rather than income deprivation. It addresses deprivation of human capabilities in terms of people's capabilities to convert income or any commodities into valued functionings in the context of one's life. Ultimately, however, the conception of poverty is not based upon economic deprivation only rather on deprivation of basic needs and deprivation of human capabilities in terms of the lives that people can actually lead and the sufficient freedom they actually have.

Generally, the concept of poverty can perceived through vanous approaches and some of these perceptions are basic and necessary to understand the phenomena of poverty. In this way different people have different ideas of what poverty meant to be. There are three approaches of poverty that helps to understand the complexities of poverty. These are namely:

1. Economic Poverty
2. Basic needs Poverty
3. Capability Poverty.

Firstly, the economic poverty refers to a deficiency in the amount of income a household has to meet its basic needs to survive. It is a condition in which people's financial resources are insufficient to meet their minimum requirements of a healthy and productive life. Further economic poverty can be defined in either absolute or relative terms. The absolute poverty is severe poverty where individual is unable to meet his/her basic rights i.e. food, health, education etc. Mowafi and Khawaja argues, "Absolute poverty refers to the set of resources a person must acquire to maintain a minimum standard of living for survival. It is therefore a matter of acute deprivation, hunger, premature death and suffering".[65]

It can be argue that absolute poverty is a state of inability to access basic necessities of human survival. On the other hand, relative poverty is concerned with how poor an individual is with respect to others in the same society. "Relative poverty does not necessarily reflect vulnerability to mortality or acute suffering, but rather the level of inequality in a given context. In such a circumstance, the inability to access goods or services that are considered norm could render a person poor".[66] However relative poverty does not concerned with people's severe deprivation that make them very poor. It is concern for comparative deprivation of resources at which individuals are unable to participate in social life.

Secondly, basic needs aspect of poverty concerned with deprivation of material goods for minimally acceptable fulfillment of human needs such as food, housing, sanitation, clothing, education and including other important areas. In addition to material requirement for the satisfaction of basic needs, this approach includes a number of indicators. "They are health and health access, employment and working conditions, skills, family and social integration, ownership of property, die and nutrition, recreation and culture, security and political resources".[67] Basic needs approach to poverty includes different aspects of human life as indicators in determining the poverty. It is ahead of the economic approach to poverty to measure the quality of life in deciding what kinds of need of life people are deprived. It can be argue that, people have to satisfy some needs that are considered basic to human life. This concept of deprivation goes well beyond the lack of material goods or private income. These have to be provided by the community to prevent people from falling into poverty. It also recognizes the need for employment and participation.

Thirdly, capability approach to poverty represents the absence of some basic capabilities to function. It extends the concept of 'human poverty' in terms of deprivation of human capabilities. Against the dominant perspective on economic deprivation to as an indicator of poverty measurement, Sen and Nussbaum have insisted on the importance of people's capabilities that is what people are actually able to do and to be. Nussbaum argues,

> Today, a different approach is prominent: the capabilities approach, represented in *Human Development Report* of UNDP. As the late Mahbub Vl Haq wrote in the first of those reports, in 1990t that the real wealth of a nation is its people. And the purpose of development is to create an enabling environment for people to enjoy long, and healthy and creative lives. This simple but powerful truth is too often forgotten in the pursuit of material and financial wealth. Amartya Sen of course, has been the primary architect of this approach; I have also developed it, focusing particularly on women's poverty and the relationship between poverty and sex inequality.[68]

Nussbaum says, "Sen and I argue that if we ask not about GNP only, but about what people are actually able to do and to be, we come much closer to understanding the barriers societies have erected against full justice for women and the poor". Amartya Sen argues in analyzing human poverty, "There is a strong case for judging individual advantage in terms of the capabilities that a person has, that is, the substantive freedoms he or she has reason to value".[69] For Sen, poverty can assess in terms of capability deprivation because people's capabilities enhances the understanding the nature and causes of poverty. According to Nussbaum,

> Sen has long argued that poverty is best understood as capability failure, not just as shortage of commodities or even of income and wealth. Poverty involves heterogeneous failures of opportunity, which are not always well corrected with income; moreover, people in positions of social exclusion may have difficulty in converting income into actual functioning, so income is not even a good proxy for capabilities. In general, income is a means to an end, and capabilities are the end. One particular difficulty with measuring poverty through income is that available income measures pertain to the household; a focus on income therefore encourages the neglect of sex bias in nutrition, health care, and other aspects of poverty. Looking at poverty in terms of capability failure, by contrast, encourages a focus on how each person is doing and spotlights distributional inequalities in the family.[70]

For Sen, capability aspect of poverty does not concentrate on *means* or in terms of people's income rather to *ends* that they have reason to pursue. It can be argued that income is not the only instrument in generating people's capabilities. The capability approach reconciles the notions of absolute and relative poverty since relative deprivation in income and commodities can lead to an absolute deprivation in minimum capabilities.

These approaches to poverty and its impact on human life have been a major cause and concern. However, when the incidence of poverty comes to women's lives, it can be calculated in double, triple or multiple folds. Martha Nussbaum argues about economic growth is an unsatisfactory indicators to assess people's quality of life and their vulnerability. "Growth is a bad indicator of life quality because it fails to tell us how deprived people are doing; women figure in the argument as people who are often unable to enjoy the fruits of a nation's general prosperity".[71] Women are identified as the most vulnerable because of their high risk of poverty. Inaddressing women's poverty, many questions can be raise relating to the incidence of income or consumption poverty among female compares it to that of male counterparts.

> One of the major factors predisposing women to grater poverty are the limited opportunities, capabilities and empowerment in terms of access to and control over production resources of land, labour, human capital assets such as participation at various levels, legal rights and protection. Gender gaps in access to, ownership and control over resources make women more vulnerable to poverty than men.[72]

It is a fact that women's access to resources has been substantially less than men. Due to gender disparity to access less social benefits and opportunities has been suggested a key to understand women's vulnerability and their subordinate position in society. The question arise: Are women compared to men having higher incidence of poverty? Are women's poverty is more severe than men? Is the incidence of poverty among women is increasing compared to men? It can be argue that there are various reason women are poorer than men not because of sufficient income, but the result of the deprivation of basic capabilities and preferential treatment by the society. This includes the lack of women's choices and opportunities to have the capability to lead a long, healthy, and creative life on the one hand and on the other, to enjoy basic human rights like freedom, respect, and dignity. Sen argues in "Poverty as Capability Deprivation",

> Distribution within the family raises further complications with the income approach to poverty. If the family income is used disproportionately in the interest of some family members and not

others (for example, if there is a systematic "boy preference" in the family allocation of resources), then the extentof the deprivation of the neglected members (girl in the example considered) may not be adequately reflected in terms of family income.[73]

Due to poverty, women in their family have been deprived of basic education, healthcare, nutritious food, and good sanitation etc. However, it can be argued that poverty leads to gender inequality because women's poverty is not an accident but the result of systematic discrimination on the ground of sex and sexuality between men and women. Poverty makes women more vulnerable because it leads women are less nourished than men, less healthy than men, less educated than men and more vulnerable to physical violence and sexual abuse. Nussbaum regards when poverty combines with gender inequality, the result is severe deprivation of women's capabilities to live a dignified life. Hence, poverty in general and women's poverty in particular has been one of the major issues in the world today that need to address because thousands of people are dying and most of these are women. It affects mostly women because of unequal wage and unemployment opportunities and low educational level of women with care responsibilities in the private realm push them to work in the informal sector such as unpaid family work.

As a result of this huge participation in the informal sector, women are more prone to poverty and being denied access to social opportunities including health, education, and other basic capabilities. Thus "poverty affects many aspects of women's lives such as dignity and self esteem and it causes them to remain silent about the inequalities and violence they face in their lives".[74] Moreover, poverty strongly correlates with gender disparity between men and women.

Gender inequality is due to unequal opportunities between men and women relating to education, health care, and other basic capabilities. Indeed Dorius and Glenn have pointed out in "Trends in Global Gender Inequality", "Gender inequality exists when men (or women) enjoy a disproportionately large share of some valued good".[75] Martha Nussbaum has also tried to show gender inequality in the absence of women's capabilities. "Women in much of the world lack support for fundamental function of a human life. They are less well nourished than men, less healthy, more vulnerable to physical violence and sexual abuse".[76] It is fact that many women have been treated unequally and lag behind men in education, employment opportunities, and even in basic nutrition and health care etc which undermined the progress of women. In other words

Martha Nussbaum argues, "Many women all over the world find themselves treated unequally with respect to employment; bodily safety and integrity, basic nutrition, health care, education, and political voice".[77]

For the conceptualization of gender inequality and its assessment, Ingris Robeyns proposes the following list of capabilities:

> Life and physical health, mental well-being, bodily integrity, social relations, political empowerment, education and knowledge, domestic work and nonmarket care, paid work and other projects, shelter and environment, mobility, leisure activities, time autonomy, respect, religion.[78]

The capability approach provides the most satisfactory way of looking at inequality between men and women and shows how gender inequality can assess? Moreover we can find various aspect of gender inequality in the fallowing capabilities and these are namely:

1. Gender inequality in Life and Health:
   As a matter of fact gender based inequality in women's lives and health is widespread in today's world. "Women's lives are unequally at many parts of the world. Statistics continue to show that women suffer unequally from hunger and malnutrition and from unequal access to basic health care".[79] Moreover gender based violence and inequalities deprive women's life through sex selective abortion on the one hand and differential treatment of women's health on the other to reduces women's life expectancy. For instance, preference for boys over girls child leads to sex selective abortion and infanticide are the major causes of gender inequality. Take an example of "sex ratio" which has been decreasing because of preference over male child than girls child. "Census 2011 revealed that, the population ratio in India is 940 females per 1000 of males".[80] As Amartya Sen's work on "missing women" shows, sex ratios in many countries indicate that large numbers of women the world over have died because they have received unequal treatment- whether outright infanticide is involved, or as is, more common, unequal nutrition and health care". However, it can be argued that "sex selective abortion and infanticide, together with undernutrition of girls, are major causes of female death around the world".[81] These inequalities perpetuated on women's life and their health is due to cultural tradition and social practices that played an important

role in perpetuating gender inequality and undermined the value ofwomen's life and health.

2. Gender Inequality in Bodily Integrity:

   It is one of the important aspects of human being; however, women bear severe threat on their bodily integrity. "No woman in the world is secure against violence. Throughout the world, women's bodies are vulnerable to a range of violent assaults that include domestic violence, rape, honor killing, trafficking and forced prostitution, female infanticide, and sex selective abortion".[82] In all these ways, the ongoing gender-based violence perpetuates injustices which greatly diminish women's capabilities. Nussbaum regards, bodily integrity includes "being able to move freely from place to place", and that almost no woman really has this capability to the same extent that men have it". The persistent threat of violence diminishes human capabilities".[83] "Women suffer many abuses that violate their bodily integrity. These include rape, marital rape, other sexual abuse, domestic violence, and genital mutilation".[84] Ingrid Robeyns also said, "This capability is adversely affected when people experience all sorts of personal violence, such as attacks on street, domestic violence, rape, sexual assault, or stalking".[85] Moreover, the capability ofbodily integrity has a gender dimension because women experience all sorts of violence at home as well outside. This capability has gender has gender dimension: studies suggest that women bear a greater incidence of and more severe sexual violence than men, while men experience more physical violence of other kinds. For women, the most common place of violent attacks is their home and the most likely offender is their partner, whereas for men this is not the case.[86]

3. Gender Inequality in Respect and Dignity:

   Justice demands that human being "respected and treated with dignity", however, gender based discrimination between men and women undermine this capability. Nussbaum regarded, human beings have a dignity that deserves respect from laws and institutions. But human dignity is frequently violated on grounds of sex or sexuality. Many women all over the world find themselves treated unequally with respect to employment, bodily safety and integrity, basic nutrition and health care, education, and political voice. In many cases these hardship are caused by their being women, and in many cases laws and institutions construct or perpetuate these inequalities.[87] Gender inequality in the capability of respect and dignity accorded to women. For example, women's domestic work has limited recognition by the society because such work is unpaid and receives less respect. However, "feminists have argued that the root of our society is the fact that women are systematically devalued and not considered fully human. Some radical feminist like Mac Kinnon, for instance give the example of pornography, prostitution, or other acts that treat women as sexual objects"[88].

4. Gender Inequality in Education:

   Nussbaum regarded "nothing is more important to women's life chances than education. With literacy, a woman may consider her options and to some extent shape her future. She may question tradition and discover how women in other parts of the world are managing to live and able to achieve well in many of life's functions".[89] However, gender affects a broad range of inequalities in our world, particularly in relation to education and schooling. Across the world, around 65 million girls are not schooled and two thirds of the world's 774 million illiterate adults are female. To address these issues, the education for all children across the world and identified six goals including the goal of eliminating gender disparities and inequalities to be met by 2015."[90] Further the author mentioned that "only 69% of countries are estimated to have reached gender parity at the primary education level, and this figure drops to 48% in secondary education. This shows there is still a long way to go towards achieving gender equality.[91] Gender inequality in the case of India has been severe because female literacy rate in India is lower than the male literacy rate. For instance, compared to boys, very less girls are enrolled in the schools and even many of them are being drop out. Such educational disparity in urban India is less but rural India has more disparity because girls continue to be less educated than the boys. Due gender disparity in education, literacy rate of India in 2011 is 74.04% while the male literacy rate is 82.14% and female literacy rate is 65.46% according to Census 2011.

5. Gender Inequality in Workforce-participation:

   Nussbaum argues, "Women should have the right to seek employment outside the home without intimidation or discrimination. CEDAW states that the rights to seek employment, to nondiscrimination in hiring, to free choice of occupation, and to equal pay for equal value are all fundamental rights that women enjoy equally with men".[92] In However women have less participation in workforce at globally and in the case of India. For instance, "Census 2011 clearly stated that, total women's labour force participation rate in India is 20.5% women are employed in the organized sector in which 18.1% female are working in the public sector and 24.3% female in the private sector respectively. According to, International Monetary Fund and its working paper, India has been one of the lowest female labour force participation rates among emerging markets and developing countries. Such gender disparity in workforce participation is due women's less education, household activates and cultural tradition impedes women to work outside of the house which is counted as paid labour.

6. Gender Inequality and Religion:

   As Nussbaum argues, "men and women should have the same freedom to practice or not to practice religion. In addition, men and women should have the same freedom to debate and determine how their religion develops and to shape religious practices. But several religions reserve the right to interpret the holy books and to make religious statement only for men"[93]. Take an example of "Shani Shignapur Temple" in Bombay, "Sabrimala Temple" in Kerala, and "Haji Ali Dargah" in Bombay. In these temple and mosque, women are not allowed to enter because of certain religious and cultural tradition. Such unequal gender implications of religious practices raises an ethical and moral concern that how women can be deprived of religious exercise.

7. Gender Inequality in Family Laws:

   Nussbaum argues, "Family law is an especially complex area of women's inequality; religious norms and laws playa direct role in it. Religious system of family laws, Islamic, Hindu, Jewish, and other, may severely limit women's degree of choice in and consent to marriage, their rights to control the lives of their children during a marriage and a child custody if the marriage ends., their access to divorce and the type of evidence required to get a divorce".[94] Take an example, India provides us an institution of secular marriage on the one hand while secular option is not available in the case of divorce. It may be argued that a couple must appeal for divorce to religion of their birth. Nussbaum exposed the famous "Shah Bano Case relating to the issue of maintenance under Muslim Personal Law in India poses a serious question of survival. In Madhya Pradesh, India, 1975, a Muslim woman named Shah Bano was thrown out of her home by her husband after forty three years of marriage and five children. As required by the Islamic personal law, he returned Rs. 3000 which had been her marriage settlement from her family in 1932". As a result she was awarded Rs. 180 per month. "Rather than accept this settlement, inadequate for her survival, she sued for maintenance under Section 125 of the Criminal Procedure Code which requires a person of adequate means to protect relation from destitution and vagrancy".[95] Her husband, however, appealed this "judgement to Supreme Court of India, holding that as a Muslim he was bound only by Islamic Law. However in Supreme Court held that the provision of criminal procedure code regarding maintenance of destitute relations was applicable to members of all religions and that the person should not lose by simply being a Muslim". Hence, the demand of change in personal laws is essential because personal laws directly affect woman's life in terms of marriage, divorce, maintenance, inheritance, succession, guardianship and adoption. In this case, gender based inequality within family laws raises ethical and moral concern for gender justice.

Thus, poverty in terms of capability deprivation has continued to shape ethical and moral concerns about the way human have been living in the society. History bears that poverty is an urgent concern of humanity, because it diminishes human dignity and makes them to live like an animal. However, when the incidence of poverty comes to women's lives, it can be calculated in double, triple or multiple folds because they are more likely to be vulnerable and poor than men. More than half a billion women in developing countries have no reasonable income, no health care and no security is the major cause of poverty. Hence extreme poverty and vulnerability is female which leads them to hunger, disease, no education, no ownership and no secure access to water and energy. Women also have been facing limited opportunities owing to isolation, exclusion from decision-making processes, low mobility, overwork and violence. Moreover, due to poverty, women in their family have been deprived of basic education, healthcare, nutritious food, and deprivation of other opportunities leads to gender inequality. In other words, poverty makes women more vulnerable because it leads women are less nourished than men, less healthy than men, less educated than men and more vulnerable to physical violence and sexual abuse. Nussbaum regards when poverty combines with gender inequality, the result is severe deprivation of women's capabilities to live a dignified life. In other way poverty strongly correlates with gender inequality between men and women raises ethical and moral questions that how women should attain dignified life. Hence, people's capabilities is an urgent need because capabilities approach of Amartya Sen and Martha Nussbaum provides us a benchmark to address the multiple forms of poverty and inequalities in the lives of women who are situated in different historical, religious, cultural and political contexts and have been experiencing several kinds of injustice.

Part - III

Capability and Gender Justice

The concept of gender justice with reference to Martha Nussbaum's capability approaches is not as a procedural justice but as an outcome-oriented approach that gives an impartial account of justice. As a matter of fact, capabilities approach serve as a normative space for addressing people's real opportunities in life that are worthy for human dignity. In other words, capabilities approach has focused on the inequality of women. It address the real lives of women that how they becomes victims of gender discrimination, oppression of cultural practices and traditions. More importantly, it concern about which type of valuable freedoms is necessary to provide women with lives that they value and choose. Hence, "Nussbaum's capabilities based gender justice" seeks to minimize injustices from the feminist perspective because gender discrimination has been experienced by women only. "Women in much of the world lack support for fundamental functions of human life. They are less well nourished than men, less wealthy, more vulnerable to physical violence and sexual abuse. They are much less likely than men to be literate and still less likely to have professional or technical education".[96] It is a harsh reality that women have been treated unequally in every society for ages and India is no exception of it. Moreover, the status ofwomen in society in general and the family in particular has been vulnerable and unrecognized. In other way, the status of women in society in general and the family in particular has been vulnerable and unrecognized. It is a fact that, women works are often confined to domestic sphere. She had to do all house hold works, which are not recognized and unpaid. Women have been depriving of economic resources which lead them to dependent on men for their living. Nussbaum argues, "In many nations women are not full equals under the law: they do not have the same property rights as men, the same rights to make a contract, the same rights of association, mobility and religious liberty".[97] Due to these unequal social and political circumstances gives women have less opportunity than men and even failure of women's capabilities. Indeed Martha Nussbaum argues in her essay entitled "Challenge of Gender Justice",

> Women are unequal to men all over the world, unequal in basic opportunities and life chances of the sort that lie at the heart of the idea of social justice. Take education. In forty-three countries, male literacy rates are fifteen or more percentage points higher than the female rate; this comprises one fourth of the nations in the world.[98]

There are various countries in the world today have failed to keep up with their promises of equal opportunities from land rights, political participation, basic education and more importantly access to professional and managerial position etc. are the urgent issue of basic justice. Hence, recognizing equality of opportunities between men and women and believing their capabilities are essential for gender justice.

Nussbaum uses capability approach to mmmuze inequality and gender discrimination from the feminist perspective because women have been facing discrimination at every stage. She tried to bring equal opportunities of all human being through human capabilities irrespective of their gender and brought feminist notion of justice. Nussbaum writes in *Sex and Social Justice,* "Women's capabilities approach focuses on women's abilities to do and be certain things deemed valuable. The approach is concerned with capability to function, rather than functioning itself, because it emphasizes the role of practical reason and choice in exploiting the capability".[99] It helps to evolve an equitable just society to evaluate gender disparity and the curtailment of women's capability imposed by family, culture and tradition and nation. Thus, the capability approach is not as procedural but as an outcome-oriented approach that provides us a vision of women welfare not in terms of human rights but to make them capable to use certain rights to lead a good life.

The human rights approach to justice has been criticized by Nussbaum for being male-centered, and for not including as fundamental entitlements some abilities and opportunities that are fundamental to women in their struggle for sex equality. For instance, right to bodily integrity, the right to be free from violence in the home and from sexual harassment in the workplace etc has not been address by human rights approach. Nussbaum argues, "Capabilities are very closely linked to rights, but the language of capabilities gives important precision and supplementation to the language of rights. The idea of human rights is by no means a crystal-clear idea"[100]. The conception of human rights have been understood in many different ways; firstly, people differ about what the basis of a rights claim is: rationality, sentience, and mere life have all had their defenders. Secondly, people differ about whether rights belong only to individual persons, or also to groups. Thirdly, they differ about the relationship between rights and duties. Take for example, if "A has a right to B", then does this mean that there is always someone who has a "duty to provide B", and how shall we decide who that someone is? Finally, people also differ, about what and how rights are to be understood? It can be argue that, human rights are primarily rights to be treated in certain ways: are rights to a certain level of achieved well-being?, rights to resources with which one may pursue one's life plan? And rights to certain opportunities and capacities with which one may make choices about one's life plan etc. However, Nussbaum argue that the best way of thinking about what it is to secure to people, is to think in terms of their capabilities.

> The right to political participation, the right to religious free exercise, the right of free speech - these and others are all best thought of as secured to people only when the relevant capabilities to function are present. In other words, to secure a right to citizens in these areas is to put them in a position of capability to function in that area. To the extent that rights are used in defining social justice, we should not grant that the society is just unless the capabilities have been effectively achieved.[101]

Take for instance, people may have a political right that has not yet been recognized or implemented; or it may be recognized formally and yet not implemented. However, by defining the securing of rights in terms of capabilities we make it clear that a people in country C don't really have an effective right to political participation. For example, a right in the sense that matters for judging that the society is a just one, simply because this language exists on paper: they really have been given a right only if there are effective measures to make people truly capable of political exercise. Women in many nations have a nominal right of political participation without having this right in the sense of capability.

In short, thinking in terms of capability gives us a benchmark as we think about what it is really to secure a right to someone. Nussbaum believes that the advantage of the capabilities approach to address inequalities that women suffer inside the family such as inequalities in resources and opportunities, educational deprivations, the failure of work to be recognized as work, insults to bodily integrity. Human rights approach to justice has neglected the issue of people's capability which focuses on what people are actually able to do and to be.

In general, Nussbaum's argues "that the best approach to this idea of a basic social minimum is provided by an approach that focuses on human capabilities, that is, what people are actually able to do and to be - in a way informed by an intuitive idea of a life that is worthy of dignity of the human being".[102] It can be argued that, capabilities approach takes into account individual's uniqueness on the one hand and pluralistic account of what we need on the other to pursue once own well-being. According to Nussbaum,

> Sen bases the case for capabilities on individual's varying needs for resource, and also on their varying abilities to convert resources into functionings. Variations in need, he insists, are pervasive features of human life: children need more protein (an expensive nutrient) than adults, for example, and pregnant or lactating women need more nutrition than nonpregnant women. So the question of variation cannot be postponed; it is omnipresent[103].

It shows that the need to focus on capability becomes clear when we consider cases in which individuals in general and women in particular are vulnerable in various ways by the very structure of their society. For instance, any culture that traditionally discourages women from becoming educated and empowered would require more resources to female literacy than male literacy. Moreover, Nussbaum's capabilities approach, "provide the philosophical underpinning for an account of basic constitutional principles that should be respected and implemented by the government of all nations, as a bare minimum of what respect for human dignity requires".[104] Moreover she has pointed out that,

> Capability in question should be pursued for each and every person, treating as an end and none as a mere tool of the ends of others: thus I adopt a principle of each person's capability, based on a principle

> of each person as end. Women have all too often been treated as the supporters of the ends of others, rather than as ends in their own rights; thus this principle has particular critical force with regard to women's lives.[105]

It makes clear that, the purpose of capabilities is to provide pluralistic account of need so that each person can be treated as end and not as means to pursue his/her wellbeing. However Nussbaum has pointed out that,

> Dignity: Aristotelian and not Kantian. Kant contrasts the humanity of human beings with their animality. The capabilities approach, by contrast, sees rationality and animality as thoroughly unified. Taking its cue from Aristotle's notion of the human being as a political animal, and from Marx's idea that the human being is a creature 'in need of a plurality of life activities' it sees the rational as simply one aspect of the animal, and at that, not the only one that is pertinent to a notion of truly human functioning. More generally, the capabilities approach sees the world as containing many different types of animal dignity, all of which deserves respect.[106]

Nussbaum's capabilities approach incorporates dignity in various activities of life i.e. health, bodily need and including the need of care etc. with which human being engages in their life. "The capabilities are not understood as instrumental to a life with human dignity: they are understood, instead, as ways of realizing a life with human dignity, in the different areas of life with which human beings typically engage".[107] Its purpose is to address different areas of life that is on their capabilities of life, health, bodily needs, and so on. It addresses various aspects of human needs and to ask, in each of these areas in which we live and act. Moreover it bring out, what would be a way in which human being can able to live with basic entitlement that is compatible with human dignity.

In general, "capability approach based on 'functioning and capability' was pioneered in development economics by Amartya Sen".[108] Although Nussbaum's version of capabilities approach developed "with Amartya Sen at World Institute if Development Economics Research beginning in 1986".[109] The capability approach philosophically, focuses on people's capabilities to the extent on what people are 'able to do and to be, that is, on their capabilities'. In other words, capabilities address to what extent people in general and women in particular have the real opportunities to achieve the things that he/she has reason to value. In this way, both Amartya

Sen and Murtha Nussbaum have adopted 'capabilities approach' to assess people's quality of life. However, it is important to explain their distinctive perspective on capability approach and to see what commonality is and what differentiality is in respective approaches. Martha Nussbaum has pointed about Sen's perspective about people's capabilities,

> Sen's primarily uses the notion of capability is to indicate a space within which comparisons of quality of life (or, as he sometime says, standard of living) are most fruitfully made. Instead of asking about people's satisfactions, or how much in the way of resources they are able to command, we ask, instead, about what they are actually able to do or to be. Sen has also insisted that it is in space of capabilities that questions about social equality and inequality are best raised.[110]

It can be argued that Sen's capability is primarily focuses on people's functionings and their capability that have reason to value. In other way Sen has emphasized on the role of people's capabilities under the space within which the people's standard of living can be evaluated. On the other hand, Nussbaum's capabilities is to go "beyond the merely comparative use of the capability space to articulate an account of how capabilities, together with the idea of a threshold level of capabilities, can provide a basis for central constitutional principles that citizens have a right to demand from their governments".[111] In Nussbaum view, idea of 'threshold level of capabilities' than Sen's idea of 'full equality of capability' is an indispensable for each person as a human being.

To understand Nussbaum's capabilities approach, it is important to see and analyze how women have been socially and culturally placed in India and several developing countries all over the world. Nussbaum has explained the situation of women in India by exposing the vulnerable situation of poor women whose name is 'Vasanti and Jayamma' in her essay "Two Women are Trying to Flourish"[112] in her book that is *Women and Human Development: The Capabilities Approach.* Nussbaum argues that "Vasanti and Jayamma have very different lives. However, it is very important to see how their lives are socially and culturally placed in particular religion, caste and regional circumstances. One is the poor edges of the lower middle class, and one is at the very bottom of the economic ladder because she is extremely poor. According to Nussbaum,

> Both have been raised in a nation in which women are formally the equals of men, with equal political rights and nominally equal social

> and employment opportunities. And both suffer to some extent from general problems of poverty that are not caused exclusively by their being women. Both, however, have also suffered from deprivations that do arise from sex discrimination, and sex discrimination is such a pervasive factor in these women's experience of poverty that it would be wrong to say that any aspect of their poverty is fully understandable without taking it into account."[113]

It can be argue that the vulnerability of women like Vasanti and Jayammais due to their social situation in which both have placed in their respective religion, caste, religion, and regional circumstances. However, the problem faced by both is due to lack of education, lack of skills, lack of economic and other opportunities which makes them poor and vulnerable. According to Nussbaum,

> Vasanti and Jayamma, like many women in India and in the rest of the world, have lacked support for many of the most central human functions, and that lack of support is at least to some extent caused by their being women. But women, unlike rocks and trees and horses, have the potential to become capable of these human functions, given sufficient nutrition, education, and other support. That is why their unequal failure in capability is a problem of justice. It is up to all human beings to solve this problem. I claim that a universal conception of human capability give us excellent guidance as we pursue this difficult task[114]

Nussbaum's capabilities approach can be "defined as an approach to comparative quality of life assessment and to theorizing about social justice. It holds that the key question to ask, when comparing societies and assessing them for their basic decency or justice, is, "what each person able to do and to be?[115] In other words, it takes into account each person as an end including men and women. More importantly, "the approach is concerned with entrenched social injustice and inequality, especially capability failure that are the result of discrimination or marginalization. It ascribes an urgent task to government and public policy to improve the quality of life for all people, as defined by their capabilities".[116] Hence, capabilities approach play an important role in constructing the notion of gender justice because it is primarily focus on what women are effectively able to do and to be, that is, on women's functionings and their capabilities. It can be pointed out Nussbaum's view on gender justice takes a political direction because she argues for fundamental entitlements secured for each person being a male and female under the constitutional arrangement. She argues that,

> Capabilities approach is not, "How satisfied is this women? or even How much in the way of resources is she able to command? It is, instead, What is she actually able to do and to be? Taking a stand for political purposes on a working list of functions that would appear to be of central importance in human life, we ask. Is the person capable of this, or not? We ask not only about the person's satisfaction with what she does, but about what she does, and what she is in a position to do (what her opportunities and liberties are). And we ask not just about the resources that are sitting around, but about how those do or do not go to work, enabling the women to function in a fully human way.[117]

The central part of Nussbaum's capabilities approach is that it focuses on how women are "capable to do and to be, that is, what is Vasanti actually able to do and to be?" It serves as space for evaluating women's life and their opportunities in their life. It is concerned with people's opportunities and freedoms so that each and every person can convert resources into valuable achievements. As Nussbaum argues, "The intuitive idea behind my version of the capabilities approach is twofold:

> Firstly, "there are certain functions that are particularly central in human life, in the sense that their presence or absence is typically understood to be a mark of the presence or absence of human life".[118]
>
> Secondly, "this is what Marx found in Aristotle- that there is something that it is do these functions in a truly human way, not a merely animal way".[119]

It is well known fact that women's lives has been so impoverished that they are not treated as worthy of the dignity of being human. For instance, women have been living in the conditions of poverty, undernourishment, educational deprivation; health deprivation and more importantly violence etc. These gender injustice deprives women's life in which women goes on living, but more or less like an animal because they unable to develop their exercise their functioning and capabilities.

Nussbaum's capabilities approach is not a procedural justice but as an outcome-oriented approach that gives an impartial account of justice. The capabilities approach is considered to be a "noncontractarian account of care[120] where justice is not understood in terms of procedural approach rather an outcome oriented approach. In other words, capabilities distinct itself from social contract theories and human rights approach because it provides moral and ethical care and concern for those who are marginalized and suppressed like women and disable and others. Moreover it concentrates on people's freedom and opportunities that is what and how men as well as women actually "able to do and to be to pursue their wellbeing. According to Nussbaum,

> Thinking well about care means thinking about wide range of capabilities on the side of both the cared-for and care-giver. Good care for dependents whether children, elderly, women etc, on support for capabilities of life, health, and bodily integrity. Care plays in the lives of the cared-for; we have to say that it should address the entire range of the central human capabilities.[121]

Good care recognizes all the needs which any individual either men or women lacks. Nussbaum emphasised that all human beings including men and women are free to develop their capabilities without any constraints. Her main concern is to show how human beings be it men or women become capable to lead their lives in dignified manner. It may be pointed out that capabilities approach underlies the idea of social justice in general and human dignity in particular. With this vision human capability is an essential requirement of a life with dignity. In Nussbaum's capabilities approach, these central human capabilities are considered to be an important entitlement for a life with full human dignity. These are, namely: "Life, Bodily health, Bodily integrity, Senses, imagination and thought, Emotions, Practical reason, Affiliation: friendship, respect, other species, Play, Control over one's environment includes political and material"[122]. These capabilities form the core concept in the notion of gender justice because it analyse and interpret the lives of women. It entails that all human beings whether men and women should have equal opportunity to acquire these capabilities in order to live a good human life. Following are the list of central human capabilities.

1. "Life: Being able to live to the end of a human life of normal length; not dying prematurely, or before one's life is so reduced as to be not worth living.[123]
2. Bodily Health: Being able to have good health, including reproductive health; to be adequately nourished; to have adequate shelter.[124]
3. Bodily Integrity: Being able to move freely from place to place; to be secure against violent assault, including sexual assault and

domestic violence; having opportunities for sexual satisfaction and for choice in matters of reproduction.[125]

4. Senses, Imagination, and Thought: Being able to use the senses, to imagine, think, and reason - and to do these things in a truly human way, a way informed and cultivated by an adequate education, including, but by no means limited to, literacy and basic mathematical and scientific training. Being able to use imagination and thought in connection with experiencing and producing works and events of one's own choice, religious, literary, musical, and so forth. Being able to use one's mind in ways protected by guarantees of freedom of expression with respect to both political and artistic speech, and freedom of religious exercise. Being able to have pleasurable experiences and to avoid non- beneficial pain.[126]
5. Emotions: Being able to have attachments to things and people outside ourselves; to love those who love and care for us, to grieve at their absence; in general, to love, to grieve, to experience longing, gratitude, and justified anger. Not having one's emotional development blighted by fear and anxiety.[127]
6. Practical Reason: Being able to form a conception of the good and to engage in critical reflection about the planning of one's life.
7. Affiliation: Being able to live with and toward others, to recognize and show concern for other human beings, to engage in various forms of social interaction; to be able to imagine the situation of another. It also concern for having the social bases of self-respect and being able to be treated as a dignified being whose worth is equal to that of others. It entails provisions of nondiscrimination on the basis of race, sex, sexual orientation, ethnicity, caste, religion, national origin.[128]
8. Other Species: Being able to live with concern for and in relation to animals, plants, and the world ofnature.[129]
9. Play: Being able to laugh, to play, to enjoy recreational activities.[130]
10. Control over one's environment: Political and Material: Being able to live with and towards others, to recognize and show concern for other human beings, to engage in various forms of social interaction; to be able to imagine the situation of another and to have the compassion for that situation; to have the capability for both justice and friendship. Protecting this

> capability means protecting institutions that constitute and nourish such forms of affiliation, and also protecting the freedom of assembly and political speech".[131] The control over one's environment including material includes having the social base of self respect and non humiliation; being able to be treated as a dignified being whose worth is equal to that of others. This entails protections against discrimination on the basis of race, sex, sexual orientation, religion, caste, ethnicity, or national origin".[132]

The intuitive idea behind lists of capabilities is the basic entitlements that are essential for women being a human. Women deserve dignity and respect, and proper nourishment to be able to fulfill their capabilities in a truly human way. Nussbaum lists of capabilities are needed for gender justice because it offers feminist framework to assess the experience of gender injustice around the globe. These central human capabilities are therefore essential for women's life. These capabilities forms foundational principle under which gender injustice in the form of poverty, inequality, discrimination and capability deprivation can be analyze and interpret the lives of women. It allows women to get equal opportunities in every spheres of life to pursue their wellbeing. Moreover, the core of central human capabilities is that women are entitled to a wide range of capabilities to function, those that are important to a flourishing life that is a life worthy of dignity of each person. "According to Firdeves Melis Cin",

> Nussbaum's approach and list offers a feminist framework for researchers because the theory starts from the experience of gender injustices around the globe. Her list includes all the fundamental entitlements that are central to women in developing countries as to western women. Her lists also address intra household inequalities in non market labour such as care responsibilities, unequal distribution of domestic responsibilities, or domestic violence, and integrates private sphere as well public sphere into her lists of capabilities.[133]

In other way, these capabilities are the basic entitlement and are therefore essential for women's life in order to elevate them to an equal place in the world. In other words, these capabilities open a pathway for women to live fulfilled life that is not influenced by traditions that enable injustice to continue against women. In order to fight against injustice, women must be allowed possess self-creativity in terms of their thoughts, emotions and imagination, including that of practical reason to live truly well in human way. They need to be heard, choose their own career, and plan the kind of life they want to live. Thus capabilities approach constitute an important aspect of gender justice because it recognize each person including marginalized, suppressed and socio economically deprived women under the constitutional arrangements. More importantly, it is the responsibility to institutions and government to preserve and secure to each and every person as at minimum threshold. Hence, for Nussbaum, gender justice is meant to secure the lists of basic list of capabilities as a political entitlement.

To bring this chapter as en end, I would say women's rights have been violating. The issues of women's rights as human rights, poverty and gender inequality have been continued to shape ethical and moral questions about the way women have been treating by the society. History bears that women have sadly treated unequally and their rights are undermined all over the world because of their gender. It has been argue that gender is a common term where as gender discrimination is meant only for women, because females are the only victims of inequalities. There are certain cultural traditions have perpetuated various forms of injustices in the lives of women who are situated in different historical, religious, cultural and political contexts. Women have been experiencing several kinds of injustice since a long time and it continue to persists depending on where a women lives. These issues continue to shape the ethical and moral questions about the way women have been treated. How can we solve such ethical problems and apply a universal concept that would allow women to attain dignified and equal throughout their lives. Therefore, Nussbaum's capabilities approach provides us a benchmark to address the multiple forms of inequalities in the lives of women who are situated in different historical, religious, cultural and political contexts and have been experiencing several kinds of injustice since a long time.

References

Nussbaum, C Martha. "Women's Bodies: Violence, Security, Capabilities". *Journal of Human Development* 6, no. 2, 2005. pp.167: 183.

Nussbaum, C Martha. *Sex and Social Justice.* New York: Oxford University Press, 1999.

Sen & Jean Dreze. *An Uncertain Glory: India and its Contradictions.* USA: Princeton University, 2013.

Vats, and Mudgal Shakuntla. *Women and Society in Ancient India.* Faridabad: Om Publications. 1999.

Jayapalan, N. *Indian Society and Social Institutions.* Volume 1. New Delhi: Atlantic Publication, 2001.

Nussbaum, Martha. *Frontiers of Justice: Disability, Nationality, Species Membership.* New Delhi: Oxford University Press, 2006.

Charlesworth, Hilary. "Human Rights as Men's Rights" in *Human Rights: Critical Concepts in Political Sciences.* Edited by Richard Falk, Hilal Elver and Lisa Hajjar. London: Routledge Taylor and Francis Group, 2008.

UNDP. "Women's Political Participation and Good Governance: 21st Century Challenges". http://www.onlinewomeninpolitics.org/beij ing 12/wpp_gg.pd

Martha Chen. "A Matter of Survival: Women's Right to Employment in India and Bangladesh," in Women, Culture, and Development, edited by M. Nussbaum and J. Glover. Oxford: Clarendon Press, 1995.

Bunch, Charlotte. "Women's Rights as Human Rights: Toward a Re-Vision of Human Rights". *Human Rights Quarterly* 12, no. 4,1990, pp. 486-498.

United Nations Publications. "Women's Rights as Human Rights". United Nations Human Rights. Office of the High Commissioner. New York and Geneva, 2014.

ABC, Teaching Human Rights, United Nations Report, https ://www.eda.admin.

Universal Declaration of Human Rights, adopted 10 December 1948, G.A. Res. 217A (III), U.N. Doc. A/810 (1948)

Singh, R.P. "Globalisation and Human Rights". *Applied Ethics and Human Rights A Conceptual Analysis and Contextual Applications.* edited by Shashi Motilal. New Delhi: Anthem Press, 2010.

Human Rights Today : UN Briefing Papers, U.N Department of Public Information New York

Cook, Wiesen Blanch. "Eleanor Roosevelt and Human Rights: The Battle for Peace and Planetary Decency". *Women and American Foreign Policy: Lobbyists, Critics, and Insiders*. Edited by Edward P. Crapol. New York: Greenwood Press, 1987.

Human Rights: The International Bill of Rights. Fact Sheet No. 2, United Nations.

Report Prepared by the Secretary General on the Global Consultation on the Realization of the Right to Development as a Human Right. UN Doc E/CnA/ 1990/9.

Peggy Antrobus, paper presented to the World Women's Congress for a Healthy Planet, Miami, FL, November 9-12, 1991.

Beil, Charistine, *Human Rights: An Agenda for the 21st Century.* London: Cavendish Publishing Ltd, 1999.

United Nations Publications. "Women's Rights as Human Rights". United Nations Human Rights. Office of the High Commissioner. New York and Geneva, 2014.

Nussbaum, C Martha. *Women and Human Development The Capabilities Approach.* U K: Cambridge University Press, 2000.

United Nations Human Rights Report. "Women's Rights are Human Rights". Office of the High Commissioner.

Nussbaum. C Martha. *Creating Capabilities The Human Development Approach.* Ranikhet: Permanent Black, 2011.

Nussbaum, C Martha. "Capabilities as Fundamental Entitlements: Sen and Social Justice". *Capability freedom, and equality Amartya Sen's work from gender perspective.* Edited by Bina Agarwal, Jane Humphries & Ingrid Robeyns. UK: Oxford University Press, 2006.

Charlesworth, Hillary. "Martha Nussbaum's Feminist Internationalism". *Ethics* 111, no. 1. 2000. pp. 64:78.

Nussbaum, C Martha. "Poverty and Human Functioning: Capabilities as Fundamental Entitlements". *Poverty and Inequality.* Edited by David B. Grusky & Ravi Kanbur. California: Stanford University Press, 2006.

M. Mowafi and M. Khawaja. "Poverty". *Journal of Epidemiology and Community Health* 59, no. 4. 2005. pp. 260: 264.

Bhanushali G. B. *Poverty Scenario in Indian Subcontinent.* New Delhi: Bookwell, 2007.

Nyiwul Mabughi and Tarek Selim. "Poverty as Social Deprivation: A Survey". *Review of Social Economy* 64, no. 2. 2006. pp. 181: 204.

Dorius F. Shawn and Firebaugh Glenn. "Trends in Global Gender Inequality". *Social Forces* 88. no. 5. 2010. pp. 1941: 1968.

Firdevs, Cin Melis. *Gender Justice, Education and Equality Creating Capabilities for Girls and Women's Development.* UK: Palgrave Macmillan, 2017.

http://www.census2011.co.in/sexratio.php

Kirti Singh. "The Constitution and Muslim Personal Law," in *Foreign Identities: Gender, Communities, and the State in India.* Edited by Zoya Hasan. Delhi and Boulder, CO: Westview Press, 1999.

Nussbaum. "Challenge of Gender Justice" in *Against Injustice: The New Economics of Amartya Sen.* Edited by Reiko Gotoh and Paul Dumouchel. USA: Cambridge University Press, 2009.

Nussbaum, "Women's Capabilities and Social Justice". *Journal of Human Development* 1, no. 2, 2000, 230: 290.

Notes

1. Nussbaum, "Women's Bodies: Violence, Security, Capabilities". *Journal of Human Development.* Vol. 6, No. 2, July 2005. p. 167.
2. *Ibid.*, p. 6.
3. Nussbaum, *Sex and Social Justice.* p. 8.
4. *Ibid.,* p. 6.
5. Sen & Jean Dreze. *An Uncertain Glory: India and its Contradictions.* p. 213.
6. *Ibid.*, p. 82.
7. Nussbaum. *Sex and Social Justice.* p. 19.
8. Vats, and Mudgal Shakuntla. *Women and Society in Ancient India.* Faridabad: Om Publications. 1999. p. 1.
9. Jayapalan, *Indian Society and Social Institutions.* p. 146.
10. Nussbaum, *Frontiers of Justice : Disability, Nationality, Species Membership.* pp. 224-25.
11. Charlesworth, Hilary. "Human Rights as Men's Rights" in *Human Rights: Critical Concepts in Political Sciences.* p. 135.

12. UNDP. "Women's Political Participation and Good Governance: 21st Century Challenges". p. 4.
13. Nussbaum. *Sex and Social Justice.* p. 30.
14. *Ibid.,* p. 29.
15. Martha Chen. "A Matter of Survival: Women's Right to Employment in India and Bangladesh," *Women, Culture, and Development.* pp. 37-57.
16. Bunch, "Women's Rights as Human Rights: Toward aRe-Vision of Human Rights". pp. 486-498.
17. United Nations Publications. "Women's Rights as Human Rights". p. l.
18. Nussbaum, *Frontiers of Justice: Disability, Nationality, Species Membership Frontiers of justice.* p. 13.
19. *Ibid.,* p. 13.
20. ABC, Teaching Human Rights, United Nations Report, p. 5.
21. *Ibid.,* p. 5.
22. Universal Declaration of Human Rights.
23. Singh, R.P. "Globalisation and Human Rights". *Applied Ethics and Human Rights A Conceptual Analysis and Contextual Applications.* p. 182.
24. Human Rights Today: UN Briefing Papers. p. 7.
25. Bunch, Charlotte. "Women's Rights as Human Rights: Toward a Re-Vision of Human Rights". p. 487.
26. Cook, Wiesen Blanch. "Eleanor Roosevelt and Human Rights: The Battle for Peace and Planetary Decency". pp. 98-118.
27. Charlesworth, Hilary. "Human Rights as Men's Rights" in *Human Rights: Critical Concepts in Political Sciences* . p. 138.
28. Human Rights: The International Bill of Rights. p. 7.
29. Charlesworth, Hilary. "Human Rights as Men's Rights" in *Human Rights: Critical Concepts in Political Sciences* . p. 138.
30. *Ibid.,* p. 138.
31. UN Doc. E/CN.6/WG.2/1992 /L.3 (3 September 1992).
32. Charlesworth, Hilary. "Human Rights as Men's Rights" in *Human Rights : Critical Concepts in Political Sciences.* p. 139.
33. Charlesworth, Hilary. "Human Rights as Men's Rights" in *Human Rights : Critical Concepts in Political Sciences.* p. 139.
34. *Ibid.,* p. 140.
35. *Ibid.,* p. l40.
36. *Ibid.,* p. 140.
37. Report Prepared by the Secretary General on the Global Consultation on the Realization of the Right to Development as a Human Right. p. 15.
38. Charlesworth, Hilary. "Human Rights as Men's Rights" in *Human Rights: Critical Concepts in Political Sciences.* p. 135.
39. Peggy Antrobus, paper presented to the World Women's Congress for a Healthy Planet. pp. 9-12.

40. Bunch, Charlotte. "Women's Rights as Human Rights: Toward a Re-Vision of Human Rights". p. 489.
41. Beil, Charistine, *Human Rights: An Agendafor the 21st Century,* p. 45.
42. Charlesworth, Hilary. "Human Rights as Men's Rights" in *Human Rights: Critical Concepts in Political Sciences.* pp. 138-139.
43. Bunch, Charlotte . "Women's Rights as Human Rights: Toward a Re-Vision of Human Rights". p. 487.
44. United Nations Publications. "Women's Rights as Human Rights". p. 1.
45. Nussbaum. *Women and Human Development The Capabilities Approach.* p. 24.
46. United Nations Human Rights Report. "Women's Rights are Human Rights". p. l.
47. Bunch, Charlotte. "Women's Rights as Human Rights: Toward a Re-Vision of Human Rights". p. 493.
48. *Ibid.,* p. 493.
49. *Ibid.,* p. 494.
50. *Ibid.,* p. 494.
51. Bunch, Charlotte. "Women's Rights as Human Rights: Toward a Re-Vision of Human Rights". p. 495.
52. Nussbaum. *Creating Capabilities The Human Development Approach.* p. 146.
53. Nussbaum. Capabilities as Fundamental Entitlements: Sen and Social Justice". *Capability, Freedom, and Equality Amartya Sen's work from Gender Perspective.* p. 39.
54. *Ibid,* p. 40.
55. Charlesworth, Hillary. "Martha Nussbaum's Feminist Internationalism". pp. 64-78.
56. Nussbaum, "Poverty and Human Functioning: Capabilities as Fundamental Entitlements". *Poverty and Inequality.* p. 51.
57. Nussbaum, "Capabilities as Fundamental Entitlements: Sen and Social Justice". *Capabilities, Freedom, and Equality: Amartya Sen's Workfrom a Gender Perspective.* pp. 55-56.
58. Nussbaum, *Sex and Social Justice.* p. 5.
59. M. Mowafi and M. Khawaja. "Poverty". pp. 260-264.
60. Bhanushali G. B. Poverty Scenario in Indian Subcontinent. p. 10.
61. Nyiwul Mabughi and Tarek Selim. "Poverty as Social Deprivation: A Survey". pp. 181-204.
62. Nussbaum, C Martha. "Poverty and Human Functioning: Capabilities as Fundamental Entitlements". *Poverty and Equality.* p. 47.
63. Sen, *Development as Freedom,* p. 87.
64. *Ibid.,* p. 87.
65. *Ibid.,* p. 260.
66. *Ibid.,* p. 260.
67. Bhanushali, *Poverty Scenario in Indian Subcontinent.* p. 54.

68. Nussbaum, "Poverty and Human Functioning: Capabilities as Fundamental Entitlements". *Poverty and Equality*. pp. 47-48.
69. Sen. *Development as Freedom*. p. 87.
70. Nussbaum, *Creating Capabilities The Human Development Approach*. p. 144.
71. Nussbaum, C Martha. "Poverty and Human Functioning: Capabili ties as Fundamental Entitlements". *Poverty and Equality*. p. 49.
72. Awumbila, Mariama. "Gender equality and poverty in Ghana: Implications for Poverty reduction strategies". Geo Journal. Vol. 67. No. 2(2006). Pp. 149-161.
73. *Ibid.*, p. 89.
74. Firdevs, Cin Melis. *Gender Justice, Education and Equality Creating Capabilities for Girls and Women's Development*. p. 41.
75. Darius F. Shawn and Firebaugh Glenn. "Trends in Global Gender Inequality". pp. 1941-1968.
76. Nussbaum, "Women's capabilities and Social Justice". p. 15.
77. Nussbaum. *Sex and Social Justice*. p. 5.
78. Robeyns, Ingrid. "Sen 's Capability Approach and Gender Inequality Selecting Relevant Capabilities". pp. 81-82.
79. Nussbaum. *Sex and Social Justice*. p. 89.
80. http://www.census20ll.co.in/sexratio.php
81. Nussbaum. "Women's Bodies: Violence, Security, Capabilities". p. 165.
82. *Ibid.*, p. 167.
83. *Ibid.*, p. 172.
84. Nussbaum. *Sex and Social Justice*. p. 90.
85. Robeyns, Ingrid. "Sen 's Capability Approach and Gender Inequality : Selecting Relevant Capabilities". p. 88.
86. *Ibid.*, p. 89.
87. Nussbaum, *Sex and Social Justice*. p. 5.
88. *Ibid.*, p. 94.
89. *Ibid.*, p. 100.
90. Cin Melis, Firdevs . *Gender Justice, Education and Equality: Creating Capabilities for Girls'* and Women's Development. p. 3.
91. *Ibid.*, p. 3.
92. Nussbaum. *Sex and Social Justice*. p. 92.
93. *Ibid.*, p. 94.
94. *Ibid.*, p. 98.
95. Kirti Singh. "The Constitution and Muslim Personal Law," in *Foreign Identities: Gender, Communities, and the State in India*. pp. 96-107.
96. Nussbaum, *Women and Human Development: Capability Approach*. p. l.
97. *Ibid.*, p. l.
98. Nussbaum. "Challenge of Gender Justice" in *Against Injustice: The New Economics of Amartya Sen*. p. 94.
99. Nussbaum. *Sex and Social Justice*. pp. 39-44.

100. Nussbaum, "Capabilities as Fundamental Entitlements: Sen and Social Justice", pp. 33-59.
101. *Ibid.*, p. 38.
102. Nussbaum, *Women and Human Development: the Capabilities Approach.* p. 5.
103. Nussbaum, *Frontiers of Justice: Disability, Nationality, Species Membership.* pp. 164-165.
104. Nussbaum, *Women and Human Development: the Capabilities Approach.* p. 5.
105. *Ibid.*, pp. 5-6.
106. Nussbaum, *Frontiers of Justice: Disability, Nationality, Species Membership.* p. 159.
107. *Ibid.*, p. 162.
108. Nussbaum, *Women and Human Development: the Capabilities Approach.* p. 11.
109. *Ibid.*, p. 11.
110. *Ibid.*, p. 12.
111. *Ibid.*, p. 12.
112. *Ibid.*, p. 15.
113. *Ibid.*, p. 20.
114. *Ibid.*, p. 110.
115. Nussbaum. *Creating Capabilities: The Human Development Approach.* p. 18.
116. *Ibid.*, p. 19.
117. Nussbaum, *Women and Human Development: the Capabilities Approach.* p. 71.
118. Nussbaum, "Women's Capabilities and Social Justice". p. 230.
119. *Ibid.*, p. 230.
120. Nussbaum, *Frontiers of Justice: Disability, Nationality, Species Membership* . p. 155.
121. Ibid, p. 168.
122. Nussbaum, *Women and Human Development: the Capabilities Approach.* Pp. 79-80.
123. Nussbaum, Creating Capabilities: The Human Development Approach. p. 33.
124. *Ibid.*, p. 33.
125. *Ibid.*, p. 33.
126. *Ibid.*, p. 33.
127. *Ibid.*, p. 33.
128. *Ibid.*, p. 34.
129. *Ibid.*, p. 34.
130. *Ibid.*, p. 34.
131. *Ibid.*, p. 34.
132. *Ibid.*, p. 34.
133. Firdevs, *Gender Justice, Education and Equality: Creating Capabilities for Girls and Women's Development.* p. 57.

Chapter - 5

Conclusion

In the conclusion, I shall summarise the main arguments concerning the concept of justice on the basis of four problematic, firstly, contending claims on social contract theory and the emergence of perfect justice. Secondly, an attempt is to analyse Rawls' position on justice to bring out its shortcomings in two fold manner; first the way Rawls has criticized his own earlier position in his later work and secondly the way his successors like Sen, Martha Nussbaum and others have criticized the positions of Rawls. Thirdly, to analyse discrepancies between institutional arrangement and realisation focussed approach i.e. *Nitti* and *Nyaya* approach to justice in Sen. In other words its attempt is to bring out the discrepancies and the implications between collective well-being and individualistic happiness to substantiate minimizing injustice in Sen. Fourthly, attempt to address the questions concerning minimizing injustice in terms of discrimination, particularly gender discrimination in the cultural practices of different women on the one hand and legal, political, social and economic status of women on the other to reach an inclusive notion of justice where justice has to be understood in terms of feminist concern and sympathetic understanding of capabilities. In order to acquire just society, these lists of capabilities would be institutionally arranged and constitutionally implemented to elevate humanity at the level of progress to pursue a dignified life.

In order to substantiate perfect justice, I have attempted social theory on the one hand and human autonomy and dignity in terms of Kant's enlightenment rationality and morality on the other to repudiate unjust society in the form of feudal monarchy and aristocracy. As a matter of fact, social contract theory has been the dominant theory which turns out to be the most appropriate normative model which rejected traditional repudiates unjust society in the form of feudal monarchy and aristocracy.

It played an important historical role in the emergence of the idea that political authority or institution must be derived from people's consensus and not by divine rights. Moreover, since ancient times the social contract theory has been used as a progressive intellectual tradition that has questioned authority in all its guises on the one hand and on the other hand. Social arrangements were not the products of nature but based upon people's consent and contract to create a just society from unjust.

However, in modem times, social contract theory propounded by Hobbes, Locke and Rousseau on the nature of political authority and how justice to be delivered within social institutions to make a just society. However, I have analysed social contract theory is in itself contested in the emergence of what a perfect society ought to be? Is social contract theory is necessary to establish a just society? Is an institutional arrangement or social force, customs and historic continuity and people's struggle is sufficient to create a just society? To address such questions, I have examined Hobbes's conception of political authority and monarch who gives justice because people lived in state of nature where social condition is a condition of war where everyone was against everyone. In such situation, people wanted a ruler of a sovereign or political body in order to be able to live peacefully in a civil society.

Hence, for Hobbes, justice lies in the hands of the Monarch whereas for Locke justice underlies in individual rights related to life, freedom and property. For Rousseau, it is the general will or moral collective will of the individuals in the society will shape the laws of institutions. Indeed the social contract theory was repudiated by Hume on the ground that there is no historical evidence to any contract, original or otherwise and his conception of justice is based on convention and customs. In this way, a just society is not based upon institutional arrangements rather it developed from social force, customs and historic continuity. For example, the question of justice will comes when a society's wealth and possessions would be moderate and then the society framed rules of distribution which recognise and redistribute to all. That is why, for Hume, justice is convention whose usefulness is directly proportional to the situation and circumstances wherein people are placed. Hegel was also anti-contracterian and believed a just society does not need any institution mechanism and justice is based on individual's efforts and struggle for their rights.

Despite of all criticism and contestation about social contract theory in the emergence ofjust society, I have developed social contract as an indispensible for justice and indeed Kant has also argued about the contractual basis for a just society which is based on the fallowing three principles, namely, firstly, the freedom of every member of a society as a human being, secondly, the equality of each with all the others as a subject, and thirdly, the independence of each member of a commonwealth as a citizen[1] where freedom, equality and autonomy of each individual is absolutely equal and no members of the society would have hereditary privileges as against others. A just society ought to be based on a fair system of cooperation among free and autonomous beings and the function of social contract is to protect individual's autonomy *for all and not for* few.

> We find a union of many individuals for some common end which they all share. But a union as an end in itself which they all ought to share and which is thus an absolute and primary duty in all external relationships whatsoever among human beings (who cannot avoid mutually influencing one another), is only found in a society insofar as it constitutes a civil state i.e. a commonwealth.[2]

Hence, Kantian perfect justice underlies at the centre of individuals concern and how humanity understands their relations with one another in terms of autonomy and dignity aspect. In other way, it shapes the very foundation of enlightened society where each and every person becomes autonomous and sovereign to act rationally and morally to construct an institutional principle of justice that how *justice ought* to be rather than *what is just* for one's own betterment and the betterment of the society as well. Moreover in perfect society, enlightened and moral being inculcates the habit of tolerance to live peacefully by respecting others' dignity, right and autonomy which promotes social justice to live and get along with others.

In contemporary times, Kant's philosophical insight into perfect justice has been carried forward by John Rawls. He combines several criteria of justice under the idea of contract in the form of 'original position' or 'hypothetical situation' by modifying social contract theory to explain the principle of distributive justice with reference to institutions. Then the question arises: is justice, the realization of institutions and rules or principles or is it concerned with the society as well? Is fair distribution of social goods is sufficient to substantiate the notion of justice? Is institutional approach to justice is fair to address justice for all? While attempt to address these questions, I have analysed Rawls's position on original position which can understood as a hypothetical contract and not as a historical contract to make political institutions ought to be just under all circumstances. In other way, laws and institutions no matter how efficient and well arranged must be reformed if they are unjust.

In Ralws, the purpose of justice is to arrange a 'basic structure of society' where the major social institutions distribute fundamental rights and duties and determine the division of advantages from social cooperation.

In order to substantiate Rawls's distributive justice, "equal distribution of social goods so that each citizen adequately develop and fully exercise their moral powers".[3] These social goods are, namely,

1. Basic liberties and rights
2. Freedom of movement and free choice of occupation against a background of diverse opportunities.
3. Powers and prerogatives of offices and positions of responsibility in the political and economic institutions of the basic structure.
4. Income and wealth.
5. The social bases of self-respect.[4]

Our society suffers from a very unbalanced distribution of wealth which creates inequality between rich and poor. Rawls, combines several criteria of justice under the idea of contract in the form of 'original position' or 'hypothetical situation' under an innovative device of 'veil of ignorance' which enables the contracting parties to choose principles of Justice without prejudice so that no one is advantaged or disadvantaged in the choice of principles by the outcome of natural chance and social circumstances. The two principles are chosen behind a veil of ignorance to determine the basic institutions of a society as to what is fair or just are:

> Firstly, each person is to have an equal right to the most extensive basic liberty compatible with similar liberty for others.
>
> Secondly, social and economic inequalities are to be arranged so that they are both (a) reasonably expected to be to everyone's advantage, and (b) attached to positions and offices open to all.[5]

Moreover, Rawls's distributive justice and its fair distribution of goods is not sufficient to deliver justice. It does not acknowledge genuine information concerning individual differences in converting resources with equal efficiency. It is a fact that, people's life plan is not only determined by 'primary goods' that he/she has at his/ her disposal, but there are various factors that determine to what extent he/ she can utilize these primary goods into valuable states of being and doing. However, Rawls himself criticizes on the position of justice fairness by arguing that fair institutional arrangement for the distribution of social goods as a political conception and it is justified by reference to political values and should not be presented as part of a more comprehensive moral, religious, or philosophical doctrine.[6] In other way, Rawls' own criticism of his earlier position still amounts to the fairness of the institutions with liberal values. It may be emphasized that, there is still a lack of the realization of the sense of Justice not as a matter of judging institutions in terms of fair distribution but minimize injustices at individual and social level.

In this way, Rawls's innovative device of "ignorance model" helps us to reach at fair institutional arrangement, where justice has to be seen in terms of impartiality. Moreover, ignorance model helps us to reach at fair institutional arrangement where justice is to be seen in terms of impartiality, however, it detach us from perpetuating injustices from the society. Inother words, Rawls's veil of ignorance as a hypothetical contract is not sufficient to distribute fairly on the basis of two institutional principles. The communitarian criticizes about Rawls' position on veil of ignorance which prevents us from getting the complete information of the subject matter of justice. Alasdair MacIntyre believes that, ignorance model separates individuals from their background, tradition and community which are indispensible aspects of their life.

Furthermore, distributive justice does not provide any information on other aspects of human life such as education, gender inequality and women's freedom and opportunities. Moreover, it is not sufficient to deliver justice because Rawls's two institutional arrangement on fair distribution of social goods seems to take little note of the diversity of human beings. As Sen has rightly pointed out that, if people were basically very similar, then an index or primary goods might be quite a good way of judging advantage and doing justice. However, people seems to have very different needs varying with health, longevity, climatic conditions, locations, work conditions, temperament, and even body size. So, index of social goods and its fair distribution unable to acknowledge people's differences to convert these goods into valuable functionings. For example, someone, who is being handicapped or crippled, would require extra care and concern to enable them to achieve the same functioning in terms of mobility as an able-bodied person. In this way, when a person lacking the opportunity to achieve some minimum level of functionings on the one hand and on the other fails to convert these opportunities or resources into valuable achievements then he/she may be considered as poor. Hence, resources do not have an intrinsic value; instead their value derives from the opportunity to convert these resources into valuable achievements.

There are number of ways where systematic forms of injustice related to social discrimination between rich and poor, caste, races, and gender persist in a society which can be difficult to recognize through institutional approach to justice. Moreover institutional approach to justice in one way or another contributes serious injustices relating to social, political and economic sphere. Sen argues in *Hunger and Public Action* that, there is no law against dying of hunger.[7] Even history bears that severe famines continue to occur in various regions, denying to millions the basic right to survive. For example, poverty, poor economic opportunities, lack of public facilities and social care like lack of nutritional food, health care, basic education and other social and economic security etc. deprives person's basic freedom to survive a life that is worthy of human dignity. These social injustices have been dominated since a long time and the only way to confront this menace through Amartya Sen's 'social realizations' or Indian tradition of *Nyaya* rather than 'institutional arrangements' or *Niti* approach to justice where justice cannot be indifferent to the lives of people.

In order to minimise individual and social injustice, *Nyaya* or realisation approach to justice is an urgent requirement so that we can move from 'less unjust society' to 'more just society' where people's well-being can be achieved in terms freedom and capabilities. The capability approach tackles the issues of injustices by highlighting that human being has a dignity with their ability to pursue their own ends. Instead of institutional mechanism or *Niti* approach to justice which governs collective choices, capability approach to justice tries to seek social outcomes through people's well-being "that a person actually has to do this or be that - things that he or she may value doing or being".[8] In other words, capability approach does not concentrate on just institutions and the means of primary goods but minimizes injustices by removing obstacles in actual opportunities in day to day life. It makes each and every individual to act on his/her choices and the kind of life that they have reason to value.

I have analysed Sen's capability approach on freedom as the means and end of human well-being. People's substantive freedom played an important role because it concerned about elementary capabilities like being able to avoid such deprivations as starvation, undernourishment, escapable morbidity and premature morality, as well as the freedom being associated with being literate and enjoying political participation and uncensored speech and so on.[9] In this way, people's substantive freedom plays an important role in terms of individualistic (intrinsic) and social role of freedom (instrumental) in justice as welfare. On the one hand, intrinsic idea of freedom ensures individual's well-being in the form of wellnourished, gets provisions for health care, enjoys good education and also given the chance to participate in social and political process. Inother way, in absence of people's intrinsic freedom, there would be degradation of human life, suffering and their injustice etc. On the other hand, freedom is also valued for instrumentally because it concerned about the way different kinds of rights, opportunities, and entitlements contributes collective well-being as a whole in any society.

Moreover, capability approach is closely linked with the opportunity aspect of freedom which focuses on person's functioning of what *hel* she wants to do and be what they want to be. In other words, people's functionings and capabilities bring out an enabling society where each individual becomes capable in terms of various activities that helshe can undertake in their day to day life. In other words, individual's functioning is the subject of the capabilities which assess their opportunities in terms of what and how people are capable in various acts of doing and being. For example, working as a rickshaw puller and being well nourished. Furthermore, capability is an opportunity to achieve a particular functioning, the opportunity to work as a rickshaw puller if one so chooses. It reflects how efficient a person can succeeds in converting bare resources into its valuable characteristics according to their purposes. For instance, a person has raw materials for food such as rice, millet and vegetable etc. and he knows (functioning) to convert these resources into its characteristics i.e. nutritional meal. So with the help of functioning, for instance, a carpenter with his skill can convert bare wood into valuable item such as chair, table and other wooden items. Sen's welfare approach in terms of people's capabilities is paradigm shift in welfare mechanism where justice concern for human beings and their well-being to be the central focus. Its concern is not to focus on material welfare (people's well off) rather to promote on human welfare (people's well being). in other way, it conceives human freedom and the ability to make decisions that affect one's life as central to human agency and their dignity. As Sen has given a very fascinating example where he distinguishes between a starving child and fasting monk, since both of them are kept away from food in terms of functioning level. However, the starving child does not have freedom of choices and opportunities to eat while monk has, but does not choose to eat. In such case the starving child does not have freedom of opportunity as well as agency freedom to choose what he has reason to value. Furthermore, capability approach to justice evolved out of ethical consideration of human welfare in terms of human functioning and capabilities that highlights human being has a dignity with their ability to pursue their own ends to foster an enabling environment where each individual becomes capable to make decision about issues that affect their lives and minimize injustice to that extent. It does not concern for people's happiness, desire fulfilment, and commodity but what can they do or achieve in terms of various functioning. It can be argue that, human welfare occurs in their opportunities and capabilities to achieve a certain level of functionings by virtue of the alternative combination of functionings relating to their nourishment, safety, security, health, longevity, literacy, recreation, comfort, housing, transportation and social relationship etc. For instance, being happy, being well-dressed, being well-nourished, being educated, being employed, being safe, being calm, having dignity and other activities that inculcates various aspects of functioning of person's wellbeing.

Hence, Sen's idea of freedom and capabilities enhances individuals and collective well-being because agency oriented capability approach assesses which capability is valuable for them, or how well they are doing but it also look at the agency of individuals to see whether he/she decide on what matters to him/her. Sen's capability bring about public enlightenment to see themselves as agents to take individual responsibility for one's own well-being and take collective responsibility for the well-being of society at large. Thus an agent is an individual who is willing to have a shared responsibility for share a process that ensures public enlightenment in terms of everyone's capabilities to decide, to self determine and to bring about change in the society.

In other words, Martha Nussbaum attempts to establish an inclusive society which not only incorporates the basic philosophic visions of Kant, Rawls and Sen, but also transcends it. In order to minimize gender injustices, we must incorporate the violation of women's rights in terms of capability deprivation. Although, women constitute an important role in transforming the family and society so their rights should be protected yet women have been facing many disadvantageous situations due to the existence of gender differences and biases. Hence, without protecting and preserving women's basic rights in terms of capabilities, no society can claim to have an established and just social order.

Since the foundation of United Nations Organization, the concept of human rights has provided a normative framework to address human rights violation for all human being irrespective of caste, creed, sex and gender. Moreover, for a long period, gender based violations were not considered as human rights violation because crimes against any person other than women would be recognized as a gross violation of the victims' humanity. For instance, there are many international human rights law and national human rights law is inherently biased against women. Such law operates primarily in the public spheres which is traditionally associated with men's life. On the other hand it does not operate in the private sphere of home and family which is generally regarded as the province of women. Thus, the failure to respect and recognize women as human led to the claim of 'Women's Rights as Human Rights'. The concept of women's rights refers to legal norms on gender based non-discrimination and includes women's rights into traditional approach to human rights to achieve equal rights, equal treatment and equal opportunities for both men and women being a human. Nussbaum believes human rights approach to justice has neglected the issue of women's capability which focuses on what women are actually able to do and to be. In short, thinking in terms of capability gives us a benchmark to think about what it is really to secure a right to women.

Women are more prone to capability deprivation which leads them to poor. Moreover, women's poverty in terms of capability deprivation has continued to shape ethical and moral concerns about the way women have been living in the society. History bears that poverty is an urgent concern of humanity, because it diminishes human dignity and makes them to live like an animal. However, when the incidence of poverty comes to women's lives, it can be calculated in double, triple or multiple folds because they are more likely to be vulnerable and poor than men. More than half a billion women in developing countries have no reasonable income, no health care and no security is the major cause of poverty. Hence extreme poverty and vulnerability is female which leads them to hunger, disease, no education, no ownership and no secure access to water and energy. Women also have been facing limited opportunities owing to isolation, exclusion from decision-making processes, low mobility, overwork and violence. Moreover, due to poverty, women in their family have been deprived of basic education, healthcare, nutritious food, and deprivation of other opportunities leads to gender inequality. In other words, poverty makes women more vulnerable because it leads women are less nourished than men, less healthy than men, less educated than men and more vulnerable to physical violence and sexual abuse. Nussbaum regards when poverty combines with gender inequality, the result is severe deprivation of women's capabilities to live a dignified life. In other way poverty strongly correlates with gender inequality raises ethical and moral questions that how women should attain dignified life. Hence, people's capabilities is an urgent need because capabilities approach of Amartya Sen and Martha Nussbaum provides us a benchmark to address the multiple forms of poverty and inequalities in the lives of women who are situated in different historical, religious, cultural and political contexts and have been experiencing several kinds of injustice.

Capability approach is an outcome-oriented approach which emphasised on the list often central capabilities: Life, Bodily Health, Bodily Integrity, Senses, Imagination and Thought, Emotions, Practical Reason, Affiliation, Other Species, Play and Control over one's environment are essential for women's life. The list of Martha Nussbaum's capabilities provides conceptual lenses for thinking about women's poverty, inequality and to bring about gender equality and justice. In other words, these capabilities open a pathway for women to live fulfilled life that is not influenced by traditions that enable injustice to continue against women. In order to fight against injustice, women must be allowed possess self-creativity in terms of their thoughts, emotions and imagination, including that of practical reason to live truly well in human way. They need to be heard, choose their own career, and plan the kind of life they want to live. Thus capabilities approach constitute an important aspect of gender justice because it recognize each person including marginalized, suppressed and socio economically deprived women under the constitutional arrangements. To conclude the chapter, I would argue capabilities approach based gender justice is very essential because it address women's issues and facilitates women should be allowed to possess self-creativity in terms of their thoughts, emotions and imagination, including that of practical reason, in order to live truly well. More importantly, it is the responsibility to institutions and government to preserve and secure to each and every person as at minimum threshold. Hence, for Nussbaum, gender justice is meant to secure the lists of basic list of capabilities as a political entitlement.

To sum up, while acknowledging the antithetical nature of perfect justice and minimising injustice and its distinct nature of the philosophical visions of Immanuel Kant, John Rawls, Amartya Sen and Martha Nussbaum, I have argued that justice in the perfect sense of the term is required as an ideal to be attained and minimizing injustice would be the process to achieve the same in terms of capability building, well-being and gender equality. For example, the philosophical concepts of dignity, autonomy, perfection and fairness, etc. in Kant and Rawls, welfare in Sen and women's equality and entitlement in Nussbaum are the exemplifications of the vision of justice. Moreover, the vision of perfect justice is foundational and unified with principles; whereas minimising injustice emerges out of the struggle against deprivation, ill health, illiteracy etc in general and various forms of injustice related to women in particular.

References

Kant, Immanuel. "The Contractual Basis for a Just Society". in *Justice: Alternative Political Perspectives.* James P. Sterba, Canada: Wodswortl Thomson Learning, 2003.

Rawls, John. 1996. *Political Liberalism.* New York: Columbia University Press. Rawls, John. *A Theory of Justice.* Cambridge: Harvard University Press, 1971.

Rawls, John. *Justice as Fairness A Restatement.* Edited by Erin Kelly. USA: Harvard University Press, 2001.

Sen, Amartya and Dreze, Jean.. *Hunger and Public Action.* Oxford: Clarendon Press, 1989.

Sen, Amartya. *The Idea of Justice.* London: Penguin Books, 2009.

Notes

1. Kant, Immanuel. "The Contractual Basis for a Just Society". p. 102.
2. *Ibid.,* p. 102.
3. Rawls. *Justice as Fairness A Restatement.* p. 57.
4. Rawls. A *Theory of Justice.* p. 92.
5. Rawls. *A Theory of Justice.* p. 60.
6. Rawls. *Political Liberalism.* p. 20.
7. Sen, Amartya and Dreze, Jean. *Hunger and Public Action.* Oxford: Clarendon Press. 1989. p. 20.
8. Sen, *The Idea of Justice.* p. 233.
9. *Ibid.,* p. 36.

Bibliography & Webliography

Primary Sources

Kant, Immanuel. "An Answer to the Question: What Is Enlightenment? (1784)", What is Enlightenment Eighteenth-Century Answers and Twentieth-Century *Questions.* Edited by James Schmidt. 58-64. London: University of California Press, 1996.

Kant, Immanuel. *Critique of Practical Reason.* Translated by Lewis White Beck. New York: Liberal Arts Press, 1956.

Kant, Immanuel. *Groundwork of the Metaphysic of Morals.* Edited by Lewis White Beck. Indianapolis: Bobbs-Merrill, 1959.

Rawls, John. *A Theory of Justice.* Cambridge: Harvard University Press, 1971

Rawls, John. *The Law of Peoples.* Cambridge: Harvard University Press, 1999.

Rawls, John. *Political Liberalism* . New York: Columbia University Press, 1996.

Rawls, John. *Justice as Fairness A Restatement.* Edited by Erin Kelly. USA: Harvard University Press, 2001.

Nussbaum, C Martha. *Frontiers of Justice: Disability, Nationality, Species Membership.* New Delhi: Oxford University Press, 2006.

Nussbaum, C Martha. *Sex and Social Justice.* Oxford: Oxford University Press, 1999.

Nussbaum, C Martha. *Women and Human Development: Capability Approach.* UK: Cambridge University Press, 2000.

Nussbaum. C Martha. *Creating Capabilities The Human Development Approach.* Ranikhet: Permanent Black, 2011.

Sen, Amartya. *The Idea of Justice.* London: Penguin Books, 2009.

Sen, Amartya. *Development as Freedom.* Oxford: Oxford University Press, 1999.

Sen, Amartya. *Inequality Reexamined.* Oxford: Clarendon Press, 1992.

Sen, Amartya. *Poverty and Famines: An Essay on Entitlement and Deprivation.* Oxford: Oxford University Press, 1999.

Sen, Amartya. *Rationality and Freedom.* Oxford: Oxford University Press. 2005.

Sen, Amartya. "Capability and Well-being" in A K Sen & M. Nussbaum, *The Quality of Life.* Oxford: Clarendon Press, 1993.

Sen, Amartya. *The Argumentative Indian.* London: Penguin Group, 2005.

Secondary Sources

ABC, Teaching Human Rights, United Nations Report, https://www.eda.admin.

Aristotle. *The Nichomachean Ethics.* Translated by J.A.K. Thomson. U.K: Penguin Books, 2004.

Aristotle. *The Ethics of Aristotle.* Translated by J. A. K. Thompson. London: Penguin Books, 1958.

Audard, Catherine. *John Rawls.* Stocksfield: Acumen Publishing Limited, 2007.

Audi, Robert. *Practical Reasoning.* London and New York: Routledge, 1989.

Barry, Brian. *Justice as Impartiality A Treatise on Social Justice, Volume II.* Oxford: Clarendon Press. 2002.

Beck, Lewis White. *A Commentary on Kant's Critique of Practical Reason.* Chicago: Chicago University Press, 1960.

Beil, Charistine, *Human Rights: An Agenda for the 21st Century.* London: Cavendish Publishing Ltd, 1999.

Bentham, Jeremy. *An Introduction to the Principles of Morals and Legislation.* Oxford: Clarendon Press, 1907.

Berlin, Isaiah. "Two concepts of Liberty," in *Four Essays on Liberty.* Oxford: Oxford University Press, 1970.

Bhanushali G. B. *Poverty Scenario in Indian Subcontinent.* New Delhi: Bookwell, 2007.

Charlesworth, Hilary. "Human Rights as Men's Rights" in *Human Rights: Critical Concepts in Political Sciences.* Edited by Richard Falk, Hilal Elver and Lisa Hajjar. London: Routledge Taylor and Francis Group, 2008.

Condercet. *Outlines of an Historical View of the Progress of the Human Mind.* London: St. Paul's Church Yard, 1795.

Cook, Wiesen Blanch. "Eleanor Roosevelt and Human Rights: The Battle for Peace and Planetary Decency". *Women and American Foreign Policy: Lobbyists, Critics, and Insiders.* Edited by Edward P. Crapol. New York: Greenwood Press, 1987.

Firdevs, Cin Melis. *Gender Justice, Education and Equality Creating Capabilities for Girls and Women's Development.* UK: Palgrave Macmillan, 2017.

Fleischacker, S. On Adam Smith's Wealth of Nations: A Philosophical Companion. Princeton: Princeton University Press, 2004.

Freeman, Samuel. *Introduction: John Rawls- An Overview.* Cambridge: Cambridge University Press, 2003.

Hart, H.L.A.. "Rawls on Liberty and its Priority," In Norman Daniels (Ed.), *Reading Rawls.* New York: Basic Books, 1975.

Hobbes, Thomas. *Leviathan.* Edited by Richard Tuck. UK: Cambridge University Press, 1991.

Hume, David. *Political Essays.* New York: The Liberal Arts Press, 1953.

James P. Sterba, *Justice: Alternative Political Perspectives.* Canada: Wodswort/ Thomson Learning, 2003.

Jayapalan, N. *Indian Society and Social Institutions.* Volume 1. New Delhi: Atlantic Publication, 2001.

Johnston, David. "Kant's Theory of Justice," *A Brief History of Justice.* Edited by David Johnston. 143-165. United Kingdom: Willy Blackwell, 2011.

Kamenka, Eugene. "What is justice?" *Ideas and Ideologies: Justice.* Edited by Eugene Kamenka. London: Edward Arnold Ltd., 1979.

Kant, Immanuel. "What is Enlightenment?". *On History.* Edited & translated by Lewis White Beck. New York: Macmillan, 1963.

Kant, Immanuel. *Perpetual Peace.* Edited by Lewis White Beck. Indianapolis: The Bobbs-Merrill Company Inc, 1967.

Kant, Immanuel. *Science of Right.* Translated by W. Hastie. *e: Books Adelaide* 2009.

Kant, Immanuel. The *Doctrine of Virtue Part II of Metaphysic of Morals.* Translated by Mary J. Gregor. Philadelphia: University of Pennsylvania Press, 1964.

Kirti Singh. "The Constitution and Muslim Personal Law," in *Foreign Identities: Gender, Communities, and the State in India.* Edited by Zoya Hasan. Delhi and Boulder, CO: Westview Press, 1999.

Kristjansson, Kristjan. *Justice and Desert - Based Emotions.* England: Ashgate Publishing Limited, 2006.

Kymlicka, Will. "Liberal Equality". *Contemporary Political Philosophy An Introduction.* New York: Oxford University Press, 2002.

Levine, Andrew. *The General Will: Rousseau, Marx, Communism.* USA: Cambridge University Press, 1993.

Locke, John. *A Letter on Toleration.* Edited by Raymond Klibansky &Translated by J. W. Gough. Oxford: Clarendon Press, 1968.

Locke, John. *First Treatise on Civil Government.* Edited by Richard Ashcraft. London: Rutledge University Press, 1991.

Locke. John. *Second Treatise of Civil Government.* Edited by Laslett Peter. UK: Cambridge University Press, 1960.

Macintyre, Alasdair. *After Virtue.* London: Duckworth, 1985.

Macintyre, Alasdair. *Whose Justice? Which Rationality?* London: Duckworth, 1988.

Martha Chen. "A Matter of Survival: Women's Right to Employment in India and Bangladesh," in Women, Culture, and Development, edited by M. Nussbaum and J. Glover. Oxford: Clarendon Press, 1995.

Martin, Rex. *Rawls and Rights.* Kansas: University of Kansas Press, 1985.

Marx, Karl. *Economic and Philosophical Manuscripts of* 1844. Translated by Martin Mulligan. Moscow: Progress Publishers, 1959.

Masters, D Roger. *The Political philosophy of Rousseau.* New Jersey: Princeton University Press, 1968.

Mill, Stuart John. "Utilitarianism". *On Liberty and Other Essays.* Edited by John Gray Oxford: OUP, 1991.

Nussbaum, C Martha. "Women's Bodies: Violence, Security, Capabilities". *Journal of Human Development* 6, no. 2, 2005. pp.167: 183.

Nussbaum, C Martha. "Capabilities as Fundamental Entitlements: Sen and Social Justice". *Capability, freedom, and equality Amartya Sen's work from gender perspective.* Edited by Bina Agarwal, Jane Humphries & Ingrid Robeyns. UK: Oxford University Press, 2006.

Nussbaum, C Martha. "Poverty and Human Functioning: Capabilities as Fundamental Entitlements". *Poverty and Inequality.* Edited by David B. Grusky & Ravi Kanbur. California: Stanford University Press, 2006.

Nussbaum. "Challenge of Gender Justice" in *Against Injustice: The New Economics of Amartya Sen.* Edited by Reiko Gotoh and Paul Dumouchel. USA: Cambridge University Press, 2009.

O'Neill, Onora. *Constructions of Reason: Explorations of Kant's Practical Philosophy.* USA: Cambridge University Press, 1989.

Passmore, A. John. *Perfectibility of Man.* Indianapolis: Liberty Fund, 2000.

Plato, *Republic.* Translated by Desmond Lee. England: Penguin Groups, 1987.

Pogge, Thomas. *Realizing Rawls.* Ithaca: Cornell University Press, 1989.

Posner, A. Richard. *The Economic of Justice.* Cambridge: Harvard University Press, 1981.

Raphael, D.O. "Liberty and Authority". *Problems of Political Philosophy.* Britain: Macmillan Press Ltd, 1990.

Rawls, John. *Lecture on the History of Moral Philosophy.* Edited by Barbara Herman. USA: Harvard University Press, 2000.

Rees, John. *Equality.* New York: Praeger Publishers, 1971.

Rosen. D. Allen. *Kant's Theory of Justice.* Itchaca: Cornell U.P, 1993.

Rousseau, Jacques Jean. *The Social Contract.* Translated by Maurice Cranston. England: Penguin Books Limited, 1968.

Sandel, J Michael. *Liberalism and the Limits of Justice.* USA: Cambridge University Press, 1998.

Schmidt, James.. *What Is Enlightenment? Eighteenth Century Answers and Twentieth-Century Questions.* London: University of California Press, 1996.

Sen & Jean Dreze. *An Uncertain Glory: India and its Contradictions.* USA: Princeton University, 2013.

Sen, Amartya and Dreze, Jean.. *Hunger and Public Action.* Oxford: Clarendon Press, 1989.

Sen, Amartya. "Equality of What?" in S. McMurrin, ed. *Tanner Lecture on Human Values, Volumel.* Cambridge: Cambridge University Press, 1980.

Sen, Amartya. *Resources, Values and Development.* Cambridge, MA: Harvard University Press, 1984.

Sen, Amartya. *Commodities and Capabilities.* Amsterdam: North Hol- land, 1985.

Sen, Amartya. *On Ethics and Economics.* Edited by John M. Letiche. Oxford: Oxford University Press, 1990.

Singh, R P. "Justice and Secularism A Conceptual and Cross-Cultural Analysis". *Morality and Social Justice.* Edited by Abha Singh. Decent BOOK: New Delhi, 2010.

Singh, R P. *Freedom and Causation with Special Reference to Hegel's Overcoming of Kant.* New Delhi: Om Publication, 2000.

Singh, R P. *A Critical Examination of Immanuel Kant's Philosophy.* New Delhi: Intellectual Publishing House, 1987.

Singh, R P. *Freedom and Causation with Special Reference to Hegel's Overcoming of Kant.* New Delhi: Om Publications, 2000.

Singh, R.P. "Globalisation and Human Rights". *Applied Ethics and Human Rights A Conceptual Analysis and Contextual Applications.* edited by Shashi Motilal. New Delhi: Anthem Press, 2010.

Smith, Adam. *Theory of Moral Sentiments,* Edited by D. D. Raphael, A. L. Macfie. Oxford: Oxford University Press, 1976.

Sterba P, James. *Justice Alternative Political Perspectives.* U.K: University of Notre Dame. 2003.

Strike, Kenneth A. *Liberal Justice and the Marxist Critique of Education.* New York: Routledge, 1989.

UNDP. "Women's Political Participation and Good Governance: 21st Century Challenges". http ://www.onlinewomeninpolitics.org/beij ing 12/wpp gg.pd

United Nations Publications. "Women's Rights as Human Rights". United Nations Human Rights. Office of the High Commissioner. New York and Geneva, 2014.

Universal Declaration of Human Rights, adopted 10 December 1948, G.A. Res. 217A (III), U.N. Doc. *A/810 (1948)*

Vats, and Mudgal Shakuntla. *Women and Society in Ancient India.* Faridabad: Om Publications, 1999.

Williams, David. *Condorcet and Modernity.* Cambridge: Cambridge University Press, 2004.

Wollstonecraft, Mary. *A Vindication of the Rights of Women: With Structures on Political and Moral Subjects.* USA: Dover Publication Inc, 1792.

Articles and Journals

Anand, Paul. Hunter, Graham. Smith, Ron. "Capabilities and Well-Being: Evidence Based on the Sen-Nussbaum Approach to Welfare". *Social Indicators Research* 74, no. 1. 2005: 9-55.

Andrew, J Reck. "The Enlightenment in American Law III: The Bill of Rights," *The Review of Metaphysics* 45, no. 1, 1991: 57-87.

Antoon. Braeckman, "The Moral Inevitability of Enlightenment and the Precariousness of the Moment: Reading Kant's "What Is Enlightenment?," *The Review of Metaphysics* 62, no. 2, 2008: 285-306.

Barnett, E. Randy. "A Consent Theory of Contract". *Columbia Law Review 86,* no. 2, 1986: 269-321.

Beckley, Harlan. "Capability as Opportunity: How Amartya Sen Revises Equal Opportunity". *The Journal of Religious Ethics* 30, no. 1. 2002: 107-135.

Benjamin, Radcliff. "The General Will and Social Choice Theory," *The Review of Politics* 54, no. l, 1992: 34-49.

Besant, Annie. "Liberty, equality, fraternity", *Bristol Selected Pamphlets, 1880.* URL: http://www.jstor.org/stable/

Bookman T John. "Locke's Contract: Would People Consent to It"? *American Journal of Economics and Sociology* 43, no. 3, 1984: 357-368.

Boot, Martijn. "The Aim of a Theory of Justice". *Ethical Theory and Moral Practice* 15, no. 1. 2012: 15 100.

Charlesworth, Hilary. "Martha Nussbaum's Feminist Internationalism". *Ethics,* 111, no. 1 2000: 64-78.

Cohen, R. Morris. "The Basis of Contract", *Harvard Law Review* 46, no. 4, 1933: 553-592. Cormick, Me Peter. "Social Contract: Interpretation and Misinterpretation," *Canadian Journal of Political Science,* 9, no. 1, 1976: 63-76.

Crowder, George. "Two Concepts of Liberal Pluralism," *Political Theory* 35, no. 2, 2007: 121-146.

Cupit, Geoffrey. "Fraternity and Equality". *Philosophy* 88, no. 2, 2013: 3003-05.

Curti, Merle. "The Great Mr. Locke: America's Philosopher 1783-1861". *The Huntington Library Bulletin,* no. 11,1937: 107-151.

Daniels, Norman. "Equality of What: Welfare, Resources, or Capabilities?" *Philosophy and Phenomenological Research* 50, 1990: 273-296.

Daniels, Norman. "Society Equality of What: Welfare, Resources, or Capabilities?" *Philosophy and Phenomenological Research* 50, 1990: 273-296.

David, Gauthier. "The Social Contract as Ideology", *Philosophy &Public Affairs* 6, no. 2, 1977: 130-164.

Deveaux, Monique "Toleration and Respect", *Public Affairs Quarterly,* Vol. 12, No. 4, 1998, pp. 407-427.

Darius F. Shawn and Firebaugh Glenn. "Trends in Global Gender Inequality". *Social Forces* 88. no. 5. 2010. pp. 1941: 1968.

Edward A Harris. "From Social Contract to Hypothetical Agreement: Consent and the Obligation to Obey the Law," *Columbia Law Review* 92, no. 3,1992: 651-683.

Eisenberg, Avigail. "Context, Cultural Difference, Sex and Social Justice by Martha C. Nussbaum". *Political Science,* 35, no. 3. 2002: 613-628.

Franceschet, Antonio. "Sovereignty and Freedom: Immanuel Kant's Liberal Internationalist 'Legacy," *Review oj International Studies,* 27, no. 2, 2001: 209-22.

Francis, Edward Devine. "Absolute Democracy or Indefeasible Right: Hobbes Versus Locke", *The Journal of Politics* 37, no. 3, 1975: 736-768.

Frediani Apsan, Alexandre. "Sen's Capability Approach as a framework to the practice of development". *Development in Practice* 20, no. 2. 2010: 173-187.

Freeman, Samuel "Reason and Agreement in Social Contract Views," *Philosophy & Public Affairs* 19, no. 2, 1990: 122-157.

Gilman, Ives Benjamin. "What is Liberty When Two or More Persons are concerned?" *International Journal of Ethics* 32. no. 2. 1922: 124-128.

Gombert Tobias, "Foundations of Social Democracy". Berlin: Friedrich-Ebert-Stiftung. 2009.

Harpham, Galt Geoffrey. "So What Is Enlightenment? An Inquisition into Modernity," *Critical Inquiry* 20, no. 3, 1994: 524-556.

Harris, A. Edward. "From Social Contract to Hypothetical Agreement: Consent and the Obligation to Obey the Law". *Columbia Law Review* 92, no. 3, 1992: 651-683.

Haydn, Mason. "The European Enlightenment: Was It Enlightened?," *The Modern Language Review* 94, no. 4, 1999: pp. xxvii-xxxviii.

Herman, Lebovics. "The Uses of America in Locke's Second Treatise of Government," *Journal of the History of Ideas* 47, no. 4,1986: 567-581.

Human Rights Today: UN Briefing Papers, U.N Department of Public Information New York

Human Rights: The International Bill of Rights. Fact Sheet No. 2, United Nations. Huntley, L Wade. "Kant's Third Image: Systemic Sources of the Liberal Peace," *International Studies Quarterly* 40, no. 1, 1996: 45-76.

Jeffrey, Reiman. "Towards a Secular Lockean Liberalism," *The Review of Politics.* 67, no. 3 2005: 473-493.

John F. Tomer. "Human Well-Being: A New Approach Based on Overall and Ordinary Functionings". *Review of Social Economy* 60, no. 1. 2002. pp. 23-45

Kemp, J. "Kant's Examples of the Categorical Imperative," *The Philosophical Quarterly* 8, no. 30, 1958: 63-71.

Kulkarni P, Subodh. "Justice as Freedom": Do We Have a New Approach to a Firm's Enterprise Strategy?" *Business &Professional Ethics Journal,* Vol. 28, No. 1/4 (2009), pp. 3-26.

L. Shannon Jung, "Autonomy as Justice: Spatiality and the Revelation of Otherness," *The Journal of Religious Ethics* 14, no. 1, 1986: 157-183.

L. W. Sumner . "The Subjectivity of *Welfare". Ethics.* 105, no. 4. 1995. pp. 764-790

Ladenson, F Robert. "A Theory of Personal Autonomy," *Ethics* 86, no.1, 1975: 30-48.

Lakoff, Sanford, "Autonomy and Liberal Democracy," *The Review of Politics 52,* no. 3, 1990: 378-396.

Larry M. Preston, "Recovering the Social Contract by Ron Replogle." *The American Political Science Review* 84, no. 2, 1990: 640-641.

Lessnoff H, M. "Justice, Social Contract, and Universal Prescriptivism". The *Philosophical Quarterly* 28, no. 110. 1978: 65-73.

Lewis, D H. "Is There a Social Contract? I", *Philosophy* 15, no. 57, 1940: 64-79.

Lewis, D H. "Is There a Social Contract? II", *Philosophy* 15, no. 58, 1940: 177-189.

Lewis, D H. "The Original Contract", *Ethics* 50, no. 2, 1940: 193-205.

M. Mowafi and M. Khawaja. "Poverty". *Journal of Epidemiology and Community Health* 59, no. 4. 2005. pp. 260: 264.

Makuwira, Jonathan. "Development? Freedom? Whose Development and Freedom?". *Development in Practice.* Vol. 16. 2006. pp. 193-200.

Micah, Schwartzman. "The Relevance of Locke's Religious Arguments for Toleration," *Political Theory* 33, no. 5, 2005: 678-705.

Michael, Keeley. "Continuing the Social Contract Tradition", *Business Ethics Quarterly* 5, no. 2, 1995: 241-255.

Murphy G Jeffrie. "Hume and Kant on the Social Contract", *Philosophical* Studies: An International Journal Jor Philosophy in the Analytic Tradition 33, no. l, 1978: 65-79.

Murphy, G Jeffrie. "Kalin on the Categorical Imperative," *Ethics* 79, no. 2, 1969: 163-164.

Myers, C Peter. "Between Divine and Human Sovereignty: The State of Nature and the Basis of Locke's Political Thought," *Polity* 27, no. 4, 1995: 629-649.

Nayak B, Pulin. "On Equality and Distributive Justice". *Economic and Political Weekly* 26. no. 11/12. 1991. 583-585+587+589-590.

Noone, John B. Jr. "The Social Contract and the Idea of Sovereignty III Rousseau", *The Journal of Politics* 32, no. 3, 1970: 696-708.

Nussbaum, "Women's Capabilities and Social Justice". *Journal of Human Development* 1, no. 2, 2000, 230: 290.

Nyiwul Mabughi and Tarek Selim. "Poverty as Social Deprivation: A Survey". *Review of Social Economy* 64, no. 2. 2006. pp. 181: 204.

Pankaj K Ashok. "Review of Idea of justice". *Social Scientist.* Vol. 39. No. 1/2. (2011), pp. 74-77.

Paul Anand, Graham Hunter, Ron Smith, "Capabilities and Well-Being: Evidence Based on the Sen-Nussbaum Approach to Welfare". *Social Indicators Research,* Vol. 74, 2005. pp. 9-55.

Peggy Antrobus, paper presented to the World Women's Congress for a Healthy Planet, Miami, FL, November 9-12, 1991.

Peterson, Jonathon. Enlightenment and Freedom. *Journal of the History of Philosophy* 46, no. 2, 2008: 223-44.

Prendergast, Renee. "The concept of freedom and its relation to economic development- a critical appreciation of the work of Amartya Sen". *Cambridge Journal of Economics* 29. no. 6. accessed on 21-01-2016.

Reck, J Andrew. "The Enlightenment in American Law III: The Bill of Rights," *The Review of Metaphysics* 45, no. 1, 1991: 57-87.

Rein'l, L Robert. "Comparative Philosophy and Intellectual Tolerance," *Philosophy East and West* 2, no. 4, 1953: 333-339.

Report Prepared by the Secretary General on the Global Consultation on the Realization of the Right to Development as a Human Right. UN Doc E/CnA/ 1990/9.

Robert A Holland. "A Theory of Establishment Clause Adjudication: Individualism, Social Contract, and the Significance of Coercion in Identifying Threats to Religious Liberty". *California Law Review* 80, no. 6, 1992: 1595-1694.

Roemer E, John. "Egalitarianism against the Veil of Ignorance" *The Journal of Philosophy* 99, no. 4. 2002: 167-184.

Ruth, W. Grant. "Locke's Political Anthropology and Lockean Individualism, *"The Journal of Politics* 50, no. 1, 1988: 42-63.

Schossberger, Cynthia "Raising a question: Coercion and Toleration in Kant's Politics", *Ethics, Florianopolis* 5, no. 2, 2006: 165-171.

Scott, T John. "Politics as the Imitation of the Divine in Rousseau's "Social Contract", *Polity* 26, no. 3, 1994: 473-501.

Sen, Amartya. "Capability as Opportunity: How Revises Equal Opportunity". *The Journal of Religious Ethics* 30. no. 1. 2002. 107-135.

Sen, Amartya. "Development as Freedom: An India Perspective". *Indian Journal of Industrial Relations* 42, no. 2. 2006: 157-169.

Sen, Amartya. "On the Status of Equality". *Political Theory* 24. no. 3. 1996.394400.

Sen, Amartya. "Welfare, Freedom and Social Choice: a Reply". *Louvain Economic Review* 56, no. %. 1990: 451-485.

Sen, Amartya. "Well - Being, Agency and Freedom: The Dewey Lectures, 1984". *Journal of Philosophy* 82, no. A. 1985: 169-221.

Sen. "Equality of What?". In *Tanner Lectures on Human Values.* edited by S.M. McMurrin. Salt Lake City: University of Utah Press. 1980. pp. 215- 216.

Sen. "Standard of Living". *The Tanner Lectures on Human Values,* Delivered at Clare Hall, Cambridge University. March 11 and 12, 1785.

Sonenscher, Michael. "Enlightenment and Revolution," *The Journal of Modern History* 70, no. 2, 1998: 371-383.

Stacey, Simon. "A Lockean Approach to Transitional Justic e," *The Review of Politics* 66, no. 1, 2004: 55-81.

Strum, Arthur. "What Enlightenment Is," *New German Critique,* no. 79, *Special Issue on Eighteenth -Century Literature and Thought,* 2000: 106-136.

Taylor, S Robert. "Kantian Personal Autonomy," *Political Theory* 33, no. 5, 2005: 602-628.

United Nations Human Rights Report. "Women's Rights are Human Rights". Office of the High Commissioner.

Walsh, Vivian. "Amartya Sen on Rationality and Freedom". *Science &Society* 71, no. 1. 2007: 59-83.

Websites

http://www.census20ll.co.in/sexratio.php

http://www.jstor.org/stable retrieved on 01/01/2014.

http://en.wikipedia.org/wiki/Capability approachretrievedon 02/02/2014.

http ://en.wikipedia.org/wiki /Justice retrieved on 01/12/2013.

http ://en.wikipedia.org/wiki/Kant retrieved on 30/01/2014.

http ://en.wikipedia.org/wiki/Rawls retrieved on 01/01/2014.

http ://en.wikipedia.org/wiki/Amartya Sen retrieved on 02/0 1/ 2014.

http: //en.wikipedia.org/wiki/Martha Nussbaum retrieved on 04/2/2014.

http://www.jstor.org/stable retrieved on 01/01/2015.

http://en.wikipedia.org/wiki/Capability approachretrievedon 02/02/2015.

http ://http://www.iep.utm.edu/Ju stice retrieved on 01/12/2015.

http://en.wikipedia.org/wiki/Amartya Sen retrieved on 30/01/2014.

http://stanford.edu/Capability Approach retrieved on 01/01/2014.

http ://en.wikipedia.org/wiki/Amartya Sen on Well being retrieved on 02/01/ 2014.

Index

A

Able-bodied person, 129
Adam Smith, 112, 128
Adaptation and mental conditioning, 126
Alasdair MacIntyre, 205
Aristotle, 17, 69, 139
Assessment of poverty, 135
Autonomous human being, 39

B

Basic education, 117, 127
Basic liberties and rights, 79, 204
Basic liberties of citizens, 84
Basic needs Poverty, 172
Basic structure of society, 76
Battle for Peace, 158
Behavioral correctness, 116
Beings and doings, 130
Blanch Wiesen Cook, 158
Bodily Health, 190, 210
Bodily Integrity, 191

C

Capabilities approach, 125, 128, 132, 136, 187
Capability approach to justice, 132
Capability Poverty, 172
Caste restrictions, 150
Central objective of development, 130
Charlotte Bunch, 156
Child sexual abuse, 150
Civil and political freedoms, 121
Civil and Political Rights, 159, 165
Civil matters, 152
Civil society, 33, 34
Climatic conditions, 205
Community structure, 94
Concept of poverty, 171
Concept of tolerance, 51
Condorcet, 112
Consumption based, 171
Contextual factors, 134
Contractarian approach, 77
Critical exposition of perfect justice, 104
Critical rationality, 29
Cultural traditions, 155
Cultural traditions and practices, 150

D

D. D. Raphael, 82
Democratic institutions, 133
Different nationalities, 94
Dignified life, 209
Distribution of primary goods, 85
Distribution of wealth, 85
Distributional indifference, 126
Distributive justice, 68, 75, 81, 83
Domestic responsibilities, 192
Domestic violence, 178, 192
Domestic work, 177
Dominant theory, 37

E

Economic arrangements, 120

Economic facilities, 121
Economic Poverty, 172
Economic security, 120
Education and knowledge, 177
Edward Harris, 31
Elementary health care, 127
Emotions, 191
Employment and participation, 173
Enlightened and moral persons, 54
Enlightened man, 61
Enlightened society, 58
Enlightenment, 47
Environmental characteristics, 124
Equal political rights, 187
Equality and fraternity, 151
Ethical problems, 193
European Enlightenment, 109

F

Fair institutional arrangement, 113
Female genital mutilation, 150
Female infanticide, 150, 178
Financial condition, 122
Financial resources, 173
Forced prostitution, 178
Forms of social injustices, 107
Formula of universal law, 53
Foundation of law, 113
Foundational elements, 131
Foundational pillars, 48
Free choice of occupation, 79, 204
Free will, 42
Freedom of movement, 79, 204
Freedom of opportunity, 123
Freedom of speech and assembly, 90
Freedom of the person, 90
Freedom of thought and liberty, 91
French Revolution, 87
Fundamental problem, 33

G

Gender inequalities, 152, 170
Gender Inequality and Religion, 180
Gender Inequality in Bodily Integrity, 178
Gender Inequality in Education, 179
Gender Inequality in Family Laws, 180
Gender inequality in Life and Health, 177
Gender Inequality in Respect and Dignity, 178
Gender Inequality in Workforce-participation, 179
Gender injustice, 154, 189
Gender justice, 151, 170
General conception, 69
General conception of justice, 69
Geoffrey Cupit, 95
Geographical location, 83
Global Gender Inequality, 176
Good education, 206

H

H J Paton, 55
Health care, 117, 120, 206, 209
Health facilities, 106, 107
Hilary Charlesworth, 161, 168
Hillary Clinton, 153
Historical date, 83
Historical evidence, 38
Honor killing, 178
House-keeping, 153
Human behaviour, 48
Human development, 119
Human freedom and the ability, 132
Human rights violation, 160, 208
Human welfare, 120
Human will, 43
Humanity and dignity, 47
Hunger and deprivation, 104
Hypothetical imperative, 46

I

Ignorance model, 83
Ignorance model of fairness, 86
Imagination, 191
Important forms of injustices, 106
Income and wealth, 80, 204
Individual and social level, 107
Inner freedom, 39
Institutional arrangement, 97, 202
Institutional mechanism, 37, 94
Institutional principle of justice, 92
Institutional requirement, 93
Institutionalizing fraternity, 96
Intellectual autonomy, 135
Intellectual tradition, 31
Internal consistency of choice, 135
International human rights law, 209
International law, 156
International legal definition of torture, 164
Interpersonal comparison, 140
Invisible injustice, 107
Isaiah Berlin, 89
Islamic invasion of Babur, 153
Islamic personal law, 181

J

James Schmidt, 28
John Locke, 16, 17, 31
John Mandle, 83
John Rawls, 13, 19, 23
Jonathan Peterson, 43
Juridical responsibility, 28
Justice and morality, 40
Justice and Secularism, 94

K

Kantian perfect justice, 37
Karl Marx, 112
Kenneth Arrow, 114

L

Lack of agency, 150
Lack of education, 106, 107, 188
Lack of genuine information, 127
Lack of leadership qualities, 150
Lack of nutritional food, 117, 120
Lack of skills, 188
Latin American women, 158
Leader of Opposition, 153
Less healthy than men, 176
Less nourished than men, 176
Liberal tradition, 17
Liberty and equality, 87
Liberty of conscience, 90
Life and physical health, 177
Limited opportunities, 209
Linguistic identities, 94
Lok Sabha, 153

M

Madhya Pradesh, 181
Major causes of female, 177
Marianne T. Hill, 132
Martin Rex, 94
Mary Wollstonecraft, 112
Masculine dominance, 153
Maximization in general, 137
Medieval extremism, 15, 29
Mental reaction, 125
Mental well-being, bodily integrity, 177
Metha Bai, 155
Missing women, 177
Monique Deveaux, 51
Moral codes, 52
Moral ingredient, 47
Moral law, 54
Moral laws, 42
Moral principles, 58
Mughal Empire, 153

Muslim Personal Law, 181
Mutual toleration, 60

N

National human rights law, 209
National law, 156
Natural liberty, 17
Natural right, 32, 43
Neglect of rights, 126
Noman Daniels, 115
Non humiliation, 192
Non-contextual view, 35
Nonmarket care, 177
Nourishment, 142
Nstitutional arrangement, 142
Nutritional meal, 207
Nutritious food, 209

O

Oliver Sensen, 43
Oppression of cultural practices, 182
Original position, 127
Original right to freedom, 49

P

Parasitic disease, 138
Patriarchal attitude, 150
Perfect duties, 54
Perfect justice, 40, 56
Perfect justice, 37
Personal autonomy, 41
Personal characteristics, 124
Personal identities, 81
Physical and mental handicaps, 115
Physical violence, 182, 209
Physical violence and sexual abuse, 176
Pleasure or displeasure, 42
Pluralistic natures, 94
Political and civil liberties, 118
Political and Civil Rights, 166
Political and economic life, 118
Political authority, 202
Political empowerment, 177
Political freedoms, 121
Political liberty, 90
Political participation, 141
Political rights, 169
Political virtue, 51
Positive freedom, 130
Poverty and malnutrition, 104
Poverty and sex inequality, 174
Poverty as Capability Deprivation, 175
Practical law, 42
Practical Reason, 41, 191, 192, 210
Premature death and suffering, 173
Primary goods, 85
Primary social goods, 140
Principle of fair equality, 93
Principle of perfect justice, 53
Principles of liberty, 84, 151
Progressive intellectual tradition, 201
Property rights, 169
Public enlightenment, 134, 135, 136
Public goods, 115
Public infrastructure, 115
Public right, 36

Q

Quality of human life, 128

R

R.P. Singh, 94
Raditional and stereotyped attitude, 170
Rajasthan state, 155
Rape and sexual harassment, 151
Rawls distributive justice, 97
Rawls principles, 83
Rawls theory of justice, 88
Rawls view, 89
Religious courts of family law, 152

Religious prohibition, 150
Right to hold personal property, 90
Rights and opportunities, 136

S

S. Vats, 153
Samuel Freeman, 75
Second-class status, 155
Self respect, 192
Self-determining agent, 58
Self-imposed laws, 46, 48, 54
Self-interest maximization, 137
Sex and gender, 208
Sex discrimination, 188
Sex selective abortion, 150, 178
Sexual abuse, 209
Sexual harassment, 151, 170, 184
Shah Bano Case, 181
Shakuntla Mudgal, 153
Social and Cultural Rights, 165
Social and economic inequalities, 85
Social arrangement, 123
Social characteristics, 124
Social choice theory, 109
Social Contract, 34
Social contract, 36
Social contract theory, 17, 19, 21, 28, 30, 31, 67, 202, 203
Social institutions, 202
Social opportunities, 122
Social relation of mutual respect, 60
Social relations, 177
Social relationships, 139
Social safety net, 122
Social situation, 188
Socioeconomic Rights, 166
South Africa, 151
Spiritual or medical state, 133, 137
Starving child, 132, 207
Subjugation of women, 106, 107
Supreme Court of India, 181
Systematic types of injustices, 106

T

The Idea of Justice, 22
Thomas Hobbes, 16, 31
Traditional accounts of justice, 169
Traditional approaches, 164
Trafficking and forced prostitution, 150
Transcendental institutionalism, 110, 111
Transcendental mechanism, 22
Transparency guarantees, 122
Transportation, 139

U

Unanimous agreement, 71
Uniform civil code, 152
United Nations, 156, 164
United Nations Human Rights, 164
United Nations International Covenants, 165
United Nations Organisations, 154
United Nations Organization, 162, 167, 208
United Nations Report, 157
United States, 151, 152
Universal autonomy, 37
Universal concept, 38, 193
Universal Declaration of Human Rights, 157, 158
Universal human rights, 164
Universal law, 44
Universal law of autonomy, 55
Universal law of freedom, 41
Universal law of nature, 55, 59
Universal principle of morality, 40, 48
Universality of morality, 53
Unjust action, 42
Unresolved agenda, 151
Utilitarian principle, 88, 127

Utilitarian theory of justice, 73
Utilitarian tradition, 18

V

Valuable state of affairs, 131
Various domestic works, 153
Various forms of injustices, 193
Vedic age, 153
Veil of ignorance, 78, 79, 127
Victims of domestic violence, 172
Victims of inequalities, 193
Violations of their rights, 56
Violations of women's rights, 155
Violence against women, 167
Violence and sexual abuse, 182
Violence committed against women, 156

W

Wollstonecraft, 112
Women in society, 183
Women integrity, 169
Women's Rights and the Law, 166
Women's rights violation, 149
Women's unequal treatment, 155
Women's unpaid labour, 153
World Women's Congress, 163

Y

Young widow, 155